MENNONITE VALLEY GIRL

CARLA ✶ FUNK

Mennonite Valley Girl

A WAYWARD COMING OF AGE

GREYSTONE BOOKS

Vancouver/Berkeley

Greystone Books Ltd.
greystonebooks.com

Cataloguing data available from Library and Archives Canada
ISBN 978-1-77164-515-7 (cloth)
ISBN 978-1-77164-516-4 (epub)

Editing by Paula Ayer
Proofreading by Doretta Lau
Jacket and text design by Jessica Sullivan
Jacket illustrations by Lana Smirnova (jeans); milart (birds); Oswald Kunstmann (embroidery) / Shutterstock
Author photo by Lance Hesketh

Printed in Canada on FSC® certified paper at Friesens. The FSC® label means that materials used for the product have been responsibly sourced.

Greystone Books gratefully acknowledges the Musqueam, Squamish, and Tsleil-Waututh peoples on whose land our office is located.

Greystone Books thanks the Canada Council for the Arts, the British Columbia Arts Council, the Province of British Columbia through the Book Publishing Tax Credit, and the Government of Canada for supporting our publishing activities.

For every female
in the family, far and wide
&
For Soopie and Sindee,
my fellow Valley gals

Why do you boast in the valleys,
Your flowing valley, O backsliding daughter?

JEREMIAH 49:4A

✗ ✗ ✗ ✗ ✗

CONTENTS

WRITING A MEMOIR is a little like Testimony Sunday. Every so often, in the church of my childhood, the preacher would invite folks to come forward and "give a testimony." Eventually, after a long and awkward silence, someone would walk slowly to the front of the sanctuary, stand at the microphone, and start to testify. The one who spoke might share a few words meant to bless or give thanks, or a "praise report" of a minor miracle occurring in our midst. Sometimes, the person told a true and simple story, confessing weakness, doubt, or the missing of the mark. Those sitting in the pews might whisper to each other, "Here she goes again," or "That's not what I heard happened," or "What must her poor mother think?" Those listening might shift in their seats as they found their own stories flashing back to them. Yes, the one giving testimony likely changed some names and altered some identifying details, to shield others from shame. She most certainly didn't tell the whole story, because some parts just weren't meant to be laid bare. Memory, like the heart, is prone to wander and full of flaws. But to tell the story with love and honesty—that's the hope, and to point toward a bigger, higher, wilder story that illuminates the valleys we pass through and the shadows that follow us, as we stumble our way out into the light.

MENNONITE VALLEY GIRL

FLASHLIGHT TAG

x x x x x x x

AS SOON AS THE SUMMER SKY deepened into dusk, we huddled in a circle and set the rules for the night. From the far side of the yard to where the driveway met the asphalt, from the pigpen to the tree fort, but not beyond the lagoon, and only to the treeline, our boundaries fell into place, marking out the limits for our game. Home base was where we started, gathered to the garage light's glow. On a patch of gravel flanked by flowerbeds, we stood—my brother and a straggle of boys from down the road, and me and the girls from the house next door. Above our heads, a windchime silvered the air, and around our ankles, the cat wove and wound its tail.

"Who's gonna be It?" my brother said. No one volunteered, and so we made our fists and held them to the center of our circle, ready for the choosing.

One potato, two potato, or *Eeny, meeny, miny, mo,* or *Engine, engine, number nine, going down to Chicago Line,* which the boys seemed to like best because it threatened with a train going off the tracks. The one who spoke the rhyme counted off the words until a final fist was landed on, and an It was picked.

1

"It"—a snitch of a word—held everything we didn't know but wanted to. In a single syllable, all the hidden secrets of the universe distilled, and all our future knowledge waited to be found. Did you see *it*? Did you hear about *it*? She did *it*. He did *it*. They did *it*. *It*'s true. *It* was the nutshell of our innocence and our hunger for experience. *It* named the shape of darkness, but not what cast the shadow.

"You're It," my brother said. He handed me the flashlight, which was the only consolation. The one who held the light, held power. To sweep the beam across a blackened panorama and find a flicker in the trees, an eyeball's shine, the neon of a shoelace, or the glint of metal bracing someone's smile—that was the mission.

I shut my eyes and started counting to one hundred, calling the numbers with a breath between each *one, two, three, four*, giving time for everyone to scatter. Though we were old enough to stay awake past dark, past when our parents went to sleep, we turned into children all over again as soon as the game began. Hollering and running through the trees, wielding sticks by moonlight, yelling curses at each other, and laughing across the acres, we could have been kids with our T-shirts whipped off, barefoot, flying wild. But now we ran with a different voltage humming in our blood, a current that sizzled in the company of other bodies. The boys were fleet and lean, all muscle and energy. They launched up trees and laddered the branches to enviable heights, while we girls stayed lower to the ground, taught to be careful in our climbing.

"Ready or not, here I come," I called into the night. I flicked on the flashlight.

When I was a child, the whole earth was filled with glory. Even a slug, sluicing a path of slime across the greenhouse glass, was a marvel to behold. The "how" and "why" of awe and curiosity fueled my thinking. I looked at the sky and wanted to know the names of what shone in it. I crouched to the dirt and studied weeds. I plucked the delicate tubes from the stalks of Indian paintbrush, sucked the nectars from their tips, and tasted the candy of what grew wild in my own backyard.

But as the body grows up farther from the ground, so the shadow lengthens. Wonder, with its soft underbelly, retreats. It goes into hiding, hushes in the dark, until the faith of childhood sounds more like a scoff than a song. The light-filled eye that scanned the dust for gold turns inward. Heats up. The body, that original house of wonder, warps and swells, holding what waits to be revealed.

I kept my footsteps slow, stalking with the flashlight held low as I listened for the silence to give up its mysteries. From somewhere farther down the road, a dog barked, its echo like a stone in water rippling. Above me, a hydro line buzzed. I swept the beam across the yard, illuminating the logging truck parked in front of my dad's shop. The chrome of the smokestacks gleamed. My body was no longer small enough to hide inside the wheel well of the truck's tire, or wedge between the mud flaps, so that my clothes and hair took on the grease and oil, sawdust and dirt, those smells driven back from the bush and clear-cut, that world of men and their machines. Now, the trailer was empty, unhitched, and the engine lay cold. Somewhere behind me, in the back bedroom of the house, my father lay snoring, my mother beside him, two cleaving sleepers bound by vows.

A snicker from somewhere in the garden swung my flashlight over and across. The seeds my mother planted weeks before grew up in tidy rows, nameable now as what they would become—the carrots with their feathery heads, the clovery leaves of radishes, the thin swordtips of onions, and the potatoes, sunk down in darkness, busting through with green. Around the corner of the greenhouse, a shape in motion. I aimed my beam.

"I see you!" I hollered but couldn't name the body, which had started now to run for the safety of home base. If that body was a boy, his speed would beat me there, but if it was a girl, I had a shot. "Soopie?" I called. "Leonard? Theresa? Richard?"

An eye above me leaning low toward the earth might have seen a single spark moving at the edges of the town, a small town poured into a northern valley full of shadows. The way a matchbox holds its future fire, my hometown held me, too, with all the elements essential for the flame. Inside its limits, inside the sameness and smallness of the place that once stoked wonder, inside a valley carved and bound by the river's bend and flow, I was ready to be shaken free, taken out. Inside a body whose bloodline sang an old, old gospel, inside a body shifting in its flesh and frame, I was learning how to burn, and what to burn, and what to keep.

Another body at my back began to move, and another rose from trees at the bottom of the driveway's slope, and then we all were running, breathing heat in the rules of our game, a game passed down to us from a time when light had been a fire, a torch held up to mark the way.

Through the garden dirt, I ran, trying not to kill what grew there, leaning toward the home-free glow above the garage. Around me, beside me, and flying ahead, shadows morphed to bodies, sweat and skin, becoming my brother, and the boys from down the road, and the neighbor girls, too, all of us breathing hard, and racing for the light.

THE KINGDOM

✕ ✕ ✕ ✕ ✕ ✕

THE MEN STAYED ROOTED on the back porch in the shade, far enough away from the kitchen so that the women, who were preparing the Father's Day meal, wouldn't complain about the smell of their smoke. Some uncles leaned against the stucco siding. Others sat on the steps with their knees bent at odd angles, their pant cuffs riding up and the white flesh above their socks glowing. My father flicked his Bic to the tip of his cigarette, then held it out to Uncle Corny, then Uncle Jake, passing down the line until all the men were breathing from the same flame.

On my mother's side of the family, cigarettes belonged in the same category as playing cards and alcohol, forbidden vices, but in the Funk kingdom, smoking was a sanctioned sin. Because Grandpa Funk had been a smoker, the habit drifted to my dad and his brothers without judgment, most of them sneaking out behind the barn to light up when they were barely teenagers. A few Christmases back, Grandma Funk had given all her sons and sons-in-law the same gift: a tin of tobacco and a home-rolling machine, ordered from the Sears Christmas catalogue. After the roast turkey and ham feast, the men had sat at the dining room table, loading tobacco into the filtered tubes and cranking out cigarettes with the quiet intensity of factory workers.

Now, in the breezy warmth of a Sunday in June, their conversation was punctuated by the tapping of ashes into the communal tin can resting on the top step. Their smoke rose to crown them with a vapor that hung a moment, then wafted away. They talked of work—life at bush camp, which logging outfit was first in the loading line, who'd bought new trucks and for what price. Their speech moved in and out of Plautdietsch, that cobbled Low German spoken by peasants and Mennonites.

Grandpa and Grandma Funk lived on the north side of the river at the top of P & H hill, so named for P & H Auto Supplies, which was situated at the crest of a short steep section of Loop Road. If I stood in their driveway, I could see across to where the shop fixed vehicles and sold ice cream sandwiches from a grubby chest freezer for forty-five cents. On summer days, Grandma would fold the coins into our palms when Grandpa wasn't watching, then whisper for us to go buy ourselves a treat. Past P & H lay Great-Grandpa Martens's house, where we butchered pigs and chickens every autumn, gatherings that had seemed in childhood like a holiday but now dragged on as long hours of work that left me smelling like blood and innards and smoke. North of the house, up another gravel road, lay the wrecking yard full of old cars and trucks, rows and heaps of metal exoskeletons rusting in various states of dismantlement and decay.

Only the boys ever made it all the way to the wrecking yard. While we waited to be called in for lunch, my brother and the other teenage males ripped up the hill on their BMX bikes, sneaking away with their stash of PVC pipe and drugstore saltpeter to see what they might blow up. The men smoked. The women cooked. The little cousins tore back and forth across the grass, chasing each other and the dogs with willow sticks, falling down, crying, getting back up, and tearing off again.

A few stands of scrappy birch and poplar trees flanked the yard, and along the edges of the large vegetable garden, raspberry canes and saskatoon and gooseberry bushes grew, flush with fruit that would be picked, washed, and cooked into jellies and jams, baked into pies, or tucked into pockets of soft dough that were deep-fried, then dusted with sugar. These were our *Roll Kuchen,* a staple of the Mennonite kitchen, which were either filled with berries or eaten plain as simple strips of dough fried to a golden crisp in a simmering pan of lard. The proper way to eat *Roll Kuchen* was to hold a slice of salted watermelon in one hand and a piece of the fried dough in the other, alternating one bite from the melon and one from the *Roll Kuchen,* which is what the uncles would do later, after they'd eaten lunch and played a few rounds of horseshoes on the back pitch. Then Grandma and the aunts would carry out a huge stainless-steel bowl of watermelon slices and a plate of still-hot *Roll Kuchen* resting on a bed of paper towels damp with grease. The men would descend, followed by their offspring, and then the women would clean up what remained.

Grandpa and Grandma's property, though too small to ever be a working farm, had a scattering of sheds and out-buildings behind the house, including the old cabin where they once lodged boarders to earn extra income. In one of Grandma's black-and-white photographs, a man smiled up from a bed that looked like a small, makeshift Conestoga wagon. The young bachelor had suffered a broken back, Grandma explained, and so had come to stay with them until he learned to walk again. "Oh, but he could build toys," Grandma said. One of the other boarders had rigged up the man's bed with a small motor so he could cruise around the property on his own, collecting tools and lumber scraps for his building projects. In the photograph, he lay on his stomach, holding a wooden dollhouse he had made, a gift for one of the girls, but which one, Grandma couldn't remember.

On the Funk side, I was the only female my age. Below me, the younger girls still played with the dolls and toys pulled from Grandma's cupboards, and the older ones had already graduated from high school, gone off to college, started full-time jobs in town, or had boyfriends who'd become husbands who'd soon make them pregnant. I was somewhere in between those worlds, meandering from room to room, trying to avoid being handed a baby or an apron or a wooden spoon.

I knew my inheritance. The Mennonite story stretched over continents and centuries and involved a lot of Bolsheviks, borscht, harsh winters, and fleeing one place for the next in search of freedom, history's slow-release chase scene with a persecuting government in pursuit. That was one way of explaining the feeling that moved through me and left me wandering inside and out, standing at the edge of the men and their hazy laughter, then bored, turning back to the house.

At the stove, at the sink, at the counters, peeling, slicing, stirring, and mixing, the women moved in the practiced choreography of the communal kitchen. Aunt Agnes poured a warm sweet creamy dressing over a bowl of shredded iceberg—her classic wilted lettuce salad. Aunt Marge stood over the steaming ham, carving slices onto a platter. Aunt Mary whisked the saucepan full of *Schmaundt-fat*—a thickened salt-and-pepper cream gravy to pour over the *Wareneki*, which Grandma was making especially for the meal.

Wareneki were our Mennonite perogies. While some families filled theirs with various kinds of meat or potato mash, the Funks filled them with either chopped fruit or with *Glums*—dry cottage cheese. I couldn't bite into *Glums* without thinking of the pitted, cleft flesh of a woman's thigh and buttocks, as if Mennonite aunts and grandmas and moms had given themselves and their cellulite to the making of the food. Whenever I tried to swallow a mouthful, my eyes watered and my throat threatened to seize, but my dad and all his siblings, even my brother and my cousins, held up their plates for seconds when the *Glums Wareneki* were passed around the table.

In assembly-line fashion, Grandma rolled out the soft sour-cream dough, cut circles from it with the mouth of a glass tumbler, then dropped a spoonful of the cottage-cheese mixture onto each round of dough. She wet her fingers in a dish of water, tapped them around half the rim of the dough circle, then folded it into a pocket and pinched the edges to seal it shut. Into a large pot of boiling water she dropped the pockets. When they floated to the surface, she scooped them out and set them on a rack.

Before she was Grandma Funk, she was my dad's mother, and before that, she was Annie Martens, a teenage bride who, at the wedding altar's *I do, I do, I will honor and obey,* became *Mrs. Henry Funk,* her name sliding behind his name, the way it did for all Mennonite women who married. But to me, she was Grandma Funk. Sometimes *Grossmama.* Always soft-bodied in a polyester dress sewn from the same pattern in various colors and prints. Always wearing thick, beige pantyhose and plain, black, lace-up shoes. She combed her thin hair straight back from her round face and wide forehead, and wore it rolled at the nape of her neck. A black mesh cap, bobby-pinned in place, covered her head. Her glasses magnified the watery blueness of her eyes. When she hugged me and pressed the smooth velvet of her cheek against my own, I smelled the rose scent of the talcum powder she sprinkled down the bodice of her dress.

Oh, bah, she said when a toddler cousin ran to her with a scraped knee. She scooped up the crying child, took his clenched fist and unfolded it, and then began to count off each finger with a rhyme whose words in Low German sounded like *yidda yidda yatcha* and had something to do with a family of mice getting their heads chopped off with a knife. *This-un one, and this-un one, and this-un one*, she'd count, pinching the tip of each little finger, and finally, ending with a tickle in the center of the child's palm, followed by a chuck under the chin. His scraped knee forgotten, the child sniffed, wriggled out of Grandma's arms, and headed back to the other cousins still running in the yard with their pointed sticks aimed high.

Though it had been over six months since he died, the ghost of Grandpa Funk seemed to linger in his corner of the dining room, a washed-out gray shadow wavering in and out of optic memory. Before the sickness, the diagnosis, and even in the months of treatment that followed, he sat at the head of the table with a blanket or quilt spread out before him. With fingers still yellowed from the decades of cigarettes, he tied off the tufts of yarn stitched to hold the wool filling in place between the two sheets of fabric. Coughing and clearing his throat, sipping his weak coffee, he knotted the yarn methodically, with the same precision he demanded in all aspects of his home and property. When he'd returned from Vancouver skinny and gray-faced after another stint of radiation, he brought back a cardboard box full of stuffed animals he'd made in the arts and crafts wing of the cancer pavilion. He arranged them on a shelf of the glass-doored cabinet in the living room so that a lineup of bear, dog, cat, lamb, and skunk looked out through the door. On the shelves above and below Grandpa's plush menagerie, Uncle Pete's models were displayed—hand-painted race cars and hot rods, and a Harley chopper ridden by a scythe-wielding grim reaper.

"What are you going to do with the stuffed animals?" I'd asked Grandpa, angling for dibs on the skunk with a fat white stripe down its back.

"I'm going to keep them," he said. "These are not toys what for playing with." He clicked the glass door shut.

That was his way—to set the rules and expect others to obey. When Grandma needed to buy new underwear, he had her tally the cost to the very cent, including tax, and then into her open palm, he counted out the exact change for the purchase. I'd heard my dad say words like *stingy* and *cheap*, and tell stories of how, as a boy, he had to give his own father ninety cents of every dollar he earned at the dairy farm.

As a four-year-old, I'd stood with my brother in the doorway of our grandparents' bathroom and listened to Grandpa Funk preach a stern sermon on how best to clean ourselves after using the toilet. He tore two squares of tissue from the roll and dangled them in front of us. "This is all what you need," he said. He showed us how to fold the tissue in half—to make another clean surface after the first wipe. Then he folded it again in half, and yet again, until the paper was as small as a sugar packet. "This way," he said, "you can wipe and wipe, and still have it clean."

When I complained to Grandma, she clucked her tongue and whispered permission for us to use "that what we needed," and then she told me how no one had any toilet paper when she was a girl.

"All what we had was old catalogues," she said, "and oh, bah—how that gave us the piles!" To avoid getting hemorrhoids, she stole the cuffs of old shirts from the ragbag whenever she was on mending duty. She saved all the fabric in a secret stash and took the rags with her to the outhouse. "And that was better for wiping," she said. "So much softer."

Even after Grandpa Funk died, his animals stayed locked in the cabinet, memorabilia of his final year on earth. Grandma couldn't bear to give them away. I didn't understand how she could have loved him so devotedly, this man who only seemed to smile when someone else was crying. When he pinched and twisted the top of my brother's ear and made him plead *ow-ow-ow* for him to quit. When he force-fed the sharpest aged cheddar to a fussing toddler, who gagged and spat it out. When my little cousin was tricked into eating hot Mexican peppers and then grabbed at his tongue and wheezed. Then—oh, then Grandpa laughed and laughed, and the laughter of my dad and his brothers followed, all of them crowding around whatever joke or mild injury had occurred. When the neighbor's dog slunk into Grandpa and Grandma's backyard and tried to pick a fight with Uncle George's pooch, the men caught the stray, grabbed it by the tail, and scrubbed its backside with a wire brush dipped in turpentine. The dog howled a chain of high-pitched vowels and dragged its butt along the grass, then streaked home yelping, while Grandpa stood on the top of the back porch, glittery-eyed and grimacing with laughter, his sons echoing below him on the steps.

When I studied my dad's face, I saw more of his mother than his father. Like hers, his eyes blurred behind thick lenses and he had to lean in close to see the words on any page. He was softer at the edges, too, always reaching into his shirt pocket for a mint to coax one of the toddlers onto his knee. He pinched the fat cheeks of babies, but gently, and did not make them cry on purpose. He fed the dog scraps of fat from his plate, and whenever his own father challenged him to a game of snooker at the basement billiards table, he knew not to boast if he beat him, and if Grandpa missed a shot, never to crack a laugh.

Before the funeral, in the foyer of the Gospel Chapel, Grandma stood alone at Grandpa's open casket, sniffling into her tissue. Head bowed, she looked into the coffin for a long moment, like she might be double-checking he was dead, no ribcage rise and fall, no whistle from his lips. Slowly, my aunts and uncles joined her, gathering around the body of their father on display. Aunt Agnes, Aunt Mary, and Aunt Marge dabbed their eyes. The uncles loudly blew their noses into handkerchiefs. My dad sat beneath the coatrack, red-eyed and shuddering with sobs over a man who hadn't ever seemed to like him, his firstborn son.

When I took my turn at the coffin, inching forward with my brother and mom, I saw a black-suited, gray-faced, gaunt-cheeked man with owlish eyebrows that even in death made him look mad. I tried to summon a memory to turn the moment warm, but all I could picture was Grandpa Funk back in his living room with his ashtray beside him as he puffed on a home-rolled smoke, his eyes forever fixed on the TV in the corner, *Wild Kingdom* flashing its animals on the prowl.

EVEN AS I studied the Funks, I couldn't find where I fit. Not with the boys and their slingshots. Not with the older girl cousins in their fresh perms and sheer pantyhose. Not with the women in the kitchen wearing aprons and wielding knives. And not with the men outside, who were waiting to be called and served and satisfied.

"Zusa," said Uncle George, calling from his spot on the porch. I was too old for the childhood nickname, a play on my middle name, "Sue," and the Low German word for "sugar." But it was better than what the uncles called my brother—"Pudel Hund," which as far I could tell had something to do with poodles or a puddle of dog pee. I sat down and scratched Pulo, Uncle George's dog.

"Sing, Pulo," said Uncle George. "Come on, you sing, Pulo."

Soon all the uncles were joining in, ordering the squat black-and-tan dog to perform his famous trick. As if unable to bear the men's chanted demands any longer, Pulo cocked back his head and shut his eyes. Mournfully, operatically, he sang, and then sang some more, howling so loudly the smallest cousins clamped their hands over their ears and begged Uncle George to make the dog stop.

"Come and eat," one of the aunts called through the back door that opened to the porch stoop.

As my dad and his brothers and all the cousins filed in from the yard, the women carried huge bowls and platters of food to the long stretch of cloth-covered tables. Crowded around the edges of the dining room, we stood, and then Grandma looked to Uncle George, the signal for him to start the song of our mealtime prayer. Our voices joined with his in a choral rendition that sounded like talking set to music, the words descending and ascending in their familiar tune. After the drawn-out, monotone *Amen*, Grandma unclasped her hands and motioned to the laden table. "And now we will eat." She waited for us all to find our seats, and then she moved to the head of the table, where Grandpa Funk always sat at mealtime, where he had sat last Father's Day, and the Father's Day before, all the way back through the years to their first table in their first home as man and wife.

They had been so poor, she told me, living in a one-room log cabin, but always God had been faithful and always He had provided. She'd birthed nine children, including two sets of twins, and even while pregnant, she helped in the farm fields and cooked and cleaned for the boarders who lived out back. Yes, sometimes the air had been so cold in winter, the wet diapers froze when they hit the bucket, but all the babies survived. Though Grandma clucked her tongue and shook her head whenever my dad and his brothers drank on the back steps, she never scolded. Grandpa had been harsh enough with them all those years, and now, she was ushering in a more peaceful realm. Once, when I asked her why she'd married Grandpa in the first place, she tilted her head a little and shrugged. Back in a small farming community in Saskatchewan, they'd met at the Mennonite church. He had been a sickly young man with lung trouble. He had been quiet and serious. "Oh, but, he would worry," Grandma said. She had felt so bad for him. I don't remember her saying anything about falling in love.

AFTER THE *Wareneki* and ham and salad and buns, the women cleared the tables and the men took to the porch again. Hunkered on the steps, the uncles picked at their teeth with wooden toothpicks and resumed their truck talk in a pattern of silence, wisecrack, low laughter, and exclamations of *"Dietschlaunt,"* the mildest of Mennonite cuss words. They wore their sideburns long, their square, metal-rimmed glasses tinted to keep out the sun. They slicked back their hair into ducktails. They slid out their dentures to get rid of a stuck berry seed or fleck of ham. They blew their noses loudly into handkerchiefs. They were good men, loyal men. Steadfast men who stood their ground. They whetted the stone, scraped the blade, swung the axe, loaded the gun, pulled the trigger. They held the keys and steered the wheel. They told us where we needed to go, and they took us there when they decided it was time.

In the kitchen, the women scraped and washed and dried the dishes, flush-cheeked and sweating in the steam and heat. But their voices chimed with the camaraderie of females and shone like the sunlight through the thin curtains that draped the window above the sink. These were women with short hair and perms. Women who wore pants. Whose husbands smoked. These were women who opened their Bibles every morning for a proverb or a psalm, and in the evenings after their children were in bed, watched *Love Boat* or *Magnum P.I.* while hemming a pair of pants or crocheting a baby blanket. They were women a little bit *in the world*, but not fully *of* it, standing on the threshold of the ancient and the new.

Standing in the doorway that led from the kitchen onto the porch and out into the yard, I could smell the yeasty tang of beer as my father and uncles cracked open their bottles. The older boys were already wandering up the road. The shrill voices of children volleyed back and forth through the trees, across the lawn. The shape of things to come lay before me and behind. I could not imagine joining myself to any other clan, but I knew the story unfolding for me. Every few months, our church bulletin printed the wedding banns announcing new pairs—the union of a Friesen and a Froese, a Giesbrecht and a Wiebe, a Thiessen and a Dyck—who'd soon become one flesh, the bride with her gauzy veil and watery eyes stepping into the arms of her stiff and sweating groom. One day, my body would be carried over the threshold of a different house, seated at a table full of strangers, and offered a drink from someone else's cup. What began as the mingling of one man and one woman would multiply to build a kingdom, seeded in the frozen fields, planted in the Prairie dust, and blooming on the north side of the river.

NAMESAKE

ᛝ ᛝ ᛝ ᛝ ᛝ ᛝ ᛝ

MY FATHER WANTED TO name me Edna, after some hot chick he knew in his fast-car days. I pictured him at the wheel of his convertible Ford Fairlane and her riding shotgun, shrieking around every hairpin curve, a gauzy scarf tied over her hairsprayed bouffant to guard against the wind. With every rev of the pedal, my father would eye Edna and take in her starlet beauty, tucking away her name like a token for the daughter who'd become me.

"It's an old-lady name," I told my dad. "Someone's grandma's name." I scoffed at the sound of it.

Ed-na. Two syllables performing a nasal thud. A name whose music conjured a thick-waisted *Grossmama* shuffling across a muddy field, her hair cinched in a bun, a black kerchief knotted beneath her chin.

"Nothing wrong with the name Edna," he always argued. "It's a good name. A pretty name." And then his eyes got that misty, far-off look, as if he were back behind the wheel of that ragtop Ford with a beehived beauty beside him and 45 vinyl record spinning on his dashboard stereo, the song skipping with every pothole in the road.

18

My mother had favored the name Shanna-Lynn, but my dad nixed it before it could stick. Too flouncy, too fancy, too strange.

"How about Karen?" my mom said to him. "How about Corrine?"

Those names, too, fell away, until I was the name that she gave me.

"It means 'strong and womanly,'" she told me, showing me the entry in a book of names and their meanings.

"Strong and womanly" sounded like my grandma Shenk, my mom's mother, a tall, large-boned lady who pinned her gray hair back into a bun and always wore a dress, even when she rode horseback or butchered the moose Grandpa hauled home from his hunting trips. "Strong and womanly" sounded like an apron tied around my waist, a knife in my pocket, my rightful female inheritance.

My mom couldn't remember what made her choose the name. It shunned the traditional catalogue of Mennonite possibilities, ensuring that I wouldn't be lost in a sea of Marys, Sarahs, and Anns. Plus, she didn't know anyone who had ever named their baby Carla, so that seemed like reason enough. But beyond its familiarity, I felt no connection to my name. It was a two-syllable cue, like the name assigned to any creature, used to beckon me to the table, in from the woods, away from the fire, out from behind my locked bedroom door.

"Carla," my mom's voice called down hallways, and out the window, and across the acres. "Carla Sue!"

Sue. A name whose exclamation sounded like a hog farmer hollering to his herd. *Sue-y*, my brother would call, and then punctuate with pig snorts. Sue. A name passed down from my mom, who shared it as her middle name. Before her, Sue belonged to her mother's mother, an Amish bride from Kansas. That single syllable, like a bead on a strand, threaded me to a line of females who came before. From the womb, I was stitched to a kinfolk by that name. In Great-Grandma Sue glowed the egg that bore my mother, and in my mother glowed the egg of me. Down through the generations, each female body opened up to yield a replica from within, like a row of nesting dolls, their shapes soft-hipped and squat from centuries of pulling weeds and bearing children. Passed down from mother to daughter, the name heirloomed me into a long line of women praised for flaky pie crusts, bountiful gardens, covered heads, held tongues, sharpened knives, and bread dough that baked into risen, golden loaves.

My name also bound me to a faith whose inheritance was God, whose bloodline was Heaven, and whose origin was eternity. Before I was a daughter, before I lay swaddled in the arms of a woman whose gray-green eyes sparked like spring and fire, before a man who smelled like whiskey, smoke, and sawdust bounced me on his knee, before I was the kid sister of a boy whose hands loaded bullets in the barrel and pulled back the slingshot's stone, I was an else-where-dreamed-up creature, unspooled from a glittering realm, and knitted by hands that already knew my name.

If I shut my eyes and gave myself to the brooding dark, I could imagine my way back into that making, see myself being scooped up from a genesis of cells and elements, raked from the clay-heavy dirt—same dirt that fed the roots of Douglas fir and aspen, black spruce and silver birch, jack-pine and lodgepole, same dirt that fattened rosehips and pussywillows, shot up into dogwood and kinnikinnick, sweetened to wild strawberries, huckleberries, and clusters of dusty saskatoons. In that dirt, I rested like a thought not yet fully formed, until, like a light turned on in a dark room, like breath breaking through the skin of deep water, the voice said, *Wake up, open your eyes. Look at where you come from.*

Above me, sky and sky and sky forever. Poplar trees in a flush of green blowing a song that rushed like water, tethering itself to the river's own singing, the current flashing with sockeye and chinook, char and Dolly Vardens, and rainbow trout in their iridescent swim. The black-capped chickadee, the crow, robin, cedar waxwing, bluebird, Canada goose and trumpeter swan—they mingled their sounds to a raucous choir taking flight, rising to blue. Down low, where I waited in the dirt, honeybees fizzed in the fireweed. On the leaves, swallowtails and skippers, coppers and whites flexed their gauzy wings.

"CARLA SUE!" my mother's voice called. "Wake up!"

Behind my bedroom door, I lay beneath a wool comforter. I opened my eyes to another morning, blinked to clear the blur. My walls were painted a breezy sky blue, except for one accent wall paneled in faux wood. I ran my fingers along a groove in the panel, letting the skin catch on the roughness. If I reached high enough, I could touch the edges of a Garfield picture tacked to the wall, the orange cartoon cat smiling with a missing front tooth and his paws in boxing gloves, the words "Reach out and touch someone" bubbled above his smug head. On each wall, a different poster with a different inspirational saying. "You're no bunny 'til some bunny loves you" above a photo of a floppy-eared rabbit. A prayer for God's help above the image of a gerbil squatting in a grassy field. A proverb on friendship beside a kitten perched on a monkey's head. When I sat up in bed, the mirror on my dresser gave back the creature of myself shapeshifting into someone new, not quite *young woman*, but more than *girl*. I flopped back to my pillow.

"I'm awake," I called back to my mother's voice. "I'm getting up right now."

Outside, the world was sunlight at my window. When I drew the vinyl curtains back, I could see the greenhouse and the backyard garden, and beyond them, past the trees, the pigpen, the sewage lagoon, and my father's shop. Parked in front of it, his pickup, and lower on the stretch of gravel that ran toward the woodshed, one of his Kenworth logging trucks. He no longer drove the trucks. Now, he hired other men to haul the logs out of the bush and to the mill. Now, he only monkey wrenched, ordered parts, kept the woodpile stacked and the shop fridge stocked with booze and Pepsi. Past the logging truck and through the stretch of pine and birch and poplar was my best friend Soopie's house, or what had been her house until she moved up the highway to a new property with a bigger house, a hot tub, and a swimming pool carved into the ground. Once summer came, I'd be floating on an inflatable island, bronzing in the heat like a sunbather on a California beach.

At Soopie's house, when we weren't goofing around in the pool, we watched as much MTV as we wanted, cranked the volume and sang along to Glass Tiger and Bryan Adams, Haywire and Honeymoon Suite. Only a few summers before, we'd spent our hours together playing with Strawberry Shortcake and My Little Pony and organizing our sticker collections, but now we snuck into her older sister

Theresa's room to read through her secret stash of flirty notes from boys who wrote things like *Girl, you're really sexy,* and *You move like a tiger in those jeans.* We stole her stacks of magazines, then lay on Soopie's bed and flipped through issues of *Teen Beat* and *Superteen,* ranking the glossy centerfolds in order of cuteness. I guessed that boys our age did the same thing, except with magazines about dirt bikes and hunting, rating engine power and a barrel's cocking action instead of a girl's eyes and the tightness of her pants.

Soopie and I practiced hairstyles in front of her bathroom vanity, crimping and curling, teasing and spritzing like the beauty columns guided us, step by step. Reflected back in the mirror, I stood short and stocky beside Soopie, who was tall, broad-shouldered, and built tough as a hockey player, except she played ringette, the girl's version of the game. Her real name was Julie Sue, but from the time she was a baby, her grandpa called her Soopie, and then everyone else called her that, too. Nicknames were a sign of affection, she said, and asked if I had one. But none of the names I'd been called by my dad—*Potlicker, Rugrat, Kjlien Schwien,* which was Low German for "short little pig"—had stuck.

My mother only ever called me Carla, the tone of my name cooling or brightening with her mood and my attitude, which seemed to darken daily, surprising even me. At Soopie's house, I could be a lighter version of my name, unhooked from all the connotations of home. "Why do you always want to go to Soopie's?" my mother said, when I begged for yet another sleepover. "If you're spending the night at her place all the time, people are going to, you know"—she cleared her throat—"start to wonder."

I couldn't explain how Soopie's house always felt like a holiday and ours like Monday, like porridge for breakfast, like chores. Even as I slid open my bedroom closet and looked at the clothes that hung—dresses that I hated, blouses too ugly to wear—I was imagining a whole new wardrobe to fit the life I was inventing for myself. Instead of *Carla*, I could be an Ashley, a Cherie, a Summer, a name whose roots sank down in more exotic ground.

By any other name, I'd wake to the sound of a different woman's voice, in a different house, in a place somewhere other than a small town in a valley surrounded by grainfields and forests, lumber mills and logging trucks, and four-by-fours revving down the main drag. Instead of a Sunday morning with the hard, wooden pews, the dusty old hymns, and a long sermon ahead, it could be an open highway all the way to the ocean and a shore sparked with sun.

These possibilities glimmered in me as I sat at the breakfast table with my bowl of oatmeal and considered my surroundings. Nothing about my mother—brown-haired, green-eyed, freckled—looked like me. Nothing about my father fit, not his love of shoot-'em-up TV Westerns and fully loaded Fords, not his zeal for casino jackpots and juicy T-bone steaks. Nothing about my brother either, whose brain was hooked to numbers and schematics and the lines of code he typed into his Tandy, whose teenage body freely ranged with a pack of guys fixed on ammo, fire, and minor explosions. By another name—Violet, Simone, Raquel— I'd be sipping sparkling juice from a champagne flute, not drinking powdered Tang from a plastic Co-op tumbler. Instead of the talk around the table being trucks, tools, fuel prices, pigs, the lawn that needed mowing, the weeds to be pulled, the conversation would rise to where on earth I'd love to go, which country I would jet to first—Italy or

France—and how the whole world was waiting with an open invitation, calling me to go forth and explore, not stay put in the place I was born.

In a town so small I couldn't find it on our globe, my life had been ordained and planned with purpose—that was the doctrine preached to me. My father's family had come from the Prairies for the government's offer of trees and cheap farmland; my mother's side, for the northern wilderness that promised a buffer from government involvement. Of all the places He could pick, God planted me in Vanderhoof. Even if I held that image in my mind—of my body being sown in the soil of our valley, in the furrow of my family line—I couldn't help but wonder what my life might look like if I'd been rooted somewhere else, and if perhaps the wondering itself was proof that I belonged to a different place and people.

I scraped the last spoonful of porridge from my bowl and rose from the table with a renewed clarity. I snuck to the living room and from the bottom drawer of an end table, dug out the album that held my baby photos. As I studied the pinkish, bald-headed, fat-cheeked creature swaddled in a white blanket and lying beside an arrangement of pink carnations, I saw a baby who didn't look like she belonged to the family that took her home. Our photo albums displayed no evidence of my mother in a hospital bed clutching the new bundle of me. Where was her stunned, post-childbirth smile, I wondered, and the shots of me among a row of glassed-in nursery newborns squalling at the light?

From beneath the album page's clear plastic shield, I pulled out pictures of my parents and held them side by side with mine: my mother's gray-green eyes, my father's hazel; her freckled skin, his sallow; her oval face, his square;

their brown, fine hair. My brother, three years older, had the same fiery eyes and shy smile as our mother, and our father's olive skin. But nothing of them rhymed with me, fair-haired, light-eyed, and pale.

"You're blonde like Aunt Agnes," said my mother, when I cornered her in the kitchen and asked why I didn't look like her and Dad.

"But she's my aunt," I said, "not my mom." I studied her face for any sign of a twitch, the dart of her eyes.

"I don't know what to tell you," she said, taking up her paring knife at the sink full of potatoes.

"But where are the pictures of you pregnant with me?"

She shrugged. "I guess I was the one behind the camera."

I took note of her tactic, that quick swerve away from any talk of my birth. It was one more clue to add to my growing arsenal of evidence, all of which pointed toward what I'd quietly suspected for years—that these people I called "Mom" and "Dad" were not my real parents. That the genes floating in my bone and blood came from a different lineage, a wholly other biology.

When I looked around at our house, at the rust-and-gold shag rug, the plastic curtains, the ceramic ashtray in the shape of a snowmobile, I had faith this was only a shadow of my real home. Surely, I belonged to rooms where floorboards gleamed like honey in sunlight. My dinner plate was meant to hold fancy foods with names like *alfredo*, *cacciatore*, *ratatouille*, not fried liver and onions. The sound pouring from the stereo should be a Mendelssohn sonata or cool jazz—anything but country, my father's chosen music.

He wanted to give me a name whose song to him was heat, and speed, and the rev of his pulse as he drag-raced on the highway, whose sound echoed with the laughter of a party girl beside him. "No," said my mother, with firmness, and she called me "strong and womanly," a name that tried to hook me to a different story. When I asked her why she'd picked it, why this name, she said, "I never knew another Carla," as if that made it clean and new, fresh as a dress never worn until she zipped me into it. But the fit felt wrong, scratchy at the neck and collar, tight at the seams. Paired with the final say of my father's family name, the syllables chafed.

From a German word for "spark," and calling forth a blacksmith's work, *Funk* swung down the hammer. To be a Funk in a valley full of Mennonites was to be a Smith in any town. Here, I was one of hundreds with that name, forged by its common fire.

"Nothing wrong with Funk," my father said. "It's a good name. It's our name."

It was his name, given to him in descent, passed man to man, and given to me the moment he slipped the wedding ring on my mother's finger and she let herself be bound to him. Whatever the flame is fed becomes the flame. What's held inside the blaze can bend or burn. My father wanted to name me Edna, meaning *tenderness*, meaning *pleasure*, the kind of name whose spark might start a fire.

*...they flowed over the mountains,
they went down into the valleys,
to the place you assigned for them.*

PSALM 104:8

IT ONLY TAKES
A SPARK

ｘ ｘ ｘ ｘ ｘ ｘ ｘ

THE FOLDED BROCHURE TUCKED IN our church's bulletin had advertised "Outdoor Summer Fun for Children and Youth of All Ages," plus a bunch of stuff about God's love and the history of the camp. Ootsa Lake Bible Camp, founded in 1957 by a Mennonite church, was designed to be a place where children could learn about the love of God and young people could actively participate in the work of the gospel. From the grainy, black-and-white smiles of the high-fiving youth on the photocopied pamphlet, Ootsa looked like fun, and like the kind of camp—built and run by Mennonites— to which my parents would say yes.

Every idea I had about summer camp came from movies and books. In library paperbacks, kid sleuths solved mystery after mystery—the howling in the haunted shack, the ghostly figure walking nightly through the woods. In vintage Disney films, slapstick hijinks led to low-level romance and a tidy resolution. Though I held no illusions about panty raids and late-night kissing contests at a camp with the word "Bible" in its name, I wanted in on the possibility of adventure. But even more, I liked the idea of being the kind of girl who'd gone to Bible camp, of coming back from summer with that status, like a badge of goodness fastened to my heart.

As I stood in line with Soopie, waiting for our cabin assignment, I took in the scope of the camp. The water's dark sheen reflected little of the birch and poplar that lined the shore, leaving the landscape washed out, tinted only by the green of the leaves and the amber of the cabins' peeled logs. The overcast sky stretched a dull pall over the property. A row of small log cabins faced the "playing field," a clay and weed-stubbled clearing flanked by various outbuildings—the arts and crafts hut, the chapel and adjoining mess hall where meals were served.

Already, a jittery rainbow of hormones and nervous adrenaline had begun to overtake the drab landscape. Boys, ball-capped and hyper, were running impromptu foot races across the field, while some of the quieter ones stood on the sidelines, arms folded across their chests, as if gauging the evolving hierarchy. I knew that stance well, that inner urge to place myself in the social structure by way of comparison, and to pray that I wasn't the loser or the freak, the one at the bottom of the rank.

Skinny, giggling girls with perms and achingly perfect teeth. Shy library girls with guileless eyes. Sporty girls in shorts and cleats who were already booting a soccer ball around the makeshift pitch. They were all here at Ootsa. Mercifully, so were the girls who hung awkwardly at the edges of every group, the asthmatic, the crybaby, the secret bedwetter. I figured I was somewhere in the middle, and saved by Soopie, because she could make friends with anyone.

"Holy cow! I know you!" A curly-haired, lipsticked teenager whose name tag said "Miss Beth" had jumped up from her seat at the sign-in table. I recognized her as one of the older girls from our church's youth group. "Awesome!" Miss Beth whooped and held up her hand for me and Soopie to high-five. "Our cabin is totally gonna be the best!"

To be the best, to win the prize, to hold the trophy and smile for the flashbulb's flare—that's what I craved. To be the one not overlooked, but seen, and seen as worthy of the light of someone's gaze—I was hungry for it, too hungry, it seemed. I could still recall the burn and flush I'd felt in first-grade circle time when the teacher announced that one student in our class had earned a week of perfect test scores. Mrs. Schroeder had smiled and tipped her chin at me, and so I pointed at my chest—*Me! Me!*—and nodded to my class-mates, shining with triumph. But then the room's mood turned. Mrs. Schroeder rose from her chair and whisked across the circle, crouched beside me, and whispered in my ear that now I'd earned my first demerit because what I'd shown was pride, and pride was sin. On the attendance sheet that bore my name, she inked a thin red mark, ruining my pure and perfect score. To be the best was tricky work, a trap sometimes. To be the girl who tried too hard or shone too brightly risked a harder fall. "You be good," my mom had said before she and my father drove away from Ootsa and left me waving at the gate with my duffel bag. I knew how to follow rules. I knew how to be good, or at least, how to appear good, even when the words that fired inside my mind were dark and mean and full of pride.

Our cabin—Cabin C—was staffed by the bouncy, loud Miss Beth, and Miss Miriam, her shy, whispery partner who seemed always to be clutching her Bible. A squat, pale girl named Laura took the bunk tucked in the corner and mutely shrugged when anyone asked her questions. Heather and Tanya, a pair of best friends from the village of Fraser Lake, moved into the bunks above Soopie and me. They were cute, dark-haired, and athletic. They leaned over the cabin's porch railing, laughing and yoo-hooing to the boys on the field, while from my lower bunk, I looked on through the cracked-open door and envied their tanned, thin legs.

When the mess hall's dinner bell tolled three times, one bunk in Cabin C had yet to be claimed. Just as we were readying to head out for supper, the clack of footsteps on the stairs announced our final roommate's arrival. The door swung open, and we turned to see the girl who'd fill the empty bunk. She wore a butter-yellow T-shirt emblazoned with Michael Jackson's face, skin-tight stirrup jeans, and red high-heeled shoes. She stood on the threshold and squinted, scanning the room, as if deciding whether or not to enter. In one hand, she held a rumpled paper grocery sack and with the other, she dragged a rolled-up sleeping bag. We couldn't help but gawk.

"You must be Gina!" said Miss Beth, holding out her hand.

The girl marched in, dropped her stuff on the floor, and without even a hello, clambered up the ladder to the final empty bunk. I looked around at my cabinmates, checking to see that we were all thinking the same thing. Pale Laura's eyes widened. Heather and Tanya stopped their chatter. I glanced at Soopie and we smirked. This new girl was weird. Like an inverse image of the Bible-camp brochure's clean and smiling faces, she wore her scowl and trouble on full display.

"Welcome to Ootsa," Miss Miriam whispered and smiled up at Gina, who swung her legs over the edge of the bunk and studied the cabin layout with a look of suspicion. The rest of us sat on our beds transfixed.

"Okay," said Gina, "What's your guyses' favorite Michael Jackson songs?" Her jaw worked a wad of chewing gum as she waited for our answer.

Miss Beth shot Miss Miriam a look that made me wonder if Michael Jackson was off-limits at Ootsa, too worldly, too secular. I'd seen him grab his own crotch in a music video on MTV, a gesture that made my mother whoosh into the living room and change the channel.

But Gina was already in motion, swinging down off the bunk. "So, you guys want to see something weird?" She jumped to the floor and pulled out her wad of gum. "You gotta come close, though." She opened her mouth. With her thumb and forefinger, as if trying to pick a piece of fuzz off her tongue, she pinched at the tip of it.

Unable to resist, I rose from my bunk. We all did, clustering close, leaning in.

"Ook," said Gina. "Thee thith?"

Her tongue puppeted left and right with the movement of her hand. Then we saw what she meant. Held taut between her thumb and forefinger was a hair, a strand that sprouted from the tip of her tongue. It was at least three inches long. As Gina tugged it, her tongue flinched and flicked.

Miss Miriam clapped a hand over her own mouth and backed away. Miss Beth flapped her hands in front of her and jogged in place on her tiptoes. Unfazed, Gina let go of the hair, jammed her gum wad back in her mouth, and shrugged.

We all fired questions at her, like how long had it been there, and didn't it feel gross to have a hair in your mouth all the time? Gina couldn't remember how long, and now she was used to it. She showed us how she could loop the hair around and around in her mouth, cinching it to a lower incisor.

Miss Beth hushed us. "You need to cut it," she said. Her voice was tight.

"No way," Gina said. She snapped her gum and climbed back up the bunk ladder.

Miss Miriam stood with her hands clasped, looking helplessly at Miss Beth. "Gina," she said. "It's not normal. What if keeps growing? You could choke on it in your sleep!"

Gina only shrugged and rolled her eyes, then flopped back on her bunk and clasped her knees to her chest. "It's my hair," she said, "and you can't make me. Now chuck me my stuff." She held out her arms.

I was in awe of her defiance, the way she so openly refused authority. In my home, that kind of lip would earn me extra chores. At Northside Christian School, a supervisor could discipline a student with a rubber stick for that level of rebellion. All my life, I'd been led to believe that being good counted, that for every gold star earned on earth, an eternal reward was being stored up for me in Heaven. But Miss Beth just picked up the paper grocery sack from the floor and passed it to Gina. I searched for signs of sternness on her face, but there was nothing, only a sweetness in her voice as she handed up the sleeping bag next and said, "Here you go."

Gina started to unpack, lifting out the sack's contents and placing them in a row along her bunk. A ratty hand-towel. A hairbrush. A single tube of lipstick that she uncapped, swiveled up, and then swiped bright red across her lips. She pulled out what looked to be a cocktail dress in a slinky black fabric, followed by a bikini, and a pair of sheer-fabric baby-doll pajamas, which she held up for everyone to see.

"My grandma let me borrow them," she said. Soopie glanced at me and raised an eyebrow and I stifled a laugh, but Gina didn't seem to notice. She began to unroll her sleeping bag on the foam mattress.

"Where's your pillow?" said Miss Miriam, her voice lilting and light.

I could see Gina taking inventory, eyeing our belongings. We had tucked all our suitcases and duffel bags beneath the bottom bunks and were pulling out our Bibles and notebooks to take along to the after-supper chapel service. I was guessing that if Gina hadn't packed a pillow, she surely hadn't brought a Bible. She blew her bangs out of her eyes with a puff from the corner of her mouth, then leveled her gaze down at both counselors. "Don't need one."

AT THE LONG plywood table in the mess hall, Gina complained about the sloppy joes. When the camp director, Mr. Toews, laid out the Ootsa rules for safety and goodwill, Gina slouched in her seat and yawned. When he reminded us that we weren't just here to follow rules, we were here to learn about the love of God, to get to know Jesus better, and to share that love with one another, I swore I heard Gina mutter beneath her breath, "Whatever." Each time she missed the mark, I couldn't help but feel the gleam of my own goodness brighten.

At the evening chapel service, we sat on wooden benches in our cabin groups as a counselor with shaggy, sunbleached hair and a trim blond mustache walked to the low podium and took his place in front of the music stand and microphone. Mr. Bryan looked like he belonged on a tropical beach or a TV cop show, not in a log-hewn chapel at a backwoods Mennonite Bible camp. In his presence, the boys seemed to straighten up, while the girls began to whisper to each other behind cupped hands. A ripple of giggles moved down the benches, girl to girl, in a strange contagion that even Soopie and I caught, unsure of what we were giggling at, and why our bodies couldn't help it.

Mr. Bryan flipped open his music book and called out the first song's number and title. As Miss Debbie at the piano chorded out the opening bars, he motioned with his hand for the boys to rise from their benches, and they obeyed. "Ladies, follow our lead!" said Mr. Bryan, and then began to sing our call to worship. On her end of the bench, Gina slouched, arms crossed over her chest, looking bored.

Back home I refused to sing in church when I stood beside my mother, choosing only to mouth the words because I knew it irked her, but seeing Gina made me want to stand. With sudden earnestness, I sang, letting my voice mingle with the others in a chorus that called down the power of God. On the other side of the room, even the boys rocked on their heels to the rhythm as they belted out the tune. Around me, the other girls swayed like the grasses at the water's edge. I knew that we were supposed to be singing for the Lord, but I couldn't help singing for Mr. Bryan, who smiled like a cool, handsome Jesus as he looked out over the choir of campers, as he looked out at me. And I couldn't help but sing for Gina, too—in spite of Gina, because of Gina—who hunched in her seat and fidgeted as she picked at her nail polish. She was here to let me rise a little higher toward the light.

BACK IN OUR cabin at bedtime, we lay on our bunks and listened to Miss Beth read our scripture passage for the week. If we memorized it, we could earn points to spend like money in the canteen that sold junk food. Cross-legged on her upper bunk, Gina sat feathering and re-feathering her hair with a plastic comb, ignoring the invitation to learn her Bible verses. In a breathy, high falsetto, she started to sing, "Thriller." She knew every song on the album by heart, she said. When she held the comb to her mouth like a microphone and closed her eyes, crooning out the lyrics, I wanted to tell her to shut up, but the words I'd been repeating, reciting—*For God so loved the world*—bridled me. While Gina lay on her top bunk and sang, Miss Beth and Miss Miriam slipped outside onto the porch to "have a little conversation." We knew they were out there talking about Gina in hushed voices. But if Gina herself knew, she didn't seem to care.

"Anybody ever French-kissed with a boy?" she said to no one in particular. Her question hung in the musty quiet of the cabin. When none of us answered, she let out a loud sigh, and then started singing "Billie Jean."

It wasn't simply that she couldn't name the twelve disciples, had no clue about the Crucifixion, the tomb, or Jesus rising from the dead, and didn't even know her Bible-story basics. Everything Gina did went against the Bible camp code. All the words I'd had washed out of me with soap were still alive in Gina's mouth and sprang vibrantly off her tongue. A *damn it* when she got a sliver in her foot from trying to moonwalk on the cabin's plank floor. *Jesus Christ* when she stubbed her toe on the bedpost. Every time she took the Lord's name in vain, Miss Beth or Miss Miriam pulled her aside for a hushed chat that probably involved the Bible verse that warned against the tongue as a deadly fire. I imagined Gina's tongue-hair sparking like a wick, drawing up the flame, illuminating our whole cabin.

Around the washhouse sinks and in outhouse lineups, Gina quickly became camp gossip, and not just because she had a hair growing on her tongue. A girl from Cabin A said she heard Gina was a foster child and Social Services had paid for her to come to Ootsa. Another girl guessed that probably Gina's parents didn't care about her. Or else they were dead. Maybe killed in a car accident or a house fire. No wonder she only had one pair of shoes.

But as Gina's mythology flourished so did her fame, as if the sadness of her story earned her extra points. "She can't help it," said one of the girls. *Poor Gina,* the other campers echoed. *Poor Gina.* Instead of leaving her at the back of the pack to solo as a loner through the week, everyone was moving toward her. She was breaking down the system that made sense to me. Her weirdness seemed to lure the other campers, not repel them. When she tried and failed to do a flip on the trampoline, they cheered for her, encouraged her to try again. At "Rise and Shine," when the rest of us jogged laps around the field, Gina sulked on the sidelines because the only shoes she'd packed were the red stilettos she'd arrived in. But instead of letting her sit by herself, one of the female counselors stayed beside her, talking with her, sometimes touching a hand to her arm with the gentleness of a mom, showing the rest of us what it looked like to *be ye kind one to another,* like the verse we sang at chapel time. In my head, I had a list of all the reasons Gina wasn't worthy of this kindness, and reasons why I was. But no counselor was patting me on the arm, or braiding a friendship bracelet for me in the craft hut, then tying it around my wrist.

"Look," Gina bragged, holding up her hand for everyone to see. "Miss Brenda made one just for me!"

When the other girls wowed at the colors and the candy-stripe design and let Gina flaunt her gift, I knew I was supposed to tell her it was pretty, too, that she was lucky and I wished I had one just like it, but what I wished for instead was a pair of scissors to snip down and cut away that bracelet, leaving her as lacking as my heart.

ON FRIDAY, the last full day of camp, Mr. Toews announced that we'd all be going on a hike up Little Ootsa Mountain. We'd leave after lunch and be back in time to clean up for the evening banquet.

Inside Cabin C, Gina was refusing Miss Beth's offer of a pair of sneakers from the lost and found.

"They don't fit," she said. "I can wear my own shoes."

No one could dissuade her, not even Miss Miriam, who offered to stay behind with her while the rest of us hiked. But Gina didn't want to miss out. She slid on her red heels and clacked out the door.

Beneath a heavy veil of cloud, we trudged in dust and heat, a small multitude on a slow ascent into the hills. Mr. Toews led with a compass and a walking stick, and the other counselors spaced themselves throughout our group. Mr. Bryan took up the rear, which meant a throng of us girls hung back, vying to be close to him.

The braver girls asked Mr. Bryan questions about his life back home. Did he have a girlfriend? Did he want to find a wife? No girlfriend, he said, and laughed, but one day, sure, he wouldn't mind getting married. I matched my stride to his, angling ever closer as we hiked, listening to everything he said. Gina, determined to keep pace, wobbled alongside me in her heels, shrieking every time a rut or stone threatened to turn her ankle, which I hoped it would so she would fall behind.

The higher we hiked, the more the hyper chatter faded, so that soon, we were a climbing chain of breath and sweat. The gravel road forked to a tire-worn trail through saplings and brush, and we turned onto a path worn down by moose, elk, and the boots of hunters. My lungs burned from the ascent, but I was determined to stick with Mr. Bryan, who took long, slow strides and kept glancing over his shoulder. Gina was lagging. Barefoot and carrying a red shoe in each hand, she stepped around the roots and rocks that knotted the terrain, calling *ouch* and muttering cusses.

"Let's wait," Mr. Bryan said. His direction echoed up the chain of hikers so that everyone slowed, and he fell to the back with Gina, until they were both behind me. Though I couldn't make out what they were talking about, Gina's shift in mood was audible, her laughter brash. When I turned around to see what was so funny, Mr. Bryan was crouched low on the trail, and Gina was climbing on his back.

"Coming through," he called out. He trekked past me, past the skinny soccer girls, and in a final sprint against the fastest boys, he piggybacked Gina the rest of the way up the hill. At the top, he set her down, high-fived her, then leaned over, his hands on his knees, to catch his breath. Gina beamed. She set her red shoes on the ground, and slipped her dirty feet back into them, then wobbled to Mr. Bryan's side for the group photo.

As we pressed together on the muggy mosquito-thick hill and posed for the camp director's camera, I felt the voltage of Gina's happiness as the snuffing of my own. Smiling beside Mr. Bryan, she stood taller and teetering in her heels, one row above me. Every day of camp, I stood on the chapel steps and flawlessly recited my memory verse. I kept a tidy bunk, made sure my sleeping bag and pillow were free of wrinkles. I did my morning chores without complaint. I followed the rules outlined by the camp. But still, the sum of all my strivings had not made my name rise. The song we sang in chapel argued in my heart: *It only takes a spark to get a fire going.* According to the chorus, that spark was God's love, an elemental force that started small and spread each time one person passed it to another. I was supposed to grab that spark, swallow it, let it grow to be a fire whose love I gave away for free, not a fire whose warmth and light I wouldn't share.

WE RETURNED to camp with one hour to gussy up for the banquet. As each girl took her turn in front of the mirror nailed on the cabin wall, combing and spritzing and feathering her hair, Gina sat on her bunk in a slinky black dress cinched at the waist, swinging her high-heeled feet and fiddling with her tongue-hair. All week, Miss Beth and Miss Miriam had been advocating for the hair's removal. Every time Gina flicked out her tongue-hair or tugged at it absent-mindedly while we sat in a circle for cabin devotions, one of us would give another reason why the hair must go, trying to convince her that it was gross and disgusting, not cool, to have a hair growing from your tongue.

Now, Gina slid down from the bunk in her dress and red shoes and planted herself in front of Miss Beth.

"Okay," Gina said. "Cut it off."

"Are you sure?" said Miss Beth. She was already rifling through her makeup bag, as if sensing she needed to seize the moment before Gina changed her mind. She held up a pair of nail clippers.

Gina opened her mouth. We crowded near—Soopie and Heather and Tanya and Laura and Miss Miriam, all of us eager to bear witness.

"Hold still," Miss Beth said, and reached for the tongue-hair, then drew her hand back. It took her a few tries to actually touch the hair, but finally, she grabbed hold of it, pinched it between her thumb and forefinger, and pulled it taut. Behind her, Miss Miriam stood on tiptoes with a hand over her mouth.

"Okay," said Miss Beth, "here goes." With the silver blades held against the taste bud from which the hair grew, Miss Beth made a single clip. At the *snick* of the clippers, she jumped back and flicked the hair from her fingers.

"Hey," said Gina, "I want it!" She dropped to her knees and ran her hands over the cabin floor, searching for the strand, but came up with only dust.

Then Gina, like the rest of us, took her turn before the smudged square mirror nailed to the wall. She opened her mouth and stuck out her tongue. She swished it back and forth inside her smile. "Weird," she said, studying her reflection as if she were looking at herself for the first time. On my bunk, I watched her smile and show her teeth. The elastic waistband of my white skirt, one my mother had sewn just for camp, dug into my gut. If the other girls were bothered by Gina's preening and delight, they didn't seem to show it, too caught up with the giddiness of a banquet where each of us would be ushered into the mess hall by one of the male counselors. I already knew who'd offer Gina his arm, who'd lead her to the table. I could hear Mr. Bryan telling her how lovely she looked in her black dress and those red shoes, as she tottered beside him toward the feast laid out for us all, a feast where the last and the outcasts and the weirdos came first, and those striving to be first fell to the back of the line.

THE LAST NIGHT at Ootsa, we lay in our sleeping bags and listened to Miss Miriam and Miss Beth pray for each one of us by name, for Heather, for Tanya, for Laura, for Soopie, for Gina, for me. May all we learned this week make a difference in our lives. Help us know that God is love and how to love each other like God first loved us. May we leave camp changed, different than when we arrived. The words they prayed floated through the cabin hush like dust sparks, and I wanted to grab them all, swallow every particle of light that fell so that the inside of me would glow. From the darkness of my lower bunk, I listened as the breathing of the other girls evened into sleep. Above my head, looped around a ladder rung, my God's-eye dangled.

"This will remind you that He's always watching you," Miss Brenda had told us, demonstrating in the craft hut how to wind and wind our rainbow-colored yarn around the popsicle-stick frame. Her words—*He's always watching you*—had sounded first like comfort, then like warning.

I felt it now, that hexagonal rainbowed eye that saw the truth in me, the words I thought before I ever spoke them, the junk that smoldered in my head and heart, that hidden world that brewed in me, a world for which I had no name. Gina, with her *Thriller* songs, her red shoes, her vulgar tongue, punched a hole clean through the pattern I thought I understood, the gospel I'd always believed, a hole down which all my trophies and gold stars flew, vanishing like garbage down the chute, trash to the incinerator. Nothing I could do would make me worthy. Nothing I could do would make me pure. That God's-eye burned.

It eased the heat in me to imagine Gina's life beyond Ootsa, to think of her returning from camp to a junky trailer park, a mobile home with battered siding and a weedy yard rusting with beater cars and broken toys. Inside, a baby cried from behind a bedroom door. In a dim wood-paneled living room, a mom sat on a chesterfield smoking while the TV blared game shows, and a dad, if she had one, smashed his fist through the wall when he came back drunk at night.

When I pictured Gina in that lowly world, I could feel a little sorry for her, sorry enough for a glimmer to begin inside me, the start of a spark that threatened to catch. I could hold still and beg for a breath to come and ember it, exalt the flame until it held me, too, and burned off all the dross, made me light enough to rise. I could yearn for that fire, for that kind of love, and let it consume me. Or I could lie in my bunk, staring through the darkness where Gina breathed, and snuff that spark. It was easier to list the ways my life was good, and to return to the world where I could earn my goodness.

Back home, I had a family to whom I belonged. Every Saturday morning, bread rose in loaves on our kitchen counter and the record player turned out hymns, not Michael Jackson. In a summer garden blooming and green, my mother knelt, pulling chickweed and quack grass, saving me from chores. Somewhere in the coolness of his shop, my father nursed a beer, but he wasn't always in a grumpy mood. Sometimes, he whistled while he monkey wrenched his trucks. Behind the woodshed, by the empty oil drum, my brother cocked his gun to load another pellet. He didn't always shoot the squirrel or the grouse. Down a trail worn through brush and deadfall, into the thickness of the forest, the empty tree fort creaked in the scrubby birch and fir, and the ladder leading higher and higher still lay waiting to be climbed.

THE CHANGEROOM

ⅹ ⅹ ⅹ ⅹ ⅹ ⅹ ⅹ

THEY HAD TOLD ME TO MEET THEM at break time in the basement. With the school field and courtyard still covered in a crust of ice that fluxed between melt and thaw, we mostly stayed indoors for recess. On the far side of the long, carpeted room, boys grappled and headlocked each other in wrestling matches. The girls stayed close to the walls, or near the cubbyholes, which was where I stood, scarfing down a cookie, when Leigh and Pearl arrived.

They were my cousins, older by only a few years, but seeming to me already like young women. They wore their hair long, pulled back with silver barrettes in the style of those I deemed most proper and pure, never inappropriate in their jokes, always saying "fluff" instead of "fart." In their presence, I wanted to stand with a straighter spine. Pearl, the eldest, had even started wearing a mesh prayer cap, a sign that she was a young woman devoted to God.

"We brought something for you," said Leigh, her voice like a secret. She glanced side to side, then reached into her cubby, pulled out a brown paper grocery sack, and clutched it to her chest.

"Come with us," Pearl whispered. "To the changeroom."

Curious and with a gut-buzz of anticipation, I followed them through the wide-open basement with its games of flying, sweaty bodies and down the hallway into the girls' changeroom. An aerosol haze of deodorant and hairspray lingered, the room smelling of baby powder and vague flowers. Usually, the changeroom was off limits to me, used only as a place to whisper with friends or hide from boys when the monitors and supervisors weren't watching. The space belonged to the girls in the upper grades. Along the walls, their vests and skirts hung on hooks, swapped for the sky-blue cotton culottes they wore as gym strip. Over in the church sanctuary, which doubled as our gymnasium, the senior girls were now doing toe-touches and jumping jacks, while the senior boys in their blue T-shirts and gray sweatpants did push-ups and sit-ups in another section of the building, the females and males separated to prevent distraction.

I was almost old enough for my own pair of culottes, which my mom, like the other school mothers, would sew from a pattern that circulated house to house. The culottes were designed to disguise the curves of the blossoming female body, belling out from the hips like a skirt for each leg, with the hemline falling well below the kneecap. Once donned, they turned every girl into the classic stick-figure drawing, her lower body angling into an isosceles triangle. During calisthenics, each girl had to clutch the excess fabric whenever she performed side leg raises, the culottes sliding up along the thighs with every lift, revealing flashes of gusset and flesh that lured the peeping boys. But no matter how much the girls complained about the culottes, they had to wear them anyway. Pants were not allowed, as stipulated by our school's governing authority, an organization based in Texas whose policies, which included daily morning chapel, scripture memorization, demerits for bad behavior, and always leaving at least six inches between male and female students, were rumored to have been inspired by the Russian prison system.

My cousins stood before me as if readying to lead me in prayer or hand me an award.

Leigh held out the brown bag to me. "Now you can open it."

Whatever I'd expected to find—homemade cookies, a few Christian comic books, or even old hair barrettes they no longer wore—was not what I saw at the bottom of the paper sack. Inside the bag lay a snaky tangle of fabric in various pastel shades.

Pearl leaned in with a hushed voice. "Our mom said we should give them to you. That it was time for you to start wearing one."

I reached into the bag and pulled out a bra. It looked like the sort my mother wore, in the same bland beige and slippery material, only smaller and with padding in the cups. "Do you want to try it on?" she said. "We can help."

I shoved the bra back in and rolled up the paper bag. "I can do it later." The idea of taking off my shirt in front of them made me nervous, and made me feel like their mother, my aunt Sharon, was watching from some peephole in the wall. I had no way of knowing if their gift was normal, if it was a tradition for females in every family to hand down their undergarments to younger cousins. I wondered if the boys did this sort of thing, too, and whether my brother had been yanked into the changeroom by the older male cousins and given his own grocery sack.

For the rest of the day at school, as I worked my way through decimals and predicate adjectives and the geography of the Canadian Shield, I couldn't stop thinking about those bras. I'd flipped through the Intimates section of the Sears catalogue enough to know that they were coming for me. I'd studied the Junior girl models whose narrow torsos sported bright white bras. With their hair combed to an otherworldly shine, they gazed with smug smiles at something outside the frame, as if they knew a secret but weren't yet willing to spill it, like the teenage girls at school who whispered to each other behind cupped hands, then gasped and laughed. I had questions, like how did breasts grow anyways, and what caused some to swell like homemade buns, while others stayed like pancakes? Why did every grade-six boy want to hook his finger around the band of every girl's bra and let it snap? What about my body made Aunt Sharon send those bras? The thought that other eyes were noticing, that I wasn't the only one studying my chest before the mirror, made me want to button up inside my winter coat and hide.

AS SOON AS I got home from school, I kicked off my shoes and raced up the stairs to my bedroom.

"Snack?" my mom called.

"Not hungry," I said, and locked my door behind me. Inside, away from my mother's eyes, I pulled the paper bag out of my backpack and dumped the contents onto my bed.

Beige and white and pink slid out. Sprigs of flowers on the fabric. Slippery bits and hooks and clasps. Amid the snake's-nest pile, a pale-blue bra with thin, scalloped straps lay coiled.

I plucked it out and held it up, inspecting the shape and structure. A bra was, I realized, nothing more than a bikini top. I'd never been allowed to wear a bikini but had always envied the girls at summer swimming lessons who paraded the pool deck in their two-piece bathing suits like beauty pageant hopefuls.

I had to turn my back on the mirror as I wrestled on the bra, embarrassed to see what I looked like as I shoved my arms through the strap loops, then twisted to fit the hook into the eye, unsure if I was doing any of it right, if I was supposed to be sweating this much, my hands tingling with pins and needles. But when I turned to face my vanity, the torso that looked back at me no longer looked mine. Soft in the paunch, thick around the middle, extra with flesh—I recognized these parts. But with the bra on, with the stretchy band digging into the fat around my ribs, and with the straps chafing my shoulders, I felt tight, hemmed in, bound up.

"Knock, knock," my mother called, her voice muffled on the other side of the door.

I whipped my T-shirt on, as if my mother's eyes might spy me through the walls and wood.

"What are you doing in there?" she said.

"Nothing," I called back. "Just changing."

After I grabbed my after-school snack, I tiptoed down the hall to my parents' bedroom. I pushed open their door and stood in front of the full-length mirror. Already, I could see the difference the bra made. I slipped the neckline of my T-shirt down over one shoulder so that the strap was visible. I turned sideways again and pulled back my shoulder blades, pushing out my chest.

"Are you wearing a bra?" My mother's voice behind me made me jump.

I tugged my T-shirt into place. "No. Yes. I guess."

When I explained where the bra had come from, and how Aunt Sharon had suggested it was time for me to wear one, my mother, for a long moment, said nothing. She peered into the paper bag full of my cousins' hand-me-down underwear. "Hmm," she said. Her mouth cinched to a tight line. "That's interesting." Then she went back to the kitchen to loudly stir the pot that simmered on the element.

I plunked down on the couch, in front of the TV and the final scene of *The Young and the Restless*, Victor and Ashley embracing again, his mustache against her ear. I wondered how she could stand the bristle and scratch of his whiskers, and what kind of bra she was wearing, and whether she let Victor see it, run his finger over the scallops and lace. I could feel the itch of my own bra knotting my ribcage. As the credits began to roll, the screen went dark. When I turned around, my mother stood with the remote control in her hand.

"But Oprah's next," I said, motioning for her to switch the TV back on.

She took a deep breath and walked over to the fireplace, then sat down on the hearth. "I want to talk to you about something," she said. Her face wore a strange, unsettling expression, like she was about to tell me that another relative had died, that someone had cancer, there'd been an accident, Dad was dead, she was pregnant.

"You're changing," she said. Her voice was brisk, authoritative. "You're going through some changes."

I felt the quick grip of panic. "What kind of changes?" A brief internal scan blinked a sequence of possibilities: wanting to sit next to Alec Horvat at the campfire, the Michael Damian cassette tape I snuck home from Ruth's house, the weird clammy smell of my armpits after a game of prisoner's base.

She picked at the knee of her polyester pants. "Puberty," she said.

My pulse jetted into my throat. In our family, we didn't speak like this—with medical terminology, with specificity and precision of language. We spoke in euphemism, with code words for the realm of hidden body parts. *Down there.* Your *"you know."* Your *"pee-ter."* The way my mother said the word *puberty* made it seem as if she were reciting the script of a pamphlet picked up from the public health unit.

"Okay?" I said, staring at the blank TV screen as if it still flashed images. Inwardly, my radar cranked to full alert, sending out a message to *deflect, deflect!*

But my mother wasn't done. "You're entering it—puberty."

Entering. As if it were a room, and I was being yarded through the doorway.

"And I wanted to talk to you about—"

"About what?" I cut her off with a mean huff meant to shut her down. I did not want to hear any of the anatomical lexicon of adolescence coming from my mother's mouth. It was bad enough when she asked me about my stomach-aches, whether or not my "bowels were moving." This was part of my inheritance—this inability to name the body and what went on beneath the skin of it. Though we could stand side by side in a church foyer and stare into an open coffin at a body prepared for burial, though we could whisper after the funeral about how orangey the pallor, how waxy the face, we could not say words like "sorrow" and "heartache" and "trauma." Instead, we said, "That's the way it is," and "Life goes on." I'd later learn that my mom had been handed the same inheritance from her mother, and my grandma from her own mother, too. There were certain words they did not say. On their Kansas farm, even the male cattle were called "papa cows," because the word "bull" was deemed too crude, too rooted in the rutting that happened on the far side of the fence. No one spoke about the body's workings. All its parts stayed hidden, unlabeled, left to speculation and guesswork, like an Old Order Mennonite bride beneath her loose, black dress.

From her perch on the hearth, my mother took a deep breath and ran a hand over one side of her face, then half-yawned, or at least pretended to, casual and nonchalant. "Your body," she said, "is changing." Before I could stop her, the words sprang forth. "You're going to—going to grow... *hair*—in places. *Different* places."

Hearing my mother talk like this was like the sound of metal scraping metal, like watching someone crying in church, like walking in on Soopie's dad hunkered on the toilet, reading the latest issue of *Outdoor Life*. I wanted to flee, to clap my hands over my ears, my eyes, to launch myself out of the room, out of my body. But I'd come to understand that a far better tactic was to keep cool, to wield the weapon of disdain. I drew in a long, slow breath, exhaled, and then rolled my eyes with the leisure of a bored soap-opera heiress at a fancy cocktail party.

"You don't think I already know?" I shook my head and forced a smirk. "Mother," I said, letting the word hang a moment, like a bubble I intended to burst. "I probably know more than you."

She dropped her chin. "Excuse me?" She leveled a scorching glare at me. "You have no clue what you're talking about," she said.

"Neither do you," I said.

And I meant it, puffed up with whatever it was that had eclipsed my sense of wonder at the world, my smallness in it. Though my mother had been alive nearly three decades longer than I, her knowledge seemed scant and out of date, while mine was newly brimming over. After all, I'd read the secret book in the school library, the unassuming paperback with the brown-and-orange cover whose title suggested nothing spectacular, just an overview of how God made the human body. During library time, when Jenny Teichroeb and I were supposed to be organizing the books in alphabetical order, we'd flipped through to the list of definitions. Past the cardiovascular and digestive systems, past the brain, and to the single page dedicated to reproduction. I huddled next to Jenny and together we parsed out the words never spoken aloud in our homes, words I'd never before heard.

"Maybe like Regina?" Jenny said. "In Saskatchewan?" She pointed to the diagram labeled "female." We sounded out the various possibilities, whispering alternate pronunciations. For the male anatomy, I was confident. "It rhymes with tennis," I said. Though both of us had questions about the terms and definitions, we knew we couldn't ask any of the monitors or supervisors. Clearly, they had no clue our four-shelf plank-and-cinderblock library contained a book with such forbidden language.

I'd remained unsure about the words until, at the bus stop, I told my first dirty joke, stolen from a movie about a man who fell in love with a mermaid. The public-school girls bent over and laughed—at the joke, I assumed. But then they kept laughing, slapping their thighs and wiping tears from the corners of their eyes. Finally, Dawn Hoggins, the grade-twelve girl whose high-top running shoes glittered with beaded friendship pins in their laces, caught her breath. "It's PEE-nis," she gasped, "not PEN-nis," and then all the girls started laughing again.

In what would become my go-to response in times of humiliation, I joined their laughter, blatting out loud *ha-ha-ha*'s as if my cheeks weren't pink with shame, as if I didn't think that God was right then doling out a custom punishment, His version of washing out my mouth with soap. Clearly, that word was dangerous, no matter how it was pronounced. "PEN-nis!" I said. "That's the joke! PEN-nis! That's what makes it so hilarious!"

In that moment of my mother trying to talk to me, to speak what had never been spoken to her before, the distance between us seemed to grow wider, longer. She sat at the far end of the living room with the fire at her back. At the opposite end, I curled away from her, my body tightening in on itself. My mother made a noise that was half cough, half sigh, then rose from the hearth, threw her hands up, and walked out of the room. I felt like I'd won the argument but lost something in the fight. The truth was that I didn't quite know what was happening to my body. Yes, the hair in *different* places, the sprouts of underarm fuzz, the eerie, errant strands of other hair, the oniony, cheese-bag smells, and that Tilt-A-Whirl feeling when Eddie Ramsay and I made eye contact across the aisle during chapel prayer.

Before I saw the word "puberty" spelled out on the page of the forbidden school library book, I heard it as "puperty," which sounded to me like a gloopy perfume, or a stage in the life cycle of a butterfly. Like the caterpillar cocooned, nestled in its pupal goo and waiting to emerge, the body, too, moved through phases, through the moistness of glands and hidden bits, through oily flesh and odors, the sudden largeness of the nose, the shine of the chin and forehead, the pox-crop of pimples and pus speckles rising, and that unnameable itch inside the bones—no, deeper than the bones, and more than an itch. It was a cinching of skin over bones, and the bones growing at odd angles, rearranging themselves from within, and the feeling that every eye in any room was staring at this metamorphosis of ordinary child into horror-clown monster-blob creature of the deep.

I didn't know if the weird gnawing sensation in my rib-cage was gallstones or cancer or only the common twist and ache of early adolescence, the launch of the flesh's betrayal. How to make it stop was anyone's guess. I'd tried plucking the strands of hair that kept sprouting in my armpits, tearing them out with my mother's tweezers behind the locked bathroom door, but those hairs grew back and brought with them more hair, leaving me to wonder if soon the hair would fuzz my face, if I'd develop the same shadow of a mustache that haunted my brother's upper lip. I couldn't tell if what I saw was normal, if other bodies looked and felt like mine. Always, I'd been taught to keep my body covered, to hide behind the drawn curtain and the locked door, and to turn away from nakedness, both others' and my own. But in the bathroom every night before bed, I stood on the edge of the tub to get a better view of my body in the vanity. The tri-fold mirror, at that height and angle, only seemed to widen and cut me into pieces, like the warp of a funhouse reflection that couldn't be trusted.

WHEN MY mother came in to recite with me our bedtime prayer, I stiffened in her presence.

"Goodnight," I said, holding the distance between us.

She bent down to kiss me on the forehead, and then paused. "Are you still wearing the bra?" she said. I pulled the blanket to my chin to hide the straps that showed beneath my nightgown. "You take off your bra when you sleep," she said. "You don't wear it all the time."

"I know that," I shot back. My head felt hot. "I just wanted to wear it to bed."

Truth was, I didn't know. I thought that once I hook-and-eyed it on, I was forever bound by the scratch and itch, the feeling of being tightly leashed around the chest. When she closed my door and left me in the dark, I sat up, wriggled out of the bra, and chucked it across the room. All night, on the carpet, its shadow-shape lay coiled.

ON THE WAY home from school the next day, instead of driving straight through town and over the train tracks toward home, my mother hung a left at the traffic light. "Let's stop at Fields," she said. "Do a little shopping."

If you didn't count the coveralls and gumboots for sale in the Co-op's hardware section, Fields was one of four shops in town that sold clothes. The boys-and-men's section lay on the opposite side of the store from the girls'-and-ladies' wear and was separated by a wide main aisle. But the underwear section was housed together at the center of the store, right outside the changerooms. That's where my mother headed when we walked through the door.

"Can I help you?" said a clerk with a name tag and a key ring, as she looked up from the stack of cardboard boxes she was unpacking.

"We're looking for a bra," said my mother, glancing from the clerk to me. She didn't need to say the word "new." Fields didn't sell secondhand clothes, but even if they did, I had the sense that used underwear was where my mom drew the line, especially if Aunt Sharon was the one to offer it. "A training bra," my mother added. Her voice sounded too big, too heavy on the word "bra," a word that seemed to hang open-jawed in the air. The clerk smiled down at me, and I wanted to go small and crawl inside the rack of shirts like I did as a kid playing shopping hide-and-seek.

She pointed us toward a rack of huge cups and thick straps in a color called "nude," the shade of beige assigned to females as they aged. Beige shoes, beige pantyhose, beige underwear, beige purse, beige tuna casserole with a can of mushroom soup, beige wall-to-wall carpet hushing the footfall in a split-level house. A message from the future whispered *beige, beige, beige*, a soft, hypnotic syllable ushering me toward womanhood and boredom. But as my mother pushed the hangers of beige out of the way, a collection of small, pastel-colored bras appeared in the colors of springtime, baby showers, and rows of bridesmaid dresses. She held a plain training bra up to my body and pressed it against my chest. I flinched.

"Just go try some on," she said, and pulled a few off the rack.

With the changeroom door shut and the lock in place, I inspected the bra. It was white with a tiny pink ribbon at the center where the quilted cups joined. The fabric felt cottony and soft. The straps, which were satiny and smooth instead of scalloped and scratchy like the hand-me-down bra I was still wearing, had a slight shine to them. On either side of me, bodies in their own changerooms shuffled, unzipped, and buttoned.

Though the partitions between the changerooms were solid, I could see socked feet, and the pants puddled around the ankles of strangers. I had the feeling that if any of us inside these rooms had Superman's x-ray vision, or a pair of those glasses advertised at the back of comic books, this place would be dangerous. What if Eddie Ramsay was on one side, I thought, and on the other, my older cousins, Leigh and Pearl, or Aunt Sharon, and the walls between us suddenly fell, so that we all stood in our skin, birthday-suited like in the beginning, before the Garden's Fall and fig leaves covering up what we were born into. What if, instead of the dumb tongue, the reddened cheeks, the turning away, we wore our bodies with boldness, all their parts named rightly, anatomy's secrets sung into the air like a chant in Latin, turning the whole room holy. Everyone in Fields would emerge new and pink inside the room's cool fluorescence. Naked and unashamed, we'd stand and face each other like clean, bright mirrors reflecting back the truth— that we were fearfully and wonderfully made.

Outside, the sun was peeling back another layer of winter's hard-packed ice. On the other side of the changeroom door, my mother called my name, asking did it fit, did I want her help, did I need her to come in? I tugged my T-shirt up over my head and dropped it on the floor. I slid the white bra off its hanger and turned toward the mirror. Above me, the store light sizzled, heating up the greener season, the unfurling of the leaf and the bud, the cocoon loosening on its twig, unraveling the stitches of its gauze and silk.

The eye that mocks a father
and scorns to obey a mother
will be picked out
by the ravens of the valley
and eaten by the vultures.

PROVERBS 30:17

⚹ ⚹ ⚹ ⚹ ⚹

THE RED APRON

x x x x x x x

IN THE MUDDY LIGHT OF the overnight bus, with dawn easing pink over the horizon, the man in the seat ahead of me lifted his head and loudly yawned. On the window, where he'd leaned his curly tangle of brown hair, an oily sheen clouded the glass with a thin smear of what looked like mayonnaise. He groaned, punched his arms in the air, and stretched, then humped around in his seat for a new position. Beside him, an older woman in a flowered dress slumped to the side, her chin tipped to her chest, her open mouth visible through the crack between the armrests. Her white hair was coiled on top of her head, braided and yellowed as a sun-frayed rope. From the way he had raised his voice at her when they first boarded, I guessed she was the man's mother. He'd been mad that she couldn't find her ticket when the driver made his way down the aisle counting passengers and tearing off stubs. The old woman had patted her son's forearm, said, "Shh, shh," like she was soothing a cranky toddler, but he'd swatted her hand away, slammed back in his seat, and muttered curses. Even after the driver helped the woman dig through her purse and they found the ticket stub, the son still sulked, already fed up with the long miles ahead, huffing at whatever his mother said to him. She only sighed back into her seat and soon dropped off to sleep.

Beside me, my mother dozed, too, curled away from me, her mouth slack and breath lightly whistling. *Just don't let me snore*, she'd said, paranoid that other passengers would hear. Into the Cariboo sunset and the shadows of the Chilcotin, through the Fraser Canyon, our bus chugged. At every small town, we pulled into the all-night station and filed out to line up for the scuzz-crusted bathrooms with empty paper towel dispensers and no soap in the pump. Then back into the bus we climbed, shuffled to our seats, and onward in darkness we moved, travelers bound together by the journey. My mother read her magazines until the sky's light drained to only moon and stars, and then she curled back into sleep. With my Walkman headphones clamped over my ears and the volume cranked to mask the engine rumble, I watched the landscape whip by like a music video montage of dense forest, farm fields, the scrub of desert hills, and the chain of tunnels carved through mountains.

We were headed for Oregon, birth state of my mother, for a big family reunion. When my mom listed all the cousins and aunts and uncles who'd be attending, some of the names sounded familiar, but I didn't really know any of them. They existed as characters in a story I'd been told was true, a story into which I was supposed to fit, too. I hadn't seen most of them since the last reunion, nearly a decade earlier. In our album photographs of that gathering, I was a four-year-old with white-blonde hair, cuffs rolled up as I waded into the Pacific. Among my cousins, I was one of the only girls wearing pants. Still, as a child, I blended in easily with the other kids, all of us sweaty-faced and filthy from digging in the sand, running into the waves. But older now, in jeans, T-shirt, and high-top running shoes, I knew I looked the part of a girl my relatives might deem worldly, especially with my hair cut short and feathered back to show off my newly pierced ears. When I twisted the silver studs, I still felt the snag of the flesh, the sting of the gun that punched the hole without my parents' permission. "You shoulda got one in your nose," my dad had said, mad at the supper table when he saw what I had done. "A ring in your nose like a pig," he said, "and then a chain hooked on to lead you around." My mom had only shaken her head and said I should be grounded.

Though the spectrum of Mennonite-ness was wide and varied in the strictness of religious views, most of the houses on my mother's side of the family were not like ours. Their living rooms were TV-free. Their coffee tables held no ashtrays. No blue-gray haze of cigarette smoke hung above the table past midnight while the playing cards were dealt. Their guests did not hold up tumblers for another round of gin or whiskey. My mother's side of the family seemed to me so good, so clean, more into prayer meetings and the Maranatha! Singers than cribbage tournaments and heartbreak honky-tonk. They were closer to the truth, or at least, to the tradition, of what it meant to be Mennonite, remembering that they were citizens of a kingdom that wasn't of this world.

As I leaned against the cool window with the tinny, driving rhythms of Night Ranger filling my head, I figured I'd need to hide my rock cassettes in my suitcase, burying them under the contemporary gospel music I'd brought to balance out the contraband. Though groups like Silverwind and White Heart were labeled "Christian rock," they at least had songs with titles like "We Will Give Him Glory" and "Sing unto the Lamb." If I needed to, I could pull out the little folded insert from the case and show off the lyrics, proving to my relatives that Jesus was in this music, that I was faithful to our family heritage and still worthy of belonging to our righteous tribe.

We'd always been an exodus people, a clan of Anabaptists on the move, pacifists dodging war, pilgrims fleeing persecution, devoted to the way of Jesus, and always on the hunt for a better promised land. Our people had always been at odds with the world, never quite fitting in with the culture of the day. That was our inheritance, I was taught, the plight of the Amish and the Mennonites. With each telling and retelling, the family narrative glowed, burnished to near-mythology as it passed down through the generations, naming our lives as meaningful within the scope of eternity and ensuring we'd never forget our roots, which sank down in holy ground. This story was my birthright, my inheritance if I claimed it and let my life be framed by it.

Great-Aunt Millie, Grandpa Shenk's older sister, was the keeper of the history. She maintained the records of births and deaths, but more than that, she wove them into a narrative that made me believe I was part of something far larger than a simple genealogy. Whenever she visited, I sat with my cousins at her feet to hear her tell stories, especially the one about the little red apron.

"Oh, yes, that one," Aunt Millie would say, her hands folded on her lap, her voice soft and reedy, her prayer-capped head nodding as she spoke.

The red apron was at the heart of all our stories, the center of the wheel that rolled our family through time and space. It was our proof of God, the emblem of our faith, the fragment of a map that showed how far we'd come. It was the shadow melody in every hymn we sang. Every time a female stood inside a kitchen and tied the strings of her apron, her body wore the story, and the story bound itself to her. The red apron was hunger and feast. It was the body and blood, womb to grave.

When Aunt Millie told the story, her voice sombered to a reverence reserved for sacred text. "In the beginning," she said, "they all lived in peace." Because Catherine the Great of Russia had offered Mennonite settlers absolute freedom for one hundred years, they migrated east from Germany into the Empire, hoping to find a land in which they could live out their convictions without fear of persecution. But over the years, as wars continued to erupt across Europe, the Emperor eventually demanded that all able-bodied men take up arms. And because our people did not believe in war, Aunt Millie explained, many were arrested, locked in prison, or worse still, shot or hanged for their refusal to fight.

The cast of ancestors was hard to keep track of, but I knew that the story's red apron belonged to Baby Elizabeth, the youngest child of Johann and Barbara Strauss, who were my mother's father's great-great-grandparents. No matter that more than a century separated us, no matter how far removed these people were from me by blood and time, they came alive in my mind's eye when Aunt Millie told the story. It was as if Johann and his neighbor Peter Kauffman were even now plotting their escape, sneaking away from their homes by cover of night, taking little Elizabeth with them, so that, without a baby to carry, the women and older children might make the journey more fleetly.

They slept in shocks of hay and in barns, hiding from anyone who might report them to the authorities. A day later, the women and children followed the same route, walking by light, sleeping in fields and barns at night, hoping to find Johann and Peter and the baby somewhere near the village of Nordenburg, in the Russian Zone.

"Imagine," said Aunt Millie, her hands on her lap smoothing out the fabric of her skirt, "how frightening that journey and how many miles they had to go."

And I could imagine it—their fear, the way my own blood-quick adrenaline spiked in a nighttime game of kick the can or capture the flag, fleeing in darkness, and holding my breath when strange footsteps or a murmur came close. As Aunt Millie told the story, I entered it, became one of the travelers in that tribe.

After almost two months of walking, the women and children had run out of food and money. On a September evening, as dusk began to deepen the sky and draw out the stars, they spotted a light in a farmhouse window. When they knocked on the door, hoping only for shelter in the barn, the German couple who lived there welcomed them in. That night, around the table of these strangers, they sat together as friends. They ate hot soup and fresh bread and slept in real beds. In the morning, sent off with kind wishes for a safe journey, the women felt a small surge of hope that they might yet see their husbands and the baby.

Later that day, as they stopped to rest by a cool stream, one of the boys called out that he could see a man walking toward them down the road. When the stranger approached, he began speaking to them in their native German, though with an accent they didn't recognize. He'd come, he said, from Russia, looking for a party of two women and six children. Were their names Strauss and Kauffman?

Yes, the women answered, yes, they were Barbara Strauss and Marie Kauffman, the wives of Johann and Peter. The man said he'd come to guide them safely to their husbands.

And here, Aunt Millie paused, leaned in, and wondered what we all were wondering. "Could they trust this man?" she said. "Would he lead them to safety or to danger? Were their husbands still alive?"

This was when the man, whose name was Katosky, pulled from his pocket a piece of cloth, and held it out to Barbara. In her grasp, the cloth unfolded—the red apron, the one she'd sewn by hand for her daughter. She wept as she held it to her face, searching for the scent of her child, her husband, home. Johann, knowing that his wife might doubt a strange man's word, had sent the apron as a sign that they could trust Katosky to lead them safely into Russia. Many days and miles later, the group walked into the village of Kovno. Johann and Peter, who had been working the fields in Katosky's absence, threw down their tools and ran to meet their wives and children. They told them of the perilous journey, but also of God's protection over them— how they'd always found shelter and food when they needed it most. And the women responded with the story of their own miraculous passage.

"And Barbara Strauss," said Aunt Millie, "your great-great-great-*great*-grandmother, held little Elizabeth in her arms and vowed that the red apron would never be worn again." That apron, she said, would be kept as a reminder of their journey and how, by the grace of God, they'd found each other once again in a new land.

WHEN THE Greyhound bus pulled into our final destination at Salem, my mother's cousin was waiting for us in the parking lot. Though the two greeted each other like long-lost sisters, the years of separation erased with a hug, this relative seemed to me a stranger except by blood and name. Over the next few days, my mother and I moved through a series of houses, sat at tables, and shared meals with an array of great-aunts, uncles, and cousins, some gray-haired and others young, and some my age, everyone explaining how we were related, how we all fit together. I was supposed to feel the connection, something sparking deep within that told me we all belonged to one another and were part of the same family story, even though some of us now wore jeans, while others still dressed in plain clothes like the Amish.

In Lincoln City, I wandered the ocean shoreline with Rachel and Susanna, daughters of one of my mother's cousins. We took off our shoes and waded into the surf, the tide foaming around our ankles. With every surge, the waves came frothing in, cold on our bare calves.

"Can we swim at this beach?" I said. "Do people do that here?"

Susanna, the auburn-haired one, said we could, if we had swimsuits, but they hadn't brought theirs along.

"We could find a store and buy some cheap bathing suits," I said.

"Dad won't let us wear the kind from the store," said Rachel, the quiet, older one.

"Even a one-piece?" I asked.

She shook her head. "We make our own. From a pattern." She explained how home-sewn bathing suits were far more modest than the ones sold in stores. I pictured the vintage photographs of swimmers at the shore. Men in striped rompers and women wearing short-sleeved, ruffle-skirted bathing dresses, more skin covered than revealed.

"But can you swim?" I asked my cousins.

"A bit," they said. "But we mostly just go wading in the shallows."

When our mothers on the sand held up their cameras, Susanna, Rachel, and I slid on our sunglasses, and I showed them how to push up the sleeves of their jackets to just below the elbow crook, which was how the models in *Seventeen* magazine wore them, but I didn't tell my cousins this. With their long hair pulled back from their clean, pure faces, they looked like girls from a bygone era, ancestors in the black-and-white photographs of our family album. I tried to picture my cousins with short hair or spiral perms. To imagine their faces with lipstick and blush and shimmery blue eyeshadow. I couldn't tell yet if they were beautiful in the way magazine girls were beautiful, but they were slender and fine-boned, their wrists delicate and their cheekbones high.

If I'd been born their sister instead of their cousin. If my mother had stayed on this side of the border instead of the other. If she'd fallen in love with someone other than my father, married a different man who stood in his wooden pew each Sunday and sang the low notes of a High German hymn, a man who loved God more than gambling. *If, if, if.* I'd be one of them, wearing cotton culottes and a long-sleeved blouse, brushing my uncut hair one hundred strokes every night to keep it shining. I'd be sewing my own bathing suit, in a modest style meant to keep away the boys. The thought of that other life cinched my breath like a collar buttoned chastely at the throat.

That night, I slept in a bedroom with Susanna and Rachel, in a sleeping bag on the floor between their twin beds. In the early hours of morning, with the light still dull and gauzy through the curtains, I woke to the sound of a woman screaming, *Help! Help!* The vowel of her cry drawn out in a long yelp, her voice like a muted trumpet, a wedge in her throat. *Help!* she cried. *Help!*

With a thud in my chest, I waited for Susanna and Rachel to bolt awake, but they slept on, their faces calm in the half-dark. *Help!* the voice called again, like a woman in peril, like a woman being hunted, fleeing the Bolsheviks. *Help!*—because the bayonet was pointed at her husband, at the baby, at her own head. *Help!*—because she couldn't hide, because the future was a room with low ceilings and small windows clouded over, because she was exhausted, because she couldn't run any longer. *Help!*—because she had to keep running. In and out of shadowy sleep, with the cries coming and going, I drifted, dreaming of the danger and the escape.

AT THE breakfast table, when I asked my cousins about the screams, about the woman crying for help in the dawn hours, they covered their mouths and laughed politely into their hands. The neighbor kept peacocks, they explained, and sometimes in the night his birds hopped the fence and wandered on their side of the property. They were so accustomed to the creatures' eerily human noises, they slept right through the *Help! Help! Help!*

We all traveled together to the grand reunion celebration, which was being held at a small Mennonite Bible college on the outskirts of Sheridan. Over the next few days, through a weekend itinerary of mealtimes, slideshows, and fellowship—which was the church-word for visiting—I sat at tables beside my mother or grandparents and listened to them put our story back together in pieces. They said things like, "So you're Reub's daughter's eldest?" and "What year did your folks move to Missouri?" Who'd been born, who died, who was widowed, who remarried, and how many kids and grandkids and great-grandkids—the conversation filled in the gaps in our family tree. Flung like seeds across the fields of generations and now rooted all over the continent were all the offshoots, transplants to other terrain. What had begun in Germany, France, and Switzerland had journeyed across the Czech borders and Ukraine, into Russia, and when the Revolution came, had sailed the Atlantic for the harbors of New York. Into Ohio, Indiana, across the Midwest states and all the way to Oregon, then up across northern borders, the ancestors had kept on moving.

ON SUNDAY morning after breakfast, before the reunion wrapped up and we left the Bible college campus, we gathered in the common room for a church service. An uncle led us in prayer from the front of the room, and various relatives took turns sharing about what God had done in their lives, how grateful they were to be part of this family, to be a blessed descendant. Someone read a passage of scripture. A girl played a solo on her violin. Our voices rose in the room, singing a hymn about the great faithfulness of a God whose mercies were new morning by morning. I wanted to believe it all, to feel that my own voice belonged inside the four-part harmony, to the song and the scripture from which its words had sprung. Back home, my life chafed inside its tightened frame, felt small, but here, surrounded by the echo of a wider history, my story swelled.

In one row, my mother stood with her parents, and behind Grandpa and Grandma Shenk, Uncle Enos and Aunt Millie with their daughters, their granddaughters. Uncle Reub and Aunt Naomi sat flanked by their own grandchildren, whose brown skin spoke of their father's ancestors, a story going back through Mississippi, Alabama, back across the waters in a vessel they did not choose to board, and back in chains to another continent they never asked to leave. My shining-haired, clean-faced girl cousins stood near Uncle Milt, who sat on the end of the row in his wheelchair, shifting the joystick back and forth as everyone sang. We were the redeemed, still here by some miraculous hand. We were a people guided by a higher compass, following an origin story more ancient than our blood.

No one knew where the red apron was now. In some girl's hope chest, it may have lain for years, folded away for decades, generations. It may have floated over some ocean to be passed down from mother to daughter again and again until the fabric faded, or until the red apron wore so many holes it could no longer be patched back together. Until it was only a scrap, a remnant to call back the old story and remind us where we belonged, and how. If we held onto it, it would prove the truth about everything we'd been told, that the pilgrim's way by which we'd traveled was the one marked out for us from the beginning. Hours from now, we'd be on the highway driving back the way we came, moving north across the border like my mother as a girl had done, loaded with her siblings into the family station wagon as they headed for their new country. In my heart, it grew— the story, the song, that red apron, God—deep and wide enough to wrap and bind me, to cover me with its blood. If I tied my body to it, no matter how wayward the road ahead, surely everything would hold.

BEFORE
AND AFTER

x x x x x x x

IN THE *BEFORE* PHOTOGRAPH, the woman stared unsmiling, her downturned mouth the drab pink of old ham. Dark circles sagged beneath her heavy-lidded eyes. Her skin betrayed every imperfection—a flush of blemishes on her nose, a tawny liver spot on her cheek. Her hair framed her face like limp curtains.

Her name was Donna. Or Kathy. Or Pat. She worked as a nurse, or a secretary, or was a busy stay-at-home mom. She was used to putting the needs of others ahead of her own. When she wasn't managing the household, cooking wholesome family meals, and driving the triplets to their team sports, she volunteered with local charities. She loved to give back to her community, but that left her little time to focus on herself. When asked what her daily beauty routine was, she laughed and said, "I'm lucky if I have a chance to run a brush through my hair."

Every female in the *Woman's World* makeover section began the same. Each week, the magazine unveiled a full-color photo spread of the chosen candidate, along with a series of small step-by-step pictures to show what happened in between her *Before* and her *After*. The makeup artist's hands swabbed and dabbed, brushed and tweezed, crimped and curled and sprayed until, in the final showcase photograph, the transformed woman emerged. Where once her gray eyes dully stared, now they widened in the wonder of iridescent blue shadow, thick black lashes, and brows arched high and narrow. Where once she frowned, now she smiled glossily with vivid lips and sudden white teeth. Hair clipped and permed. Cheekbones rouged peach. Spots and wrinkles smoothed.

"Look at what they did to her," my mother would say, pointing at who the woman used to be, then who she had become. "Doesn't even seem like the same person."

Together, we marveled at the weekly transformation, mesmerized by how a common housewife could be made to look like a soap-opera star with just a simple slash of rouge, a sleeker cut and color, and a stroke of lavender along each brow. All she had to do was give herself over to hands that knew how to alter her for good.

ON THE morning of my thirteenth birthday, after breakfast and gifts unwrapped at the kitchen counter, my mother announced that she had a surprise for me.

"You're a teenager now," she said. Her mouth smiled, but her eyes were alert with gentle dread, as if she could see past me, ahead into the future of slammed doors, sullen huffs, and rolled eyes. "I'm taking you to town," she said. "For a surprise."

We weren't a family who did surprises, unless you counted my dad's spontaneous announcements that he'd invited company over, or was hosting a cribbage tournament on Sunday, or he'd won a puppy in a card game, or had a knife salesman in the driveway and could my mother bring him the checkbook. So, by the time my mom pulled the car along the icy curb in front of the Vanderhoof Department Store, I'd grown nervous about her surprise, and curious.

I followed my mother through the store's glass doors, past the bulletin board advertising upcoming events—the Kinsmen and Kinettes Valentine's dinner and dance fundraiser, the curling bonspiel, the Ladies Hospital Auxiliary rummage sale and bazaar, and a sign for "Volunteer firefighters needed." Past the till, the round racks of sweaters, the children's nook with its wooden shelf of worn-out Golden Books and comics and hand-me-down toys, I trailed her. I suspected now that she'd planned a shopping spree, which would involve her pulling clothes off the rack and saying, "This would look nice on you," and me scoffing at the blouse, the pants, and the sweater she held up, telling her they were ugly and out of style.

Tucked in the store's back corner by the emergency exit, just outside the staff bathroom, was a wooden vanity with a lit-up mirror and a padded stool. Standing beside it was a tall, blonde, and feathery-haired woman, the kind of woman who might be featured in the *After* of a *Woman's World* makeover.

"You must be the birthday girl," she said, and held out her hand. "I'm Wanda."

I recognized her as the lady from the fabric and notions department, and looked to my mom, unsure of what Wanda had to do with my birthday.

"This is it," said my mom. "Surprise. You're going to get draped."

RUTH BRAUN was the first girl at school to wear Lip Smackers, and she had all the best flavors—root beer, Dr. Pepper, Orange Crush, and cherry cola. Because they only left a faint tint of color on the mouth, Lip Smackers were the one kind of "makeup" permitted at our Christian school. All other cosmetics were deemed worldly, believed to be tools the Devil used to lead innocent females to their downfall.

When Ruth leaned into the girls' washroom mirror and applied her Lip Smackers, I took note of her method—how she smoothed it on the top lip first, then the bottom, and then pressed them together, and finished with a *moo-wah* kiss. Even dressed in our dull gray uniform, Ruth looked like a Sears catalogue model. Her auburn hair hung thick and wavy down her back, and her hazel eyes glinted with a mischief that made the boys bumble in her company. Ruth was two grades above me, but in a school as small as ours, we found ourselves lumped into the same intermediate cohort, sharing gym class, field trips, and Friday arts and crafts.

Most of the other girls at school seemed so pure and full of Sunday-school goodness, so earnest in their desire to be saints, not sinners. In chapel, they sang as if they meant the words of our worship, closing their eyes, and sometimes even holding their hands out, palms up. *Change my heart, O God*, they sang. *Mold me, make me*, they sang. I couldn't fathom any of those girls living in a house with a television and a dad with cigarettes and a bottle of rye whiskey beneath the kitchen sink. The thought of inviting those girls into my home made me edgy with nerves. But Ruth Braun was different. She rolled her eyes at teachers, winked at the older boys during church. She laughed with her head tipped back, loud and unabashed. She knew how to toss her hair just a little to the side and smile in a way that held a boy's gaze, and she was always the one to walk away first. She was kind. Normal. Safe. The kind of friend who wouldn't whisper to the other girls about what went on at so-and-so's house.

At the end of last summer break, with my parents away at a family reunion on the prairies, Ruth came to spend the weekend. Perhaps because she was older than me, my mother felt that her presence in the house would lend an element of safety, especially on the nights my brother was working the late shift piling lumber at the sawmill. As soon as my brother's car spun out of the gravel driveway with a wake of dust and fumes, Ruth and I raced to the telephone.

"You call," she said, holding out the receiver.

Already, my pulse thudded in my throat. I took the phone from Ruth and dialed a number I knew by heart.

"It's ringing," I mouthed, clamping my hand over the mouthpiece. When a male voice answered, I shoved the phone at Ruth.

"Hey," she said, her voice steady and cool. "Is this Shawn?"

The weekend before, at the 4-H Auction, Ruth and I had sat in the bleachers of the exhibition arena and watched as Shawn Atley led his blue-ribbon steer past the stage. We'd both noticed him, this lanky dark-eyed boy older than me, older than Ruth, but I was the one who couldn't stop gawking.

"He's pretty cute," said Ruth, but she had her eye on the Mormon with the dimples and blue eyes and black cowboy hat.

On the phone with Shawn, Ruth was breezy and coy, and her flirty banter came easily. When she handed the phone to me for a turn, I tried to match the drop in her voice, the slow, low giggle, the way she asked questions, like "When's your birthday?" and "What's your favorite band?" and "Are you going to raise another 4-H steer next year?"

Even if it was me who invited Shawn to the house, told him to get in his truck and drive on over, even if it was my voice that coaxed him to put on a pair of tight jeans, throw a six-pack of beer into the cab, and start down the long rural road from his parents' farm into town, then along the tracks, and up the hill toward us—if it was me who begged him to *come on over, come on, just come,* Ruth was the reason he said yes.

Half an hour later, when we heard the crunch of gravel beneath tires in the midnight driveway, we ran to the kitchen window, unable to believe that what we'd asked for might actually be happening.

"Holy crap," said Ruth. "Shawn's here."

We couldn't let him in the house—this much I knew. Even though my brother wouldn't be home for hours, and my mom and dad were asleep somewhere in a motel on the outskirts of Swift Current, I had enough sense to not open the front door to a boy we didn't know, especially one old enough to drive his own pickup truck.

Ruth and I crept down the stairs, through the garage, and out into the front yard. We stood in the eerie cricket-quiet, clutching each other's arm, waiting for the next thing to happen. The slam of a truck door. Footsteps on the gravel. The bark of a neighbor's dog. Then Shawn came around the corner of the house with an open can of Pepsi in his hand.

"Hey," he said. "What's up?"

He didn't look at me when he spoke. He aimed his voice at Ruth, his eyes at Ruth, his whole muscled body at Ruth. She smiled back at him and cocked her head ever so slightly to the right, tipping her chin up. I'd practiced this very move in my own bedroom mirror, trying to perfect the angle.

We sat at the picnic table on the front lawn, talking about nothing important. Softball season, and Shawn played first, had hit a bunch of homers already this year. Graduation, and his plans for after he finished school, which were, he said, "loose" right now. Probably auto mechanics, maybe a welding ticket. And farming. He could always take over the family farm. He and Ruth talked cattle, meat versus dairy, how many head in the herds, the conversation edging further and further away from me.

"Cold out here," Shawn said, flexing as he rubbed his bare arms. He took another swig of Pepsi, then set the can down on the table beside his pickup keys.

It felt like he could slip away at any moment, climb back inside his truck and drive off, leaving everything the same as before he came. Beneath the picnic table, I pressed my knee to Ruth's thigh and waited for her signal, a nudge to know the next thing we should do or say to make Shawn stay, but she gave me nothing. In the dark, their eyes were hard to read, but I could see that Shawn, across from us, was grinning, fixed on her.

"Wait," I said, and told them that I'd be right back. I left them on the lawn and went into the house. From a hallway closet, I pulled some camping blankets and sleeping bags, then hauled them to the front yard, pleased with my plan.

While Shawn and Ruth watched, I unrolled the sleeping bags and spread the blankets on the damp grass. We could all keep warm together, I told them. I patted the makeshift bed.

In my mind, a picture was coming into view of how the night could go, so that the story I would tell the morning after held more thrill and glamor, but when I went to lie down in the space between Ruth and Shawn, buffering their bodies, he insisted on swapping spots with me.

"That way," he said, "I can talk to you both."

Though I was lying on the edge, with one half of my body on the blanket and the other half on the grass, I was still close enough to Shawn to feel his bare arm brush against my own. Each shift of his body made me shiver. The sugary waft of the flowerbed's evening stock mingled with the noise of crickets and the echo of the neighbor's barking dog, so that the stars above me became a movie and I was both inside the scene and watching it play out. When Shawn rolled onto his side and angled toward Ruth, coolness filled the space between us. He wanted to know what kinds of things she liked to do for fun. What I liked to do for fun was play piano, read *Sweet Valley High* paperbacks, and rent videos from Diamond Jim's, but Shawn wasn't asking me. He was asking Ruth if she had a boyfriend, and her laughter at his question sounded like it came from a different girl's mouth. I laughed, too, my breath puffing above me in a small cloud. When Shawn finally turned back to me, he didn't speak, only gave me the smallest nod, the upward jut of his chin directed toward the house, a message I immediately understood. *Go*, said his nod. *Leave us here. Just go.*

Automatic as a flicked-on switch, as if I had been waiting for this cue, knowing it would come, I scooted off the blanket, my body obeying this boy's silent command. I made some excuse to Ruth about needing to go to the bathroom, then turned to go, leaving her alone with him.

Inside, with the lights turned out in the house, I could still see them through the kitchen window. On the grass, their two shadow-shapes lay close. I hopped up on the counter, my bare feet planted in the sink, and listened. Through the screen, their voices drifted—his low and muffled, hers higher and fringed with giggling. Even after his shadow moved on top of her shadow, and the two bodies became one rolling back and forth, Shawn on top, then Shawn on the bottom, then over to their sides, I kept watching. While he clutched Ruth, and their bodies rocked across the blankets, I turned the faucet on and off, on and off, letting the cold water run over my toes, on and off, until my feet felt numb.

After Shawn drove away with the spit of gravel flying from his tires, Ruth came back inside with the rolled-up blanket beneath her arm. She was quiet, her mouth a straight line as she climbed the stairs. I wondered if he'd kissed her goodbye beneath the porch light, like in all the romance plots, his hands cupping her face, her eyelids fluttering. Outside the bathroom door, I sat and waited as Ruth scrubbed her face, brushed her teeth, and rinsed her mouth with mouthwash again and again.

WE CHANGED into our nightgowns and then crawled into my parents' waterbed, Ruth on my mother's side and me on my dad's. I could smell on the pillowcase my father's smoke-and-oil scent. For a long while, we said nothing, only let the lull and slosh of the mattress fill the quiet. The digits of my father's alarm clock bled huge red numbers into the darkness, a countdown to sunrise. In a time zone two provinces away, my parents slept in a strange bed, their bodies already dreaming the future. West down Highway 16, my brother on the green chain at L & M Lumber grabbed two-by-fours off the conveyor and stacked them into pallets. I was the one who'd wanted to call Shawn, who came up with the plan. I'd spread the blankets on the lawn, asked Shawn about baseball season, about his team, and what position he liked best, which made him laugh and say, "Never mind."

"He tasted like beer and Pepsi," said Ruth. Her voice sounded small and far away.

"Oh," I said, wanting her to tell me everything, and nothing.

"And his lips were like rubber."

"Gross," I said.

I didn't ask any questions. I didn't want to hear about his shadow locked with hers. I didn't want to hear the truth about what I already knew—that she was the one with the beauty that boys couldn't help but choose.

In the morning, before my brother came home from his mill shift, before Ruth woke, I snuck out of bed and slipped outside into the sun. Where the front lawn lay flattened from the night before, I knelt. Beneath my hands, the earth had gone cold. I combed my fingers through the grass, fluffing the blades patch by patch, so that the ground where their bodies had lain appeared unchanged, no different than before.

I'D HEARD about draping. My mom and her sisters had all been draped, one after the other. Over the phone and at Sunday gatherings, they compared the results of their drapings, talking in a coded language of color families and seasons.

"I'm an autumn," said my mother. "No silver for me, only gold. And only ivory, never white." Her closet, after her draping, began to fill with reds and browns to draw the amber flecks from her gray-green eyes. She'd stand before her full-length mirror and hold a swatch of fabric to her neck, angle her chin, pull another piece of material to her face and look herself in the eye. *Too much winter, not enough fall,* she'd say.

"Take a seat," said Wanda, patting the stool.

I sank down in front of the vanity, and Wanda swung a black salon cape over me and pinned it in place around my neck. In the mirror's frame, I looked like a doll head mounted on a plastic base, the kind that came with toy cosmetics to pretend your own beauty salon.

"Now let's get started," she said.

Wanda began by handing me a little deck of cards looped on a metal ring. Each card was like a hardware-store paint chip displaying different colors. One had bluish purples. The next held purples with a burgundy hue. She explained how the seasons worked, and how it was less about what I liked and more about what tones complemented my skin and my hair and highlighted the color of my eyes.

She could already tell by looking at me that I was definitely not an autumn. With my blue-gray eyes and my hair, which was flyaway with the dry January air and blonde as the heart of a bleached-out pine, I likely wasn't a winter either. From a cardboard box, she pulled large squares of material, which looked like scraps of fabric from the remnants bin, and began holding them up to my face, folding them around my neck and shoulders.

"See?" Wanda said, holding the orange swatch to my cheek, which suddenly sallowed to a sickly yellow tint.

"Not good." She swapped the orange for emerald green. "Better," she said, as my skin lost its jaundice. When she held a piece of sky-blue material against my face, she gave a happy, "Yes!"

After more fabric swatches and further draping, Wanda declared me a clear, undeniable summer, and showed me a color palette of pinks, pale purples, powder blue, aqua, and silver.

I wondered if any boy had ever been brought here for his thirteenth birthday, if any man had sat before this mirror to find out what season matched his face. I tried to imagine my dad or brother perched on the stool, listening to a woman tell him he was winter, he was spring, he needed to start wearing a ball cap whose color better complemented his eyes.

"Now that we know you're a summer," said Wanda, "we can really get started." She opened what looked like a fishing tackle box. Inside, on hinged tiers lined with small trays, was an array of brushes, blushes, pencils, and gloss.

My mother had always warned me away from makeup, partly because it had been forbidden when she was growing up, considered a sin that might lure a girl into lust and vanity. Sure, as a teenager, she'd washed her face with the morning dew from the grasses in the field, in hopes her freckles would fade, but that was different than lipstick or rouge. It seemed unfair to me that the very thing expected of girls—to be beautiful—could lead to hell. That a shimmer of Twilight Mist or Moonflower Blue across my eyelids could make me a target for demons, the way my brother's heavy metal could make him a kid in Satan's service, especially if the music was played backward.

On a shopping trip to Prince George, I'd bought my own palette of eyeshadow at the Sears cosmetics counter when my mother was shopping elsewhere in the Pine Centre Mall. Without her consent, I chose the palette with Dusky Lilac for its iridescent sparkle and its swoony sound, took it to the till, and bought it in secret. Later, in my bedroom, leaning into the bureau mirror, I'd practiced with the tiny wand, dragging it across each of the colors, then tracing the shades in various ways across my eyelids. A line of pale purple along the brow. A charcoal streak in the crease. In the mirror's frame, my eyes deepened their glower. I couldn't help but think of Jezebel, that wicked queen from the Bible. She was our proof text for the doctrine of cosmetics, an evil woman who painted her face and worshipped idols and fawned at herself in the mirror, and who fell to her death when the royal eunuchs pushed her out the high palace window, her blood licked up by dogs. Before my mother could catch me wearing the eyeshadow, I'd wiped the makeup off with a piece of dampened toilet paper, ridding myself of the sin.

As Wanda began to dot a peachy lotion on my face, blending it in with a small sponge, I watched my mirrored self being smeared and smoothed, aware that my mother's caution over cosmetics had taken a quick pivot. *You're a teenager now*—her words came back. She was giving me something she'd never been permitted as a girl—a shot at beauty, the chance to be the one lit up, to feel the voltage of the change.

YOU HAD to stand in front of a mirror in a room with the lights on. You had to close your eyes and turn in a circle while repeating the phrase "Bloody Mary." After you circled and chanted, you had to turn out the lights, face the mirror, and then open your eyes. *If you do all this*, said Treena, *you'll see a woman in the mirror. You'll see Bloody Mary. You'll see what your future holds.*

Treena waited with her hand on the light switch as she stood guard at the door, blocking it with her body in case one of the senior girls or a teacher tried to barge in. The rest of us girls gathered, nervous, around the bathroom vanity.

"Ready?" said Treena.

Jeanie whimpered that she didn't like this idea, not one bit. But yes, we told Treena, we were ready.

"Remember," said Treena. "Eyes shut."

In unison we turned, circling like slow, blind dervishes in our gray polyester skirts, and as we turned, we chanted, "Bloody Mary, Bloody Mary, Bloody Mary."

"How many times do we have to say it?" someone asked, but Treena said to keep going, so our voices chanted on in the pale room: "Bloody Mary, Bloody Mary."

"I don't like this," whispered Jeanie, her body pressed against mine.

"Now!" said Treena, "open your eyes!" She flicked the switch.

In the cluster of sweaty, breathing girls, I stood before the mirror, my eyes adjusting to the new darkness.

"Look in the mirror!" said a voice.

Jeanie let out a stifled, high-pitched yelp. "She's falling!

"I see her! The woman!" said Shelly.

It was hard to tell who screamed first, but soon the whole bathroom was a choir of shrieks and bodies clambering for the exit. Treena flipped on the light just as Miss Schultz pushed open the door and demanded to know what on earth the racket was all about.

We were just being dumb, we told her, playing a game. Like hide and seek, but in the dark.

Even Treena's eyes were glassy with fear, and Jeanie was shuddering by the library shelf, trying to catch her breath.

"Did you see her?" said Ruth. "Did you actually see the woman?"

In the blackout of the bathroom, with all the bodies pressed together, it was difficult to clearly see, to know for sure what the shapes actually were, but I thought I'd seen something—the woman in the mirror tumbling backward, falling off the cliff and into the darkness, falling—*Bloody Mary, Bloody Mary, Bloody Mary*—to her death, the shadow of her fluttering, a white dress with arms and legs and hair flying behind her, a white dress dipped in blood and falling.

BEFORE, I was a girl with pale, stubby lashes. Faint brows. Freckles on my nose and cheeks. A dull and downward mouth. Before, my blonde hair lay flat against my head, except for the staticky strands that floated up. Before, I did not want to meet my gaze in the mirror's bright reflection.

"Wow," said Wanda. She pulled off my cape. "Look at the transformation."

I stared at my new face in the vanity: my round cheeks pinkened with streaks blended upward toward my temples, my eyes rimmed with kohl, my brows darkened with a brownish pencil, and my lips waxy and Popsicle-pink. When I blinked, I blinked with bluer eyes, longer flutters, my lashes thick with black mascara.

Wanda leaned in behind me, smiling, her hands on my shoulders. "Do you like it?"

I smiled with a mouth that seemed too huge. I nodded and the girl in the mirror agreed. "Thank you," I said, and rose from the padded stool. Wanda handed me a deck of color-matching cards—"to consult when shopping for new summer-palette clothes," she said.

As I walked past the racks of clothing on my way out, I was sure that other customers were watching me, wondering at who I was and what had happened to make me look like this, so different than I was before. In the glass of the double doors, I caught my reflection, a blurred version of myself, a girl with shadowy eyes and lips bright as a wound, pushing into the wind and cold. Our green Grand Marquis idled ahead on the curb, my mother at the wheel, waiting, watching the rearview mirror for her daughter to appear.

BABY, BABY

✗ ✗ ✗ ✗ ✗ ✗ ✗

DEEP IN THE RURAL REALM OF TRAPLINES and ranches marked by barbed-wire fence, down a dirt road cutting through a forest of poplar and birch, and seated at a table in a stranger's log house, I studied a picture of Kirk Cameron, the teenage star of *Growing Pains*. His hair was brown and curly, cut above his ears and grazing his collar, much the way my mother wore her hair, but I shook that thought away. Instead, I let Kirk's heartthrob eyes look all the way into me, wooing with their blueness. Only nights earlier, I'd dreamed him breathing next to me. As I was paying for a pack of Juicy Fruit gum at the Stedman's checkout counter, Kirk had sidled up, taken my hand, and laced his fingers through mine. I'd seen boys and girls holding hands like this, interlocked and walking together down sidewalks and through hallways, advertising their affections and announcing to the world that they were "going out," wherever "out" was. When my dream-hand joined with Kirk's, I felt in my gut that carnival-ride quickening, a flicker that stayed upon waking, that I savored as I spooned my breakfast cereal and replayed the scene.

Now, when I looked at Kirk's glossy photo face, at his half-smirk, half-pout mouth, the same feeling hummed, as if a tiny winged thing were flitting to life in the lowest rung of my ribcage. I set down my magazine and sighed across the dining room table at Soopie. "Do you think a boy will ever like me back?"

This was the question we were asking each other these days, and one I asked myself when I stood before my bedroom vanity and tried to gauge my ranking in the league of girls I knew. Soopie peered over the top of her issue of *Tiger Beat*. She narrowed her eyes and tilted her spiral-permed head. "Hmm," she said, as she studied my face. "You're not *that* ugly."

Though I hoped she meant to console me, her words still flashed a mirror in my mind, magnifying my every flaw and fat roll. "But do you think it's possible? For a boy to actually like me?" I said, in a voice that seemed lately to be opulent with self-pity, cloying with sighs and whines. Soopie shrugged and flipped the page.

The sound of a drill buzzed beneath us, rising from the basement of the house, where Mr. Futterman had his workshop.

"He better not wake up the kids," I said. The clock on the wall still promised us an hour of naptime freedom, which was our solitary bright spot in the eight-hour day that dragged.

Soopie and I had been hired as summer babysitters for a family with three children, all of them under the age of four. Mrs. Futterman, who worked at the bank, and her husband, who ran a carpentry business, needed someone a few days a week to look after their kids. They were having trouble finding steady childcare, probably because they lived so far out of town and didn't own a television. As a team of two, Soopie and I figured we could split the twenty dollars a day and maybe even have fun looking after the kids together. It would be practice for the future, kind of like playing house, the way we'd played only a few years earlier, pushing our Cabbage Patch dolls in toy strollers down the shoulder of the road, pretending to be mothers, except this time, we'd be doing it for money.

But less than a week into the job, I hated it, dreading everything from the long drive out into the sticks to the children themselves. The four-year-old, Sammy, whined and sucked his thumb and begged to be read to, the same story over and over, the rabbit in the garden, the rabbit on the run. The two-year-old, Marlee, still sogged around in diapers, and cloth ones at that. Natalie, the baby, shrieked as soon as her mother pulled the car keys from her purse and started for the door. Mr. Futterman, a tall, thin man with a ponytail, stayed home while his wife went to work, but he spent most of the days in his basement workshop, rarely appearing, except to take his lunch from the refrigerator once the kids had been put down for their naps. He'd nod at me and Soopie, say a quiet hello, and then disappear with his sandwich to the lower floor, where the sounds of hammering, sawing, and drilling would start up again, punctuating our afternoon hours. From the moment one of our parents dropped us off at the family's house, Soopie and I tracked the slow rotations of the clock, counting down the hours until Mrs. Futterman returned from the bank to hand us our day's wages in crisp, new bills, then release us back into our childless lives.

"If I ever have kids," said Soopie, "I'm still going to have a job. There's no way I could handle being a stay-at-home mom."

It wasn't hard to picture Soopie with a diaper bag slung over her shoulder, a baby in her arms, a toddler by the hand. She was nearly six feet tall and could easily be mistaken for some kid's mom. Her height alone seemed to command respect from the Futterman children, who listened to her when she told them to stop fiddling with the radio dial, stop fussing, stop hitting your sister on the head with that wooden block.

"I don't want even one," I said to Soopie.

This wasn't completely true. In secret, I practiced writing the names of my future children. Bradley, for the boy, after a character on *The Young and the Restless*. For the girl, Ocean, after the actress who played the marine biologist's daughter on *Danger Bay*. Beyond naming them, though, I didn't want the responsibility. Bradley and Ocean could slide their way into the world, and after that, be turned loose to fend for themselves while I went off to work, like Mrs. Futterman at the bank, or even like her husband down in the basement with his power tools and plans. Babies meant sacrifice. To be a mother, you had to rise from your own sleep to comfort the crier. You had to offer the soft part of the bread, and then eat the crusts yourself. You had to be willing to run into the burning building to save your child, even if it meant death.

"No babies," I said. "No thanks."

Soopie pushed her magazine across the tabletop toward me, open to a full-color spread. "Even if Kirk Cameron was the dad?" From the photograph, Kirk aimed his dimples and white teeth at me.

A baby with Kirk was still a baby, and the thought of one clinging to me made me feel caged, claustrophobic. I couldn't fathom a baby sliding from inside me, or why I'd ever want to pull that creature to my breast and let it suck. The soft-skulled lolling head. The thrushy tongue. The drool. The rashes, and the creams that needed to be smeared. The constant wiping. Babies scared me with their unpredictability and neediness. I could dream a boy's hand in mine, imagine my lips pressed to his, his hands cupping my face, like in the *Growing Pains* episode where Kirk had his first kiss. But a baby was the complication in the romance plot, the part that turned the story into a cautionary tale.

I'd witnessed the fussing and clinging of all the babies my mother had looked after over the years. "He's just teething," or "she's just gassy," my mom would say, shushing the wailing lump tucked over her shoulder. But she was an expert. She knew how to turn her teaspoon into an airplane and blow puttering noises as she flew its cargo of mashed noodle soup toward the baby's mouth. She easily made the necessary mother sounds—the coo, the hum, the hush. She knew to swaddle tightly, how much gripe water to give for gas, and when to give it, how to test a bottle's warmth by shaking milk droplets on the inside of her wrist. When a baby fussed, screeched, wailed, or whined, she swooped in with the right reply. A kitchen sink full of cool water for the baby to splash its feet in. A clean diaper from the bag. A walk in the yard to look up at the sky, pointing the baby's gaze to the line of crows hunkered on the telephone wire. But more than her natural maternal instincts, she clearly enjoyed that babies showed up at our house, seemingly unannounced. In the doorway, a baby was passed from its mother's arms to my mom's, and after a quick goodbye kiss

on its bald, flaky head, its mother whisked away to her job
in town, or to an appointment, or simply for a break, leaving my mom as the surrogate caregiver. But eventually, the
baby's mother had to return. That cord, though severed at
birth, held fast, an invisible tether that only let the woman
range so far before it snapped her back to reality, to the diaper bag, and the kitchen dishes, and the piles of laundry
waiting to be washed.

I could tell that I was supposed to want this life, to be
willing to give up freedom for the gift and glory of being
a mother. There was no higher calling for a woman, even
though all the words attached to the role sounded like suf-
fering. Childbirth was labor, hard work, a woman sweating
and grunting with her feet in the metal stirrups while the
man sat by with a cigar ready to be lit. When I asked my
mother if having a baby hurt, she said, "It isn't fun, but it's
not going to kill you."

Long was the family lineage of women birthing baby
after baby. Grandma Funk had nine, with two sets of twins
in a row. I'd heard the stories of how she had to melt buck-
ets of snow on the woodstove just to wash the few flannel
diapers she owned. Of how Uncle John and Uncle George
slept in old banana boxes from the grocery store because
there weren't enough cribs for everyone. Of how the deliv-
eries left her so weak that the doctor prescribed her a cup
of red wine every day to fortify her blood, and she drank it,
even though alcohol was forbidden by the Church. Grandma
Shenk carried nine babies, too, the first one a stillborn son
buried in the field in a tiny casket while she lay healing in a
hospital bed. After the first death, eight births, with hardly
two years between each baby. That was the way of the Old
Order Mennonites and the Amish, which was also the way

of the Catholics and the Mormons, and all the other tribes who believed that babies were a gift from God never to be refused. But my mother and most of my aunts had stopped at two or three children, which made me wonder if our bloodline's reproductive inheritance was being divided into smaller and smaller portions as it passed from one generation to the next. Either that, or the women were quietly realizing that birth was too much work and babies were a lesson in surrender and humility, in the giving up of freedom and of fun.

"Oh, you'll change your tune one day," my mother would say when I argued my case against babies, but I didn't believe her. I didn't want to be known only as so-and-so's mom, to have my husband call me "Mother," my name after childbirth washed away like the diaper pail dregs.

I saw the way other girls my age fussed over little ones, how a baby in any given room became a magnet for their attention, causing them to coo over its tiny fingernails and downy hair, to ask if they could *please, please* hold the baby, feed the baby its bottle, or even change the baby, an act that seemed to me more penalty than prize. At family gatherings, when an aunt or older cousin offered me her baby, I felt as if I were being groomed for the future. As the infant peered up at me, it seemed we both were thinking: *you're not who I want.*

I'D HEARD about how the whole system worked, how the biological clock started ticking inside a female, which was just a cleaner way of saying her body began to crave a body with whom to make another body. At weddings, when the preacher stood with the bride and groom and spoke of them "entering into this sacred union" and "making a life together," I understood the implication. The vows. The kiss. The honeymoon. The locked bedroom door, and behind it, the breathing, heavy and ragged, like a race for the finish line. The mingling elixirs of creation, the making of a life. This was the old order of things, the way it had been since the beginning. But nothing about the diagram of the reproductive system unveiled the mystery. Nothing in *The Book of Knowledge*, our encyclopedia set—no pictures, no clues, no facts about the sperm and egg—explained the bigger question about how two bodies locked together yielded life, about how an act so hushed and shameful could be sacred.

Grandma Shenk spoke of how her grandmother had been the Amish community's midwife back in Kansas in the early 1900s, but her work was always done in secret, the man of the house and his children banished while his wife labored behind a shut door. As a young girl, my grandma remembered hearing strange noises coming all night through the floorboards. Where the stovepipe ran up through her attic bedroom from the hole cut in the kitchen ceiling below, grunts and moans rattled the tin, ghosting in and out of her sleep. In the morning, when she went downstairs for breakfast, her mom was sitting in the rocking chair, holding a baby. "This is Becky," her mother said. The new sister had appeared like a miracle, without warning or explanation, as if delivered by way of that stovepipe hole.

Even now, Grandma Shenk didn't use the word "pregnant," and if she did, she spoke it in a hushed voice. The women in our family were "expecting," or "in the family way," or simply "due" in a certain month. The women wore shapeless dresses with ruffles and bows near the neckline to distract from the belly's swell. They seemed to be embarrassed about their condition, as if something—whatever that "thing" was—had been done to them, and now, rubbing their own swollen feet and sore backs, they were stuck.

I'd heard about the pill, though I had no clue what it actually meant. I didn't know anyone who took it, who was "on it," as the girls said. To be "on the pill" was to be a certain kind of girl, that much I'd figured out. For one, it meant that you were doing "it." And if you were doing "it," then you were a fire threatening to spread your heat to any girls standing too close. If you were willing to swallow the pill, you were probably a girl willing to get an abortion, that unsayable word. Only in movies and from the public-school girls at the back of the bus had I heard it whispered, like an insult or a curse. *Coat hanger*, I heard. *Blood*, I heard.

When Justina Hiebert, one of the young women from our church, came home from Bible college in the middle of the autumn semester, something about her seemed different. She had always been the athletic type, always playing sports on local teams, cracking home runs for the town's softball league. But now she stood in her pew with her family, wearing a baggy, navy-blue jumper, a style of dress so unlike the clothes she normally wore. I couldn't help but stare. My mother noticed, too, and whispered to an aunt sitting near us. "Is she...?" She tipped her head toward Justina and raised her eyebrows. "You know?"

My aunt's lips tightened and somberly, she nodded.

Over the next few months, I caught snatches and scraps of the story, that Justina Hiebert had fallen in love with a man, but he was married, or he was divorced, or he had a terminal disease, or maybe he didn't love her at all, or she didn't love him. He was rich. He had no money. Whatever the truth, Justina had come home in a shapeless dress and without a ring on her finger. When the baby boy was born, his name appeared on the cradle-roll bulletin board like all the other church babies, his birth announcement printed on a sheet of paper cut in the shape of an old-fashioned scroll, welcoming him as the newest member of the congregation with only his mother's name as the proud parent. No one ever spoke of the father, or the situation. There was grace for whatever she had done, but never any words. In church, in the same pew she'd always sat in, she held her son in the crook of one arm and the open hymnal in her hand, singing along to the familiar songs, like "Tell Me the Old, Old Story" and "Just as I Am," her life a reminder of what could happen to any woman, any girl, to me if I ever gave away my body, let myself fall too fully into the arms of a man.

ACROSS THE table from me, Soopie pulled another magazine from our dog-eared stack and flipped it open. "Who would you rather make out with?" she said, holding up the photograph. "C. Thomas Howell or Ralph Macchio?"

Ponyboy or the Karate Kid. Rebel or underdog. Blue eyes or brown. Pick your type and see what comes next, the magazine urged.

"Kirk Cameron," I said.

Soopie rolled her eyes.

I'd rehearsed the scene already, run the script, and revised it to sleek perfection. In a dark movie theater, Kirk and I sat with our sleeves touching on the shared armrest. When I slid my hand down to my thigh and splayed it out over my knee, he slid his hand down to meet mine. Laced his fingers with mine. I leaned my head against his shoulder and smelled his leather and toothpaste and spicy cologne, like the sample bottle of *Stetson* I'd pulled from the drugstore shelf and spritzed onto the inside of my wrist. He leaned his brown curls against my blonde hair, then tipped his face to meet mine, touched my chin, pulled me forward, and pressed his lips against my lips, soft and pink and damp with his minty breath. I leaned into what he offered. *Baby,* he said. *Oh, baby.*

A muffled whimper came from the upstairs bedroom.

"Ah, shoot," said Soopie, and set down her magazine.

I looked at the clock. Even though Marlee, the toddler, was supposed to be sleeping for another half hour, she was awake, calling out. At the top of the stairs stood Sammy, the eldest, holding his blanket and his rabbit storybook. His bottom lip quivered.

"Mommy," he rasped, then plugged his thumb into his mouth.

From the basement, the sound of grinding droned through the floorboards, metal biting into wood, the machine's dust flying.

The baby started to cry.

"Your turn," said Soopie. She scooped up Sammy and carried him toward his juice and crackers.

The crying pulled me up the stairs, the way time tugged the clock hands forward through its hours, step after slow step, until I stood at the top of the landing. Through the cracked-open nursery door, I watched the baby grip the rail of her crib, press her face to the rungs, and bellow, her cry heating up. At the end of the hallway lay the master bedroom, door pulled shut. I imagined it full of furniture built by the husband, that shine of varnished pine, and the bed where they slept every night, two bodies side by side, locked together until death. On the other side of the hall, in the children's room, the little girl began to sing a loud and made-up song, calling out to me that she was awake, awake, now she was awake.

HIPPOCAMPUS

𝙓 𝙓 𝙓 𝙓 𝙓 𝙓 𝙓

ALL THAT MY MOTHER HAD LEFT of her high school days was a pair of dead seahorses. Gone were the penny loafers, the mohair sweater, the modest dresses she sewed for herself. Gone was her music, the Johnny Cash record shot to shards by her father's rifle when he found her secret stash of vinyl. Gone was her teenage life only told to me in fragments, because, she said, those memories were murky, washed away with the years.

The seahorses had been my mother's project for her ninth-grade science class. From an advertisement at the back of a *National Geographic* magazine, she ordered a pair matched for mating, all the way from Florida. While she waited for them to arrive, she read everything she could find about the creatures, searching books in the school library for details on their habitat and habits. *Seahorse*: a tropical marine fish, scaleless but equipped with bony armor. *Seahorse*: from the Ancient Greek word *Hippocampus*, meaning "horse" and "sea monster," the mingling of the known and the strange. They were solitary creatures. Poor swimmers. Good at camouflage. The dwarf variety, for which she'd sent away, were Nature's slowest-moving fish.

On the day she picked up her parcel from the Vanderhoof post office, the weather was cold—she remembered that, and I tried to see her on the sidewalk, her coat buttoned up against a gray sky's wind and early signs of winter. Up the concrete steps and through the glass door I'd shadow her, stand with her at the counter where the scowling postal ladies sorted mail, where one took the piece of paper from my mother's hand and disappeared into the back to find the package. *Florida*, I imagined her thinking, as she opened the cardboard box. *Palm trees, and orange groves, and the turquoise surf along the sand.* Inside a plastic bag filled with brine, two dwarf seahorses swam.

"Be careful," said my mother, when I lifted them to the dining room light. In a clear plastic pill bottle, twenty years later, the seahorses lay. The little fossils of their bodies clicked against the plastic as I tipped them out into my palm. They were tiny, brittle and white, delicate as lace.

She must have given them something to eat—dried flakes from a tin, whatever came packed inside that cardboard box. She must have peered into the glass to study their behavior, made notes on how the pair most days hung inside their brine as if asleep. When one of the seahorse's bellies began to swell, she knew that was the male, carrying the clutch of eggs.

Of all the facts about the creatures, this one—a reversal of the natural order—was most difficult to fathom. In the ocean shallows, after days of an acrobatic courtship dance, the female deposited her eggs in the male's pouch. While he stayed put, grazing in the sea grass and growing the brood, she swam off to wider waters, her territory more expansive.

"And when they hatched," my mother said, "the babies rode on the father."

"Yeah, right," I said, "as if."

But she insisted. They had, they really had. The babies, small as grains of rice, clung to the male's spiny back and curled tail, floating where he floated, bobbing where he bobbed.

"And then what happened?" I said.

My mother shrugged. "Then they died." Within a couple weeks, they all were floating on the surface of the brine. There wasn't any more to the story than that. She couldn't remember what mark she received on the project, but it must have been a decent one. One girl in the science class cooked a dead barn cat on the stove, stinking up the kitchen, and then reassembled the boiled bones into a skeleton. What the other students worked on for their projects, who knew? How was her brain supposed to hold all those long-gone details? She might have kept the seahorses in her bedroom at home, or maybe in her school locker. She must have marveled at the creatures hovering in that water, fluttering their dorsal fins. But my mother did recall for certain that she had been the only one to order seahorses all the way from Florida and watch them hatch their babies in a jar.

OUT.

I wanted out.

Out of the gray polyester skirt and navy-blue vest. Out of the polka-dot blouse and ribboned bow hooked around my neck.

"Look at this," I said to my mother, tugging at my collar, itching in my tights. Like most mornings at the breakfast table, I complained about my uniform, and how the public-school kids snickered when I got on the bus, how dumb I felt, how cold it was to wear a skirt on days when it was snowing.

"I couldn't wear pants to school either," my mother said. She and her sisters were never allowed, even though they'd gone to public school. Pants were for boys and men, but not for Mennonite females. "Try playing basketball in a skirt," she said.

But at least she didn't have to wear a uniform, I argued, or sit in a narrow study carrel called an "office," complete with wooden dividers to keep me looking straight ahead, never to the left or right, never whispering to my fellow students trapped on either side. She'd had a real classroom, not the panopticon-style learning center where supervisors and monitors patrolled the room, our backs to them, our faces toward the wall. No one had given her a demerit for forgetting to push her chair in, or threatened her with a rubber strap for pretending to play a badminton racquet like an electric guitar. At least, I whined, at least she got to go to public school.

From first grade, I'd attended Northside, a small church-run school on the north side of the river. All of my cousins on my mother's side attended the school, too, which meant that I was related to at least a quarter of the student population. In my early years, I'd loved Northside for its order and clarity and myriad rules, its system of demerits and rewards, levels and privileges, the morning chapel services where Miss Bueller strummed her Autoharp and Miss Hornsby trilled in piercing soprano as we sang, *O the valleys shall ring with the sound of praise.* I'd relished the blessing of being set apart from the secular realm where kids grew into teenagers who blasphemed and smoked and did not submit to authority, where they weren't even being warned that the Mark of the Beast would soon be tattooed on every unbeliever's forehead. I'd felt sorry for those public-school students abandoned to the kingdom of darkness, sorry for their ignorance.

Our school's mission from the beginning had been to provide an alternative to public education, and to train up a generation of godly young people whose faith would not yield to the fallen world's way of thinking. The brain, given too much freedom and the wrong kind of fuel, could burn the whole body into hell. The mind, opened to the wider road of darkness, would veer toward waywardness, would begin to ask too many questions, crumble into doubt and godlessness. Though the mind of God was infinite, His wisdom limitless and full of light, the human mind was weak and prone to wander.

Northside's Bible-based curriculum, designed by an organization in Texas, emphasized scripture memory, rote recall of information, and the development of Christian character, which was implemented in every aspect of school life. Even the workbooks, whether math or spelling or social studies, featured an ongoing comic strip whose characters promoted holy living. Along the bottom of our workbook pages, in the narrow frames of their cartoon world, Ace Virtueson and Sandy McMercy extolled the merits of obeying one's parents, telling the truth, and choosing an edifying activity like prayer over reading a frivolous paperback. Chunky Pudge Meekway asked forgiveness for hurting someone's feelings. Christi Lovejoy cheerfully helped her mother in the kitchen, the way a proper daughter should. "I am honoring my mother," bubbled the thought above Christi Lovejoy's head, her eyes wide, her mouth fixed in a smile as she held up the white dish towel. Only Ronny Vain and Susie Selfwill, the two unbelieving characters, showed what life outside the faith looked like. Over time, both Ronny and Susie spiraled into full rebellion. Eventually, Ronny ended up crashing his car, and Susie, who'd been riding shotgun, died as a result of his reckless driving, leaving him as an injured, guilty down-and-out.

I didn't want to slide into a life of sin and death like Ronny Vain or Susie Selfwill, but neither could I see myself in any of the other characters, who only grew in their goodness and their desire to be righteous, even as they moved from childhood to adolescence. Ace Virtueson never talked back to his parents or rolled his eyes behind his supervisor's back. Sandy McMercy never complained about her ugly uniform, or the rules about no makeup or jewelry. None of the characters ever asked the questions that bubbled in my mind, like how the lowered hemline of a gray polyester skirt determined a girl's holiness, and why on Friday afternoons the males ventured outside for archery and wilderness survival skills, while the females learned to crochet and decorate cakes. And who decided what was wrong and what was right, and why, when the principal read out a verse with the words "sexual immorality," did my ears lean forward and not away, why did my heart edge toward the flame, the line? And who drew the lines anyways? In the silent march to chapel service, why did all the other girls, whose goodness gleamed like a mirror angled straight at me, only reflect back the warp of my own heart? Where in the Bible did it say that we should stay inside our holy bunker, fearful of the world?

"There's nothing wrong with Northside," said my mother, listening to me plead and whine, and fire at her my reasons for needing to escape. "It's fine, just fine." She agreed that it didn't have a lot of fancy programs to offer, and she knew that their curriculum wasn't academically robust, that students often had to upgrade after graduation. Yes, she said, Northside sometimes seemed too strict, but the staff was trustworthy, and the school was safe, like a smaller version of our town contained within the town itself.

WHEN MY brother began to talk about studying something more than what Northside could offer, about becoming a pilot or an air traffic controller or a computer programmer, and how he'd like to try college or university, the argument heated up.

"What's wrong with driving truck?" my dad said to Richard. He wanted to convince him to take over the logging company, so they could make it a father-son business. "You don't need no college courses for that."

No one in our family, except for an older cousin on my father's side, had gone on to study after high school, beyond a year or two at Bible college, or the completion of a short course in bookkeeping or office skills. University seemed to be a realm reserved for others. That kind of education was a luxury, designed for those who didn't really like to work— at least, not with sweat and muscle.

But on the nights my dad was melancholy and blood-shot with nostalgia, he called for my mother to bring his old schoolbooks from the box in the crawlspace. As Richard and I sat with our homework at the dining room table, our dad turned the pages of his own mathematics, reading aloud the German words and recounting the numbers.

"One hundred percent," he said, pointing at the score penciled at the top of the faded page. He slid the notebook across the table toward us. Fractions, long division, and the early signs of algebra showed their work on the ruled paper. "You look here," he said. "That's perfect. I got good grades."

I knew exactly what he wanted. To prove that he'd been smart enough to do what we were doing now, solving for x, balancing our equations, working out quadratics.

"And I didn't use no calculator," he'd say, watching as we punched in numbers to double-check our answers.

I couldn't fathom my father as an almost-teenager bent over a desk, a scholar squinting at the teacher's blackboard notes. The only stories I had of him as a student weren't really stories at all, but brief remarks from Grandma Funk, who said my dad had been a quiet boy, too shy to stand up for himself when classmates chucked rocks at him in the schoolyard. The teacher hadn't liked him either, Grandma thought, but she never understood why. He obeyed, she said, and he worked hard.

When my father reached eighth grade, he left school, like all the Mennonite boys he knew, and went to work on his uncle's dairy farm. As the eldest of nine children, he was expected to earn money that helped support the family, to carry his share of the burden. How else would he learn the meaning of sacrifice, and what it took to provide for his own future wife and kids?

"You better work hard," he said, tapping the page of his notebook and nodding toward us and our homework spread out on the table, bearing formulas I didn't think he'd ever understand.

OVER THE summer, in a rare show of sibling unity, my brother and I plotted in whispers our tactics of persuasion, considering which argument would work best on which parent. We started with our dad, thinking if we convinced him first, and he thought that the switch was his idea, he'd wield his authority over our mom, smack his hand down on the dining room table and say, "I've made up my mind."

"Ask your mother," was all our father said, as if he understood that this was her domain, that she knew more than him about how best to educate. "It's up to her."

At the breakfast table, the dinner table, in the car as we drove through town, we took turns pleading for the change, trying to wear her down. It was the perfect time for me to make the switch, I said, so I could slide right into eighth grade with all the other seventh graders, not stand out as the new girl in the school. Nechako Valley Secondary was free. We could save money. Plus, they had computers and not just electric typewriters, my brother said, a real gymnasium instead of a carpeted church sanctuary with basketball hoops at either end. If we went to public school, we could graduate with real diplomas that let us go straight to college or university.

While she weeded the garden, I stood in the row and added reasons to our argument, naming all the people we knew who already attended, especially the good ones, like Soopie and Theresa, some Funk cousins, even some of the Mennonite kids from church.

My mother still gave no sign that she would bend her will to ours. By the end of August, she was letting down the hem of my gray skirt, fitting it to regulation length. On the floor of her sewing room, she knelt and pulled a straight pin from her mouth. She slid it into the fabric, saying nothing as I turned in increments away from her, pin by pin.

"But you went to public school," I pleaded. "You got to go." I wanted what she'd had, but more. "What am I supposed to do when I graduate from Northside?" I said. At the rate I was working through the curriculum, filling in the blanks and collecting my foil stars for every test completed, I'd be finished all the schooling by the time I turned sixteen. "Then what?" I said. With the limitations of the education offered by that system, I couldn't see myself beyond the town. When I scanned the Help Wanted column in our local paper's classifieds, the listed jobs were ones I didn't want. Part-time cashier at the Co-op grocery store. Childminder. Secretary/typist. Farmhand. Lumber piler. Waitress at the Village Inn. Though I didn't yet know what more I wanted, I knew I wanted more. What was wrong with that? I'd ask. My mother listened, told me that she heard what I was saying, but still, said nothing that made me think she'd ever change her mind.

Once, she'd been my age, the hemline of her dress falling well below the knee, her hair worn long, no rouge or lipstick on her face, no polish on her nails. The rules of her house held fast. But I wanted to believe that at some point in history, she was like me, aching to escape the closed-in world. She'd wanted to become a nurse, that much I knew, and had worked at the hospital after graduation as a nurse's aide, saving money for the school she'd attend in Oregon. On night shifts, when the ward was quiet, she'd crawl into an empty crib and close her eyes for a few minutes, become a child behind the metal bars, drifting over the threshold of sleep, floating there, her mind swimming out of her body, out of the room and the hospital, up from the town, spilling her into a world where anything could happen, so that she shone inside that story until a nurse walked in, or a baby cried, or someone called her name, and she had to rise from the dream.

By the time the letter came to say she'd been accepted to the college, she was dating my father. But she drove across the border and to Salem anyway. She toured the campus, seeing what her life might look like if she left, listening to the description of what classes she would take, the rigor of the two-year program, the rewards of the vocation. When she returned to Vanderhoof, she called the nursing school to let them know she wasn't coming after all. She'd changed her mind. The man she was dating had proposed. In spring, they wed. My mother laid her future plans aside. All the savings she'd deposited in her bank account she signed over to her husband, her money now theirs, now his. Instead of moving away for college, instead of a career that could have taken her anywhere—an inner-city clinic, a field hospital in the Middle East, a medical mission to Africa—she stayed to be a wife and mother, the storyline believed most worthy of a girl.

FIVE DAYS before the start of the new school year, as my brother and I sat at the table with our bowls of cereal, my mother walked up the stairs and stood on the threshold of the dining room. She'd come in from working in the garden, cleaning up the rows before the heat of the day. She looked at us, saying nothing for a moment as we ate our breakfast, studying us in a way that made me wonder what we'd done, what was coming next. Then she let out a long breath. "Okay," she said, and nodded. "It's your choice. If you really want to go, you can go."

Later that morning she drove us to the district office to sign us up for public school, then took us over to Nechako Valley Secondary to fill in all the paperwork. After she signed her name at the bottom of the forms, and my brother and I picked our classes from a list, both of us giddy and trying to hold back our joy at this sudden reversal, this release into freedom, we walked through the empty school, peeking into classroom doors.

In the art room, jars of paint and folded easels and reams of colored paper. In the music room, a dusty piano. Against the back wall of the science room, the skeleton of a horse hung from the ceiling, its bleached bones swinging with the open window's breeze. The school seemed both familiar and new, like a blueprint from a dream I'd moved through before, but with more doorways than I expected. In one room, two banks of sewing machines, where I'd sit and learn to thread the bobbin, ease the tension, and sew an apron for my final project. In another room, machinery and tools, where I'd plane and sand the wood to build a napkin holder. In the small auditorium, for drama class, I'd stand and face my partner to play the mirror game, my left hand waving as her right hand waved, her head tipping to the side as my head tipped, our bodies leading and following each other as we moved.

"It's bigger now," my mother said, as we walked a wide hallway lined with lockers. "Different than what I remember."

I tried to see her there, to let her live inside my mind before she was my mother, the woman who held our household together, who washed the walls with bleach each spring, who baked our bread, and grew our garden, and helped my father up the stairs at night. In that same building, minus the big gymnasium and the new Home Ec wing, my mother had pushed through these halls, books pressed to her chest as she headed to her next class. In one of these rooms, in a quiet row, in a desk, decades earlier, she was writing down facts and figures, names and dates, learning her generation's version of the world. It might have been in English class, or maybe mathematics, she couldn't recall exactly, but yes, late morning, near the lunch hour, the principal's voice buzzed through the PA to say that the President of the United States had been assassinated. The teacher started to weep. Students at their desks went pale. For the rest of the day, the school's mood was like a church before the funeral, boys and girls whispering at their lockers, *A man shot JFK.*

"Here, the library was here," she said, as we came around a corner at the far end of the school. Here, while the other girls flirted in the halls and the boys revved their cars in the parking lot, she'd spent her lunch hours reading story after story that swept her far from the school and the town and her life inside it. If I peered through the narrow pane of glass in the library door, I could picture it—my mother alone at a table, her long brown hair pulled back from her face, her head bowed over a book. Even if she couldn't remember those tales of intrigue and escape, the characters and plotlines and knowledge that carried her away, I could hold her there, another mystery brightening in the ever-expanding universe. She'd pick up a magazine, turn the pages and see the glossy photographs of countries whose names she'd never heard, places she'd never imagined. Her mind—valley, mountain, desert, ocean—began to dream and wander. A girl could go anywhere. The world, glowing in emerald waters and coconut palms, coral reefs and strange, miraculous creatures, spilled open.

Multitudes, multitudes,
in the valley of decision!

JOEL 3:14A

A BRIEF HISTORY OF
MENNONITE DANCE

ⰹ ⰹ ⰹ ⰹ ⰹ ⰹ ⰹ

ONLY AS CHILDREN DID WE MOVE FREELY to the music. At the front of the church, we stood facing the pews as we sang, "Father Abraham has many sons." We marched to the downbeat, the boys in their corduroy pants and button-up shirts, the girls in cotton dresses and bright white knee socks, singing, "I am one of them, and so are you, so let's just praise the Lord!" *Right arm, left arm, right leg, left leg, turn around, nod your head*—we called out the actions as we performed them, our bodies sweating to their own song.

On Tuesday afternoons in our primary class at Northside Christian School, Miss Hornsby pulled out the red vinyl record from its sleeve and placed it on the turntable that rested on a filing cabinet in the corner of the room. My classmates and I took our positions, bodies tensed and waiting for lift-off.

"Wings out!" she called. I jetted out my arms. "Airplanes," she called, "fly!"

The orchestra revved with a cymbal crash, then descended furiously before buzzing upwards. I was a biplane, a Snowbird, a B-52 bomber. I followed in the contrails of

Jeanie and Kevin and Corey and Christy, running the perimeter of the room, skyward soaring.

"Hummingbirds!" Miss Hornsby called above the music.

We all tucked in our elbows, shortening our wingspan. I whirred, fluttered my fingers, hovered on the spot, then zigged a circle with the thrumming charm of birds.

With the music to propel us, we moved as bumblebees in a choral buzz that turned the classroom to a garden lit with hollyhocks, nasturtiums, fireweed, and roses. We sucked the nectar, collected pollen, and jutted out our back-ends to threaten a sting.

In the sanctioned dancing of childhood, my body gladly took whatever tune it was given and made it play, galloping to the blare of the Irish Rovers on the living room stereo, tip-toeing to the piano-twinkle of "Music Box Dancer," and sliding across the kitchen linoleum in easy swing time to Bert Kaempfert and His Orchestra. Even my mother tapped her foot as she peeled potatoes at the sink and moved side to side to the snare-and-horn bob of "Free as a Bird."

But beyond the Sunday-school action songs and movement-to-music exercises, beyond the innocence of arms and legs mimicking the tune's rhythm and mood, dancing was discouraged, even named as sin. The mystery of its wickedness seemed to be locked in the heart of a joke told by prepubescent boys in church basements.

"Why don't Mennonites have sex standing up?" whispered Randy Ginter when the Sunday-school choir leader wasn't listening.

All of us near him leaned in at the sound of the forbidden word: sex.

"Why?" one of us whispered. "Why don't they?"

We all wanted to know. I wanted to know.

Randy smirked, his eyes in slits, and hissed the punch-line. "Because it might lead to dancing."

I didn't want to picture old Mr. and Mrs. Wiens clutching each other on the sanctuary podium, rubbing and writhing in their drab, dark clothes, but how else to make sense of the connection, two bodies moving to the music of the flesh? The punchline cinched the riddle tight. Sex and dancing, a knot impossible to undo.

DANCING WAS something done by other people, like Lutherans, the unsaved, kids in public school, and sometimes even the Mormons, but it was not done by Mennonites—unless, of course, you were a "Holy Roller," also known as "filled with the Holy Ghost," the sort of believer swept up by the Spirit. I'd seen it happen to some women in a Pentecostal church. This rare tribe swayed in their long skirts, arms raised toward the whirring ceiling fans while the flute, piano, and guitar played a repetitive chorus and the congregation sang. They moved their bodies to the music like underwater fronds in a dentist-office aquarium, pushed into motion by some mystical force beyond themselves.

To dance for any reason other than God, though, was to risk the slide into all manner of sin, which was why, when I asked my mother if I could attend the first dance of the year at my new public school, she scoffed through pursed lips.

"Pfft," she said. "The answer is no." She gripped the steering wheel and held her gaze straight ahead as we barreled down the highway into town.

In the passenger seat beside her, I flicked the radio dial to something other than local news. "But Soopie's allowed," I said. These words were my crowbar—the leveraging of my best friend's freedom in hopes that my mother, not wanting to be the un-fun parent, would yield. It had worked when Soopie and her sister signed up to raise 4-H lambs, and sometimes still worked when it came to tagging along to the movie theater and the carnival.

But my mom did not waver. "That's fine for Soopie," she said, her foot on the brake as we idled at the train tracks, waiting for the rail guards to rise.

"But *you've* gone to a dance before," I said.

And she had. The New Year's Eve party at the Legion. A dinner and dance for which she even bought a new dress from the Shirl-A-Dee Boutique, and smoothed on pink lipstick and sparkly-green eyeshadow to match the fabric's shiny emerald hue.

"That was your father's idea," she said.

This was also true. He hadn't taken "no" for an answer, despite her list of reasons why the Legion was the last place she wanted to be when midnight hit. The morning after the dance, when she sat at the dining table yawning and blinking the grit from her eyes, drinking her third cup of coffee, I'd asked for all the details, wanting to know if she and my father had actually gone out onto the dancefloor together, not able to picture the two of them doing anything in unison, other than chopping firewood or butchering chickens. Only once had I ever seen them try to dance. On my dad's birthday, after the rowdy, slurred singing of "Happy Birthday," after the candles were blown out and the cake was sliced and eaten, someone had cranked the volume on the stereo so that George Strait's baritone twang made a dancehall of our dining room. My father grabbed my mother by the wrists and dragged her along to the beat's two-step hump, his socked feet clomping as if in steel-toed boots across the linoleum, never in time to the music.

I kept pressing my mother, trying different angles for a weak spot in her resolve. "But it's just one dance," I said. "One single dance."

"We're not dancers. We just don't dance." The firmness in her voice came as a full-stop, end of sentence.

She was right, of course. The Mennonite Church as a whole had forbidden dancing, along with carnivals and movie theaters and video arcades, all of which were outlawed as worldly pleasures and thus to be avoided at peril of damnation. But card games, smoking, and drinking were on that same list, and my father partook of them all, which meant our house was already a den of iniquity, so what harm was a little dancing? Surely, somewhere back in the bloodline, a Mennonite had moved in rhythm to a beat while swinging the scythe in the barley field at harvest or hacking the axe-blade through the rooster's white neck. Surely, one of them had shushed their boots in three-four time across the barn floor in secret, waltzing to the tune of a whistled hymn.

Behind my own locked bedroom door, after I made sure that my mother was out in the yard somewhere, far enough away so she couldn't hear me, I drew the curtains, pressed "play" on my ghetto blaster, then took my place in front of the dresser mirror. When the music started, so did I. To the synth-pop of Rick Astley, to the crunch and kick of Bon Jovi, to the INXS snare-beat, I danced, practicing moves straight from music videos watched on the sly, shimmying, twirling, marching to the music, snapping my fingers with my arms above my head.

The first dance of the school year came and went. While I envied the Monday-morning hallway conversations recapping Friday night—who danced with whom, who started a fight in the smoking pit, and *Did you see Lecia MacLeod making out with Aaron Harley?*—I was already planning for the next big dance. In late November, when posters appeared on the bulletin boards advertising in swirled silver letters the Christmas Formal, I began choreographing my new moves.

At their hallway lockers between classes, girls in my grade were already talking dresses. Pamela had a shiny pouf skirt and was going to crimp her hair. Amy and Andrea were heading to the Pine Centre Mall on the weekend to find new outfits, probably at Mariposa or Ricki's, and then they'd go to Merle Norman for free makeup samples or to the Faces kiosk for cheap lipstick to match their dresses. Charlene said the Vanderhoof Department Store had a rack of fancy gowns she was going to try on after school—*Who wants to go along?*

Oh, I wanted to go along, all right. I wanted my own shiny pouf and glittery hairspray and lipstick that matched my eyeshadow that matched my earrings that matched the color of my dress, all the accessories that would move me toward the dance. Did I want to go along? Yes. But first, a different question needed to be answered, and the strategy of my asking needed stealth.

IN PAST years, when I was a student at Northside, the church-run school, December brought with it the annual Christmas concert, an evening in which the whole student body performed a play, and the parents sat watching from the pews. It was the dramatic event of the season, and always, every November, my mother had taken me to the

Department Store to pick out a pattern and fabric for a new Christmas dress. Now, at the public school and without a holiday concert to attend, our annual ritual hadn't yet been triggered. We had no reason to stand side by side in the fabric and notions department, together flipping through the fat books of Butterick and McCall's and Simplicity patterns, a mother and daughter united in a search for the right dress.

As I leaned against the kitchen counter, I tried to gauge my mother's mood. She stood at the stove, wooden spoon in the pot, stirring. She was humming along to the radio, which I took as a sign of hope.

"So, is it okay if Soopie comes here next Friday after school?" I said, keeping my voice casual.

"I don't see why not," she said.

"Or maybe I'll go there," I said, quick with the pivot. "We'll figure it out."

Unasked, I pulled out the dinner plates and started setting the table. "We have the Christmas Formal next Friday night," I said, careful to use the "we" and leave out "dance." My hands in the cutlery drawer clattered out the knives and forks.

"The what?" my mother said. She stopped humming.

"The Christmas Formal." *Fork on the left,* I reminded myself, *and knife on the right.* I went back into the kitchen for the spoons and water glasses, kept my back to my mother, and pretended to focus on my task.

"Christmas Formal?" She turned away from her stew-stirring to eye me. "If it's some kind of a dance—"

To tell the truth without telling the whole truth was tricky, like walking a fence nailed with a "No Trespassing" sign. Lose balance, and over you tip into the hellfire pit, the place where all the liars go, along with the unbelievers, the murderers, the sorcerers, and whoremongers. At least, this was how I remembered the verse from the book of Revelation, which promised a lake of flames and brimstone burning for eternity.

"Oh, there's probably music." I sluffed that detail away as fast as I could. "But it's more about the dressing up—the *formal* part. All the girls are buying fancy new dresses," I said, and then, like the garlanded star to adorn the top of the tree, finished with the words, "*Christmas* dresses."

The knee-length calico with the velvet bodice. The white-and-burgundy one with gold square buttons down the front. The blue jacquard with black frog closures and a sweetheart waist. I wished all the dresses of Christmases past to haunt my mother's memory, willing her to soften with nostalgia.

"But I wouldn't have time to sew you a dress," she said. I thought I heard a tint of wistfulness in her voice.

"Maybe I could just borrow some old skirt from Soopie, or order something from the catalogue?" I said. I carried the salt and pepper shakers to the table. Took the salad and bottles of dressing from the fridge and set those in their places, arranging all the elements with care and craftiness.

"What exactly do they mean by *formal*?" my mother said, cocking the lid on the simmering pot, then wiping her hands on the tea towel. "And when is this happening?"

BEFORE MY mother could change her mind, I picked my outfit from the Sears Fall and Winter catalogue. Instead of a dress, I chose a matching skirt and blouse modeled by a young woman who looked like a girl on the cover of a paperback teen romance, the kissable heroine of *Winter Dreams* or *Wrong Kind of Boy*. On the Sears model's body, which was tall and wispy, the clothing had an earthy, free-spirit look, the blouse trim against her ribcage and the drop-waist skirt draping loosely over her hips and falling just below the knee. When it arrived, however, the look on me was less bohemian, and more Bible study. I tried both the tuck-in and tuck-out looks, but the blouse still hung funny and the skirt's rayon clung to my hips. The hemline fell mid-calf, perfect church length.

"I like the color," said Soopie, who stood with me in her bathroom, our torsos reflected side by side.

I leaned into the mirror and swabbed a dusting of coppery shadow across one eyelid, then the next—to match my skirt and blouse, which was a shade of brown somewhere between mushroom and rust and sprigged with tiny black flowers. The collar, in scallops of cream-colored eyelet lace, itched the skin of my neck.

Next to me, Soopie looked like a teen movie star. Her mom had hired a lady in town to sew her a dress, and now she stood shining in puffy, silver princess sleeves against a black velvet bodice. The skirt of her dress rippled out in crinkly silver, the same fabric as her huge sleeves. Gripping her bangs from the root in one hand and wielding a comb in the other, Soopie teased her hair higher, higher still, before spraying it into a crusty cloud that would hold until midnight.

ACROSS THE snowy parking lot, where her mother dropped us off, Soopie and I trudged in the tire marks, trying not to slip in our faux-leather dress shoes, cursing the ice and pretending to be cool, not giddy, like we didn't care that we were going to this formal, like it didn't even matter if no one asked us to dance. We picked our way past the row of smokers sitting on the low plank fence along the front of the school, their breath and cigarette waft clouding the sharp cold air. Above us, stars pricked the black sky with studs of light. Even before we walked through the glass double doors, I heard the music, the bass heavy and pumping. Through the mingled scents of hairspray and cologne, we wove our way down the main hall and into the small auditorium.

I had never been inside a room so loud, a room whose walls vibrated with the noise from the DJ's speaker towers and made my ribcage buzz. The air hung with a dry-ice haze that smelled of cinnamon and musk. Multicolored lights pulsed, catching flashes of the gold and silver stars that garlanded the walls, and the bodies that moved like a live-action music video, lit up, then darkened in the jerky stutter of the strobes.

I took my place beside Soopie and with a cluster of other girls who stood by the bleachers touching their hair, smoothing on more gloss, whispering behind cupped hands into each other's ears.

"What did you say?" said Amy. "What?"

"Huh?" yelled Andrea.

Near the far corner exit, Tom Thiessen, an older boy I recognized from church, faced Helen Wall on the dance floor. While she did what looked like jogging in place, Tom moved side to side like a kneeless speed-skater, transferring his weight from one leg to the other and back again, but with no discernible recognition of the music's beat. His right leg swung back toward his left, touched down behind it, and then his left echoed the motion in a pendulous, on-the-spot lope.

"Look at him," I whisper-hollered in Soopie's ear. "Look at Tom dance."

I couldn't stop watching him, the long-limbed awkwardness of his movements, which seemed to work against the rhythm of the song, not with it. I was sure I could dance better than Tom, better even than Helen with her pop-jog, but I still wasn't dancing yet. No grade-eight boy had walked my way with that look—the invitation look, part bravado and part terror.

At the end of one song and start of the next, I studied the interplay of the sexes and saw the pattern. In the opening bars of the music, a girl would turn her body in the direction of the potential dance partner, and if he didn't notice her, she'd move a step or two toward him, like a doe rising out of the thicket, waiting for the buck to catch her scent. When he did notice her, he gave her a look that cast out a question mark, quick and tentative, and if the girl did not look away, if the girl smiled lightly, then the boy casually, nonchalantly—as if this was nothing, no big deal, whatever—walked over to her, faced her, jerked his head in the direction of the dance floor, and shrugged. Then the girl nodded and followed him into the bobbing, swaying horde.

But sometimes the boy walked right up to the girl, stood in front of her with a blank look on his face, as if someone had just asked his name, but in a language he didn't speak. Sometimes he just stared at the girl, the stunned way a boy was staring at me now, moving his mouth, but with no sound coming out, staring at me until finally, over the music's *thump-thump-thump*, I said, "Um, do you...want to...dance?"

"Uh, okay?" he said, this lanky, large-nosed, slick-haired boy named Norman Dyck, who was also Mennonite but attended the Gospel Chapel, the church where the women freely wore pants and earrings to Sunday services.

I followed Norman around the edge of the auditorium to the far back corner where fewer bodies were pumping their legs and arms to Billy Idol. Whenever the "Mony Mony" chorus drained down to a verse, a chant rose up from the heart of the dance floor, a choral shout of cussing that made the teachers on chaperone duty shake their heads at each other. I avoided eye contact as much as possible, letting my glance pass over Norman as I surveyed the rest of the dancers. Shaun Fincher, a grade ahead of me, punched his fist in the air and screwed up his face when he yelled the chorus, but he stomped to the beat, even thrashed his head, snaking his body as he grooved. I kept stepping lightly, side to side, tapping my left foot on the beat twice, then over to the right two times. Small steps. One step per beat. I was conscious of my hands and arms, not wanting to bump into a fellow dancer, so I tucked my elbows in and let them follow the lead of my feet, my fists clenched, fingers ready to start snapping. So far, nothing terrible was happening. Norman didn't writhe or try to rub against me. He only shuffled on the spot, shooshing his shoes around in no discernible pattern, but he wasn't a flailer or a wide-stepper, and I was grateful that we blended in, two Mennonites among a larger tribe moving to the beat.

For the rest of the evening, whenever no one approached to ask for a dance, whenever it became clear that I had no partner, whenever a country-and-western song like "Fishing in the Dark" came on and the farm and ranch kids all flooded the floor in two-stepping mania and I had no clue what moves to do, or whenever the boy we called Gopher lurked near, I did what all the other girls did. I retreated to the bathroom, making as if I really had to pee, or check my hair, or fiddle with my earrings. From behind the stall's locked door, I could listen in as one girl cried to her friends about "that dumb cow" trying to make out with Jason, hear the *ka-chunk ka-chunk ka-chunk* of the paper towel dispenser as another girl blotted her weeping black mascara. Meanwhile, strains of the dance floor thumped on, drawing us all back, drawing me back to the crush of hormones and sweat, to the bouncing crowd of girls whose high hair sank lower by the song, and boys whose cologne could hardly mask the odor wafting from their armpits.

We were into the final hour of the evening, nearing midnight, when members of the student council began to move covertly through the small auditorium, weaving in and out of the slow-dancing couples.

"Mistletoe," Soopie yelled over the music, her hands cupped around her mouth. "They have mistletoe."

One of the seniors, a girl named Claudia who played on the volleyball team, snuck up to a swaying couple and tapped the boy on the shoulder, then held a sprig of leaves and berries above the head of the boy's dance partner. Claudia grinned, winked, and waited.

Soopie and I waited, too, along with everyone else gawking from the sidelines, eager to see the next move. And it came, on cue, with only a moment of stalling from the boy, who grabbed the girl by the shoulders, abruptly pressed his mouth to hers, then released his hold. The girl shrugged, seemed to smile, and then set her hands back on the boy's shoulders to resume the dance. But now her body moved closer to his, the space between their torsos lessened, as if their belly buttons were touching, their hipbones grazing.

Like a festive virus, the effect spread quickly, the energy shifting so that more bodies moved to the music, more couples listed and bobbed, eager to be accosted by the bearers of mistletoe. By the end of the night, new couples would be formed from a single kiss, two mouths pressed together by an old tradition and a plant whose name in the German translated literally to "dung on a twig," named for the birds who ate the berries and dropped the seeds as they flew from tree to tree.

When the bars of a ballad began to arpeggiate through the speakers, the girls around me popped to attention in their taffeta and sparkles. None of us knew how long it would last, this song, this frantic chance to find a partner. As the twelve-string guitar climbed with the harmony of a flute, I saw Wendyl Quartz standing near the corner by the bleachers. Wendyl sat in front of me in Ms. MacLean's math class, and once asked to borrow my calculator, then returned it to me upside down with the word "hEll" typed on the display.

"Hey," he said. He looked at the ceiling, his tongue circling the inside of his cheek. He shrugged.

"Hi," I said, and shrugged back.

And then, not knowing who was asking whom to dance, we shuffled toward the floor, and faced each other. Wendyl's damp hands settled on the clinging rayon of my hips. My hands hovered on the sweaty cotton of his shoulders. Inside the swarm of other couples, we leaned side to side, side to side as the singer broke into the opening lyrics of "Stairway to Heaven." When Claudia pranced over with her mistletoe and hung it over our heads, Wendyl couldn't look me in the eye. He leaned forward as I tipped my head, and he pecked his dry lips against my cheek. Then those white berries trembling on their stem swung away toward the next pair of dancers.

As the song rose toward its end, the tempo shifted, and the couples began to release each other. The electric guitar crescendoed. The cymbals shimmered and crashed. Unclasped from my partner, I started to sway and turn. The singer's voice pitched higher and higher. Wendyl bent his knees, straightened up, rocked side to side, then repeated, making a pattern of his movements. Inside an auditorium full of jocks, headbangers, skaters, and band geeks, Mormons, cowboys, weirdos, and preppies, inside a crowd of dancers that even included Mennonites, the punch of the drums reverberated. The floorboards thrummed. Beneath the spinning disco ball, our faces flashed with shattered light and sweat. I felt the thumping in my ribs, the old ancestral blood-beat calling the body to move as it was made to move, dust to dust, glory to glory. First song. Last song. Under my feet, the grit of all our dancing. Above me, swinging on lines in the darkness, the stars.

SMALL TOWN
LIMITS

Ⅹ Ⅹ Ⅹ Ⅹ Ⅹ Ⅹ Ⅹ

ONLY TWO WEEKS INTO SUMMER BREAK, and we were bored. The spring flood had long receded, leaving the river lazy and low enough to walk some sections only waist deep. When the heat peaked, people floated three hours down current on truck-tire inner tubes, all the way from the Stuart Lake Highway bridge—the "new bridge"—to the "old bridge" that connected to Burrard Avenue, the main drag. But Sindee and I had no way of getting to the new bridge, and no tubes for the floating. So, instead, we stood down at the shore of the Nechako, dragging sticks in the water, talking about how lame our small town was, and trying to figure out what might happen next.

At the start of eighth grade, when the high school hallways made me feel anonymous, I'd recognized Sindee from Junior Sunday School. She had been the tiny, dark-haired girl who showed up from time to time and rarely spoke as we sat around the folding table in the church basement, filling in Bible crosswords, and listening to Mr. Wiebe tell us about Jesus. When Soopie and I tried out for volleyball, Sindee showed up, too, and because none of us made the A team, we all ended up on the same B-team court and bench. As soon as Soopie and I found out that Sindee liked Glass Tiger—our favorite band—we liked her. No one else we knew wore purple high-top Converse. Plus, Sindee knew how to fold notes in the cool way, so that the loose-leaf page tucked in on itself and formed a little envelope, small enough to be slipped from hand to hand in class when the teacher turned his back. Like us, she rolled her eyes when the popular girls traipsed past our lockers, so we knew we could trust her. By summer, we had become a trio that could split into combos of two when one of us was busy or gone, like Soopie, who had left us behind for a holiday in California.

"We could go sit on the hospital hill," said Sindee, "with paper bags on our head. And then, I don't know, wave at people who drive by, or something?"

She had tried the paper bag thing last summer, she told me, and from what she could see through the cut-out eye-holes, drivers did double takes. Some had even honked.

Above us, vehicles rumbled over the wooden bridge that spanned the river, alternating directions as the traffic light shifted from red to green, north to south. We'd planned to walk the mile into town from Sindee's house in the Vander-view neighborhood, but neither of us had money to burn, and the new *Seventeen* and *Sassy* magazines wouldn't be on the drugstore rack for at least another week.

"We could chuck stuff at cars," I said, mostly joking, but then curious about what that might look like. From there, our talk went the way it always did, fanning out into hypothetical vandalism, minor crimes and consequences. From *what if* to *and then*, we built the story, riffing on each other's ideas until, in our minds' eyes, we had already tossed the fist-sized rock at some dude's lift-kitted four-by-four, cracked his side window to smithereens, caused the guy to swerve, smash through the bridge deck, and crash into the river below. To cover our tracks, we'd jump into the water, swim out to the sinking vehicle, pull out the unconscious driver, drag him to shore, and then—well, this is where we'd get stuck, because neither of us, no matter how badly we wanted to press our lips against a boy's, had any desire to perform mouth-to-mouth on a mustached, beer-gutted stranger who smelled like muskrat and gun grease.

What we wanted—beyond that kiss from an actual boy—was for something interesting to take shape. I had the rising sense that nothing ever really happened in our part of the world, and nothing would. Nothing could. Our town was too small, too redneck, and so far, the rumor that we were getting a 7-Eleven had been just that—a rumor. All we had was the Vanderhoof International Airshow, the Nechako Valley Agricultural Exhibition and Bull-a-Rama dance, the Hooterville Hoot classic car show, and a sign that welcomed visitors to *Vanderhoof: The Geographical Centre of B.C.*

"This place is boring," I'd complain to my mother, who would respond with a list of reasons why our town was just fine. It was a good place to grow up, for one, and the people were friendly.

"It's because I'm related to half of them," I said, which was only a minor exaggeration. Never could I walk through the Co-op grocery store without seeing a cousin or aunt or great-uncle, and even if a member of the immediate family wasn't pushing a cart through the baking goods aisle, some other Mennonite inevitably would be. As the saying goes, where two or more Mennonites are gathered, a family reunion occurs.

"We have everything we need here," my mother said, which was true if all we needed was lumber, tools, fuel, a pickup truck, winter boots, sewing supplies, cowboy hats, guns, and Bibles.

There seemed to be an unofficial list of acceptable reasons for venturing outside the region, namely family reunions, cancer treatment, missionary work, or a short holiday at one of the destinations advertised in the window of Seven Seas, the local travel agency. The world beyond the borders of our town was eyed with a measure of suspicion. The general belief seemed to be that we couldn't trust what happened elsewhere because we didn't know the folks who lived there, especially if "there" was the big city, a place of perverts, gangs, and criminals. Vanderhoof was safe, cupped in a snug valley, remote enough that few strangers passed through, and when they did, hardly stayed long enough to cause a ruckus. This was home, our known world, and where we all belonged.

But home was growing smaller by the year. Even if we counted all the folks who lived on rural farms and ranches and in the outskirt boonies, Vanderhoof was still only technically a village. Our nearest city was an hour's drive east on Highway 16. Prince George boasted an indoor swimming pool, a roller rink, and the Pine Centre Mall, "the centre of it all," as the TV jingle sang. But even that city was starting to feel small. Every time we descended into Prince, as the locals called it, the septic stench of the pulp mill left me carsick.

"Look," said Sindee. She pointed her stick toward Loop Road. A woman on a bicycle was pedaling toward the bridge. "It's Miss Olofsson."

Miss Olofsson taught English at the high school. She was tall, silver haired, and wore elegant sweaters and long skirts in bright purples and vivid reds. When she passed students in the hallways, she always called out a cheery "good morning" or "good afternoon," and smiled with her huge teeth. She was the rare kind of teacher who genuinely seemed to like her students, even the slackers at the back of the class who tapped their pencils to an inaudible beat or slept with their heads on their desks while she explained the difference between expository and argumentative.

"Quick," I said to Sindee. "Hide."

Though I didn't quite know yet why we needed to take cover, it seemed the natural response to seeing a teacher while on summer break. Sticks in hands, we scrambled up the slope of the riverbank to the abutment of the bridge so that we were directly below the start of the pedestrian path.

"Should we scare her?" whispered Sindee. "Or try to tip her over?"

Both options sounded dangerous and excellent. As Miss Olofsson coasted closer, we nodded to each other, braced ourselves against the creosote-coated beam, and held our sticks up high, positioning their tips in the cracks of light that filtered through the wooden slats. The tremor of bicycle tires rumbled on the bridge. As the sound's shadow passed overhead, we rammed our sticks up hard, aiming for the front wheel, the back wheel, going for the spokes, jabbing through the slats in a stabbing frenzy until the bicycle shape wobbled past, beyond us with our useless tools.

Sweating and out of breath, we scrambled back down the slope, nervous with laughter.

"I think she saw us," said Sindee, shiny-eyed. "What if she saw us?"

"She almost wiped out," I said.

"We could have knocked her right off her bike," said Sindee.

"Right off the bridge," I said. "Into the river."

And with that, the narrative broke open into possibilities—Miss Olofsson with a broken nose, a broken leg, a full-body cast. A town-wide search for the perpetrators, while the two of us sat in her English class pretending to be innocent, writing our thesis statements in perfect blue-ink cursive, hoping our shifty eyes didn't make us look like the criminals from the Police Beat section of the local newspaper. Our story launched the way we hoped our lives might one day, too—into the unlikely and unexpected, and out of this small world.

We chucked our sticks into the river and watched the current carry away the evidence, then climbed the bank and walked the rest of the way into town. Our flip-flops slapped with every step, past the old stucco apartments where Uncle George's ex-girlfriend used to live, past St. Joe's school, the nuns' quarters, Shoppers Food Mart, Fox Ford, North Country Inn, the liquor store, and all the way to the intersection where the Reid Hotel and Frankie's Pub stood opposite the Royal Bank. Here, where Columbia Street East met Burrard Avenue, the town center began.

As a child, I believed Vanderhoof went on forever and was endlessly alive with people talking on sidewalks, parked cars lining the roads, and the stores and businesses bustling with customers. Every trip into town felt like adventure. We might see the mayor, a short, smiling bald man who said hello to everyone he passed as he limped down the sidewalk, or the woman with the black beehive hairdo and the faint hint of a shadowy mustache, or the fellow in a cowboy hat who walked around with a garbage bag slung over his shoulder. So much mystery abounded in the place and its people, so much possibility crackled within its borders. Until it didn't. Until I learned about polio, about hormonal disorders and the horrors of unwanted facial hair, about how the mysterious cowboy was just a man named Joe who once worked the rodeo circuit and now walked the ditches picking up tossed-out empties.

Like every household in the district, mine had its own copy of the locally famous book *Vanderhoof: The Town That Wouldn't Wait*. Wouldn't wait for what, I always wondered, flipping through the black-and-white photographs of the river, the Dakelh people, the fur traders and Grand Trunk Railway workers, the early pioneers and homesteaders and cattle ranchers, and Mennonites posing stoically beside woodpiles. The particulars of the town's history and all its complications failed to grip me. I glossed over the text, only looking at the pictures and wondering why, of all the places those people could have picked, they chose Vanderhoof. From as far away as Sweden, Scotland, England, and Chicago, they came for adventure and prosperity, settling in the same dull valley that now held me captive.

I was at that hinge of adolescence, easing out of the awkward, oily surge of puberty and into the cocky cynicism of youth. What had once seemed exciting, hilarious, so much fun, now was plain dumb. Our town was dumb. The drugstore was dumb because they'd tacked up a NO READING THE MAGAZINES sign, and now a clerk patrolled the aisle. The movie theater was dumb because it took months to get new releases on the screen. Fields was dumb because most of the jeans they sold were factory seconds, always too tight in one thigh, too long in the crotch. When I sulked around the house and complained about what a boring place I lived in, about how I had nothing to do, my mother would suggest better ways to spend my time. She'd say, "Why not weed the garden?" or "Babysit the neighbor kids," or "Your dad's pickup could really use a wash." But I didn't want to work. I wanted to do nothing, and to complain about having nothing to do.

During the school year, my days fell into a prescribed rhythm, but in summer, time was a sun-stoked, drawn-out wandering over the same grid of roads. Life beyond our small interior town struck me as glamorous and mythical, like a movie or a dream whose ending was inevitable. The only people who left always seemed to return, as if the bowl of our valley were impossible to escape. Try as they might to climb out—a year or two away at college, a move to the sky-scraping city of Vancouver—they'd slide back in, take a job at one of the mills or at a store in town, fall in love with a local, and start to multiply.

It made sense that my dad wanted my older brother to take over his logging business when he graduated, but the thought that I might repeat my mother's life, her mother's life, and the life of every woman in my family pinched like a pair of discount Fields jeans, cinched like a too-tight band around my waist. I didn't want to be an Agatha in a sweater set, a Tina in a tent dress, a waddlingly pregnant Mrs. Heinrich Harder dragging twin toddlers by their wrists down the Sunday-morning church aisle. Some of my aunts had jobs outside the house—Aunt Evelyn at the bank, Aunt Mary at the bookkeeper's—but I didn't want those jobs either. Neither did I dream of being a drugstore clerk patrolling the magazine aisle, or a stylist at the Hair Affair salon. I didn't know what I wanted to become, only that I didn't want to stay. At eight years old, I'd penciled in my School Days album: *When I grow up, I'll be a* DOLPHIN TRAINER, as if even then, I was plotting my way toward the coast and the ocean. On the high school career quiz handed out by the guidance counselor, I checked off "lawyer" and "psychologist" and "journalist," jobs that sounded too exotic for my hometown and would mean I'd have to leave.

As Sindee and I walked the main drag, we peered in store windows, eyeing what was going on inside to deem whether it was worth entering. Through the Department Store's window, we spied the earrings on a spinning rack beside the till, and the lingerie on the side wall, chastely lacy bras and pale nightgowns hung on display. We agreed we'd never wear that stuff, it was tacky, and probably itched like crazy.

The windows at Circle 7 Foods were still boarded up, having been smashed in a Halloween fight when Sean Byrd threw Matt Becker through the glass.

"I miss the hot fudge cones," said Sindee.

"I miss the Jo-Jo's," I said, sighing over those steaming, fat potato wedges deep-fried to a crisp.

We passed Omineca Sports and Sound, Taylor Brothers' hardware, and then stopped in front of Black Bob's Billiards. We looked to see who was shooting pool and whether we could recognize the bodies locked to the arcade games, joystick hands fiddling, screens glowing with asteroids and pixel-eating creatures. The people who hung out at Black Bob's were the type that Sindee and I regarded with fear and suspicion. They were the ones who spent weekends partying at the gravel pit, who wore leather and denim and black T-shirts crusted with Metallica and Anthrax emblems. The guys' shaggy hair covered their eyes, and they each seemed to sport one silver earring—self-pierced with a hot needle, and always hanging from the left lobe. They knew all the bootleggers in town—or were the bootleggers in town—and smoked the fifteen-cent cigarettes sold in bulk by Black Bob and his lady, who wore matching "Old Fart" and "Old Fart's Wife" T-shirts when they worked the counter together. We knew we didn't belong there. As much as Sindee and I liked the idea of being bad, we remained girls in oversized sweat-shirts and pleated chambray shorts, replicas of the Junior Miss section of the Sears catalogue. We were not the kind of girls who stood alongside the cluster of guys chalking cues or crowding around the Super Mario Bros. machine, cheering on Pinky, the red-haired high-scorer. The typical Black Bob's girl sported a high, hairsprayed wall of bangs and a thick rim of black eyeliner, and carried a black leather purse with a rabbit's-foot keychain swinging from the zip-per. This girl was the girlfriend of the boy who played the games, the female accessory who tagged along, a lady ever in waiting for her guy. She was the scrappy girl, the cuss-ing girl, the terrifying girl, the kind of girl who ended up in fights in the school parking lot and pulled out handfuls of another girl's hair. While waiting for the bus one afternoon, I'd witnessed a Black Bob's black-purse girl named Tamara tear out one of Debbie Reed's silver hoop earrings, ripping it clean through the bleeding lobe.

Sindee and I raised our eyebrows at each other, as if Black Bob's was beneath us, but really, we were too freaked out to go inside. Instead, we headed for the drugstore, to look at the makeup and sneak-read the magazines when the clerk was at the till, and maybe we'd go onward to the Co-op grocery store for jujubes and fuzzy peach gummies, or to the Deli Dish for the fancy glass bottles of fizzy Koala Springs, a drink that made us talk with Australian accents, or over the tracks and down to the Shell, where the owner, a Sikh man some of the truckers called Hindu Ken, let customers make their own "screamers," alternating layers of half-frozen soda pop from the slush machine and soft-serve vanilla from the ice cream nozzle into a tall plastic cup.

Bored. We were bored, crossing the street at the single traffic light, walking a sidewalk we'd already traveled, going back the way we'd already come.

"I heard you can derail a train if you put a penny on the tracks," said Sindee. She'd read it somewhere or seen it in a movie.

Before boredom could lead to creativity, it had to pass through the valley of monotony, to settle into that lowland groove and hunker there awhile. Before creativity, boredom had to spend some time rummaging around in the skull, digging through the odds and ends of the ordinary and the mundane, the way a kid with popsicle sticks and yarn and glue, pipe cleaners and scissors and cardboard and dried legumes might craft some strange contraption and call it a creation, call it art.

I knew from my brother that teenagers who lived in a town like ours had to learn to make their own fun, and if that fun broke the law, to not get caught while making it. If you were going to fill balloons with a stew of watered-down pig manure, for instance, and then pelt those balloons at cars driving down the main drag at night, you needed to not hit a police cruiser, or, like my cousin did, a Greyhound bus whose stunned passengers looked on from behind their spattered windows. If you were going to leave a dead chicken on the doorstep of Hazel Kafsky, Vanderhoof's animal-rights zealot, you had to go by cover of night and then run like stink when she started screaming curses from her front porch. If you snuck in darkness down your high school English teacher's driveway, and, on his front lawn, jammed into the grass a whittled spear, then stuck a bloody pig's head fresh from the butchering shed on the end of that spear, you had to be prepared to be called to the principal's office on Monday morning. You had to be ready to give an answer when your teacher asked you if you believed it was normal, healthy, remotely okay for a young girl to wake in the morning and see what she saw through her bedroom window, that dripping snouted head.

By the side of the Co-op, Sindee and I dug pennies from our pockets. In my palm, the coins sweat a coppery tang. With a fistful of pennies, I could buy a tiny paper bag full of candy, a licorice stick, a postage stamp to lick and fix to an envelope to be slid into the slot and flown away into a far-off part of the world. A few years before, I'd begun writing to Moira, a pen pal I'd found in the back of a *Tiger Beat* magazine. In her profile, Moira said she liked Kirk Cameron, Duran Duran, collecting stickers, and riding horses. Best of all, she lived in California. On a sheet of stationery adorned with a rainbow and a pair of roller skates, I wrote my first letter to a stranger, asking her about palm trees, Disneyland, the Pacific Ocean, surfing, and who was her favorite member of Duran Duran. I snuck a stamp from my mother's desk, stuck it on the rainbowed envelope, and in my neatest printing, addressed it to Moira from *Palo Alto, California*. Simply to write the name of that city, that state, made me feel significant, connected to a life beyond my small interior town. When a bright-orange envelope appeared in our mailbox two months later, my mother insisted on reading it.

"Who is this Moira from California?" she said. She took the letter from my hand, her eyes scanning left to right, left to right as she read. When she got to the part about Simon Le Bon being "soooooo sexy," she gasped and scolded my name. Then she told me I was never going to write another letter to "this Moira girl, whoever she was," even if I had told Moira I'd be her pen pal, and that I'd love to one day visit her in California when I saved up enough money for my own plane ticket.

Sindee and I stood with our pennies, stalling with tactics and plans for an exit strategy if the train crashed, until finally we worked up the nerve. We laid the coins in a row on the rusted tracks of the CN Railway, then sat with our backs against the Co-op's cinderblock wall and waited. The air was windless. The sun, as it lowered, cast the town in the warm amber light of old Polaroids. The sounds of the town slowed to the intermittent hiss of a logging truck's air brakes, a man's voice hollering across a parking lot, a car door slamming, the thrum and rev of a four-by-four at the traffic light.

The train would be traveling north. It would already have moved through Prince George, the nearest city, and before that, through the Cariboo and the Fraser Canyon, all the way from the western edge of our province, our country, our continent. When I considered the tracks that cut through our town, and how they were stitched together with the rest of the nation, and even with the rest of the world, the thought fizzed in me like shaken soda pop, like I could, at any moment, jet out my own body with the sheer force of imagined possibility of where in the world I might end up.

When the high whistle of a train finally sounded, Sindee and I jumped. From behind a stack of wooden pallets, we watched the safety guardrails descend, dinging to warn motorists. The engine pulled the cargo cars by in a blurry whoosh, the wind from its motion whiffling the air around us. But no screech of metal on metal. No fire, no sparks, no smoke. No train flew off the tracks.

"So much for that," said Sindee.

"At least nobody died," I said.

"Yeah," said Sindee. "That would suck."

We walked to the other end of town, past the Reo movie theater and Seven Seas, past the Pagoda, the Reid, the liquor store, the auto parts shop, and toward Shoppers Food Mart, where we'd trail through the aisles of grocery items, hungry for nothing in particular, hungry for everything they didn't sell. As we walked, we kept a vigilant lookout for any hint of action, for somebody or something worth paying attention to. For anything to crack through the commonplace. For a break in the pattern to yield meaning, for some sense that things could change. That we could change it. And if nothing was happening, we'd make it. We'd give ourselves a story worth telling, so that later we could say to each other, *Hey, remember the open window we climbed through, that neighbor's empty house, the double dare. Remember the breathing over the midnight phone line. The dead dog in the trunk. The campsite guy in the dark with the axe. Remember the close call, the near miss, that time we almost died, but lived to tell.*

Look at your way in the valley!
Know what you have done!

JEREMIAH 2:23B

⚹ ⚹ ⚹ ⚹ ⚹

HOLDING THE FLAME

x x x x x x x

THE SKY WAS HALFWAY BETWEEN SUNSET and darkness as we stood in the parking lot outside the bus depot. At the hinge of summer, the air hung warm and breezeless, edging on humid, and the asphalt still held the day's heat.

"Come on," my dad said, holding his arms out to me.

He clamped my shoulders in a soft bear hug. He smelled like he always smelled in the evenings: sweat, smoke, and whiskey. His stubble chafed against the side of my face, like it did when I was small and he would pull me close and say, "What you need is a good whisker-rub," then scrape his cheek against my own until my skin burned and pinkened, and I begged for him to stop.

In the openness of the parking lot, though I stiffened and arched away, my father tightened his arms around me.

"Dad," I said. "I gotta go. Now."

My mother stood a few feet back, waiting for his display to be over. "Dave," she said, his name a gentle tug.

"You never mind," he said, swatting the air in her direction. "Can't a guy say goodbye to his daughter?" His words dragged, drawing out the vowels, the way the moment would be drawn out if I pushed away his affection. So I let him hold me and press his stubbled jaw against my cheek until he shuddered, on the verge of choked-back tears.

"Dad, okay," I said, bristling. "The bus is ready to leave."

With reluctance, he let me go, but not before he pressed his lips against my cheek. I flinched, drew back, and wiped off the wet slur of his mouth.

"I guess this is goodbye," said my mom, scooting in front of my dad. She gave me a quick hug and parting benediction—*be safe, have fun, call us when you get you there*—then nudged me and my baggage toward the idling Greyhound.

I took my place in the line of passengers waiting to board the bus and watched from a distance as she guided my dad back to the pickup. He swung open the door, set a foot on the running board, and eased his body up into the passenger seat, like a man moving through water, weighed down by a strong current. He sat with the door cocked open long enough for him to unsnap his left shirt pocket and reach for his pack of Export A's. In the driver's seat, my mother gripped the wheel. As the bus rolled away from the station, I could see through the window my parents moving in the opposite direction, away from me, the red glow of their taillights heading for home.

ALL I KNEW about Camp Rainbow was that teenagers from all over the province would be attending, gathering for a week of leadership training sponsored by the Rotary Club. All I knew about the Rotary Club was that they sent students on exchanges all over the world, that they held fundraiser pancake breakfasts in town, and that the organization wasn't affiliated with any church, which concerned my mother.

"What do they teach at this camp?" she said, studying
the brochure.

"Leadership," I said. "Stuff like that."

Truth was, I had no idea what leadership training even
looked like, whether lecterns and blackboards and single-
file marching would be involved, or if, like the poster
showed, I'd be flashing a peace sign and smiling and draping
my arms over boys' shoulders all week long. The experience
of Camp Rainbow, the Rotary brochure promised, would
give each camper a new and golden opportunity, a weeklong
journey of personal development as we searched out the
treasures hidden within ourselves. But I didn't care about
my hidden treasures, my secret pot of gold. What made me
edgy with anticipation was that Camp Rainbow would take
me away from summer's monotony, away from home and all
it held.

I would be a different Carla at this camp. Here, where no
one knew anything about me except for what I told them, I
would become a Camp Rainbow version of myself, new and
improved. Instead of aloof, I would be gregarious. Instead
of clammed up, a bubbly talker. Instead of wallflowering on
the margins, I would slide my way into the group laughter.
Instead of reading and rereading the week's itinerary as I
lay on my bunk, pretending to be absorbed in the details
of the daily schedule while around me the other cabin girls
unpacked their suitcases, smiling, asking questions and
saying their names to each other the way normal people did
when they met for the first time, I would shuck my stand-
offish awkwardness and be the one who swung her head
down from the top bunk and greeted my new bunkmate.

"Hi," I said, way too brightly, to the upside-down face of
the girl below. Even as I introduced myself, the words felt

false in my mouth, scripted, as if I were playing the character of a sitcom friendly girl.

But the bottom-bunk girl smiled back. "Hey," she said. "I'm Natalie. Where you from?"

Natalie, from Osoyoos, was into soccer and volleyball, but she seemed nice enough, and more importantly, wasn't a whole lot thinner than me, which made me feel like I could trust her. Erin, the black-haired pixie girl on the top bunk across from mine, was into horses. Michelle worked as a lifeguard in the summer and wanted to be a doctor. Mandy spoke fluent French. As the cabin chattered, I reminded myself to keep smiling, keep nodding, saying things like "Awesome!" and "That's so rad!" with believable enthusiasm. Yes, I was "totally stoked" about the week ahead. No, I'd never tried line-dancing, but it, too, sounded "awesome."

The next day, as I stood in the gravel parking lot, learning the choreography to "Pink Cadillac," I slapped my ankle, dug in my heel, spun a circle, walked tall, and grapevined with my fellow campers, wondering what I was doing there, and how many dancers in that line could tell that I was faking the zeal of my hollered *Yee-haw!* In every camp activity, at all the stations and workshops, group hikes, and role-playing lessons on how to be a strong leader in your community, I felt as if I were standing at the edge of things, never in the center. It was as if some invisible tether held me back, a line stretched across the miles between camp and home.

All week long, I smiled at my fellow campers, went out of my way to say things I never said to almost-strangers, things like, "I love your sweatshirt!" and "Your hair looks so awesome!" and "We should totally be pen pals!" I tried to ignore my inner running commentary, the little asterisks that annotated my interactions with secret thoughts. *She's probably bulimic. At least I don't have dandruff. Does he think I'm fat?*

In the bathroom's morning crush of girls leaning over the communal sinks, I marveled at the camaraderie of those who shared lipsticks and blowdryers, combed each other's hair, crowded the mirror together and said things like, "You're so pretty," and "Seriously, you have the best eyes." They gave their praise with such convincing honesty, as if they truly meant what they said. At night, as we lay in our bunks with the lights out, I listened to my cabinmates confess their crushes. Natalie liked Ben. Mandy and Michelle thought Mike the counselor was cute. Erin had frenched with Jai behind the pumphouse, even though she had a boyfriend back home, and when she started crying, Michelle said, "You're not a bad person, okay? Everyone makes mistakes." When all the girls crawled out of their sleeping bags and gathered around Erin's bunk, patting her arm, stroking her hair, I stood with them, echoing their soft consolation sounds, but not knowing what to do with my hands. I felt how I always did when hearts around me overflowed and spilled, like I was close-fisted, holding back some part of myself without knowing what it was and why I held it.

IN THE evening, during free time after supper, I stood in line for the payphone and waited my turn to call home, listening in on the conversations of the campers ahead of me. Everyone, it seemed, had the same cheery script, the same bland dialogue. *Yup, I'm getting enough to eat. Yup, it's a lot of fun. Yup, everyone's really nice here.*

My mother, on the other end, sounded as small as a thumbnail, faraway as a star.

"Everything's good then?" she said. The connection clunked and my father's voice cut in.

"Who's this?" he said.

"Hang up the phone," she said, gently. "It's hard to hear."

"You hang up," he said.

I pictured him where he always was at this hour, sitting in the old rocking chair out in his shop, nursing a can of Pepsi cut with whiskey, the dirt-and-oil-smudged phone in his hand. Inside the house, in the kitchen, my mother held the wall phone, the cord stretched taut as she stood at the sink, looking out over the yard and to the road to see who came and went. This was our script—my dad in one room, my mother in another, and me somewhere else entirely, or trying to be.

"I've gotta go," I said.

"Huh?" said my dad. "Don't even have time to talk to your old man."

His words were amplified by the shared telephone line, his breathing loud and heavy in my ear.

"Other people need to use the phone," I said, my voice steely, stage-whispering to keep the boy in line behind me from hearing. My dad coughed, cleared his throat, then gruffed out the familiar dialogue. *Not even a couple minutes, huh? I guess I'm the bad guy. I guess I'm just no good.*

He was not the bad guy. He was not no good. He was some mornings the man who drove me to school, humming along to his country radio. He was some days the man who scanned my report card and then pulled out his wallet and paid me twenty dollars for every *A* earned. Sometimes he was a man hand-feeding table scraps to a dog, speaking to the animal as if it were a small child. Sometimes he was the man who swung open the front door and announced that we were going camping in two hours, so hurry up and get ready. Sometimes he was the man who sat at the head of our dining room table and in the presence of houseguests ordered me downstairs to "go play 'Music Box Dancer,'" his favorite piano tune.

"Come on," he'd say, "I bought you that piano. You go play it."

I'd grit my teeth and trudge downstairs to the far corner of the basement, flick on the piano lamp, and play the notes that conjured the twirling figurine of a slender ballerina. Around and around, the phrases turned and turned, the melody frilling and jumping an octave, the bass notes rising to meet it, crescendoing, then quieting. Upstairs the voices of the men and women at their game of cards rose and fell with laughter, and ice clinked in their glasses. The pattern repeated and repeated, until the song ended the same way it began, with the twinkling notes revolving into a fade-out. When my hands stilled on the keyboard, faint applause filtered from upstairs, and then my dad's voice, happy and hollering down to me, *Play it again. Play that song again.*

He was the sad-hearted man, breathing slow and heavy through his mouth into the other end of the line, expecting me to speak, to say what he needed me to say. That he wasn't no good. That he wasn't the bad guy. To say what other sons and daughters said into the telephone when they talked to their dads from hundreds of miles away. *Miss you. Love you. Can't wait to see you soon.* Those words, when others said them, sounded true.

"Dad, I gotta go," I said, my cheeks growing hot. "I can't talk. Goodbye."

EACH MORNING, I sat through Camp Rainbow talks designed to motivate me and all the other campers toward a more authentic life, chanting back the counselors' words until we sounded like we meant them. I had the power to make all my dreams come true. True greatness lay within. I could change my life. I'd heard these ideas preached before, except with Jesus, not me, shining at the center and able to transform me into the Carla I was destined to be. Afternoons, in color groups, we practiced being our best selves in relays and games, shouting affirmation to each other, cheering from the sidelines no matter the flubs and stumbles, as if this were the new reality, a world that we created and would take home with us when we left. Every evening, after the shuffle of meal trays and dinner-table chatter, we spilled out into free time, the structure of the day cracking open into huddles of laughter, boys and girls pairing off for secret walks, or impromptu dance parties on the front lawn, someone's ghetto blaster pumping Madonna's "Vogue" on repeat as we catwalked, spun, and struck our poses until the bell rang and called us in to "mug up," our ritual of hot chocolate and cookies before bed.

On the second-to-last night of camp, the counselors announced that we'd all be taking part in a very important Camp Rainbow tradition. They wouldn't give us any details, only that we were to meet in our color groups after the final bell, and we'd go from there. With the rest of my group, I followed the path from the camp's main hall, leaving the mauve twilit sky and entering the gymnasium with its harsh fluorescent light. None of us had a clue about what we'd be doing there, only that our itinerary placed us here for a one-hour mystery slot that would take us past cabin curfew.

"Okay, let's sit in a circle," called out one of the male leaders, marshaling us like a phys ed teacher toward our next activity.

As we claimed our spots on the scuffed wood floor, everyone chattered, still sugar-buzzed from our evening mug-up of hot chocolate and cookies. When I looked around the circle, I saw familiar strangers, teenagers whose first names and hometowns I knew only because we'd talked during mealtime or taken turns catching each other during trust falls. To look at my fellow campers was to see a cross-section of adolescence, from the popular ones with their on-trend surf shorts and neon T-shirts to the athletes, logoed in Nike and Reebok. There were the band and choir geeks, the art-class kids with dyed black hair hanging in their eyes, the girls clean-faced and combed, and the boys greasy-haired and chuckling too much. We could have been any group of teenagers, randomly selected to represent the category.

Mike the counselor told us that we were gathering in this gym to participate in a special tradition. Of all the Camp Rainbow activities, this was the most special, he said, the one that had the power to bring change. In a moment, he would turn off all the lights, and then we'd go around the circle, taking turns to share with the rest of our group.

"First of all," said Mike, "everything said in this room stays in this room. No exceptions."

We heard the gravity in his voice and somberly nodded.

Mike and the other three counselors went on to explain how the sharing circle would work. Maybe we wanted to talk about something difficult we've been going through, a struggle, they said, or maybe we wanted to share a secret we've never told another soul.

"This is a safe space," said Mike.

Part of being a strong leader, the counselors explained, was being willing to open up, to talk about your feelings. To be vulnerable. Authentic. That was what this time was all about. That was what Camp Rainbow, a place for tomorrow's leaders, was about.

Mike walked over to the doors we'd come through. His hand hovered over the bank of switches on the wall.

"Ready?" he said, then flicked off the overhead lights and covered us with darkness.

The quiet curiosity in the room quickly shifted to nervous laughter, stifled giggles, whispers and hushing. With the scratch of a match, a tiny flame cracked the blackness. As my eyes adjusted to the glow, Mike's face lit up on the far side of the circle.

"I'll pass the candle around," he said, "and when the candle reaches you, it's your turn to talk. If you don't want to share, just say, 'pass.'"

He pushed the candle in its holder to his left, and a cross-legged girl flickered in shadow, her elbows on her knees.

"Pass," she said, quickly, and giggled, then pushed the candle on.

After three or four passes and intermittent laughter, the candle stopped in front of another girl. She sat with her knees pulled to her chest and her baggy sweatshirt tugged over them. With every second that the candle remained before her, the anticipation in the room grew. Finally, after a long minute of silence, she picked up the candle and held it out in front of her.

"Um, my parents are getting a divorce?" She said it as if asking permission.

"Do you want to share anything about how that makes you feel?" said Mike. His voice was even and gentle, calm as a dentist's.

"Um, bad?" She sniffed, wiped her nose. "They argue about everything. All the time. I hate it."

"That must be really hard," said Mike. "But they love you, right? And they want you to be happy, right?"

The girl nodded and shoved the candle to the boy on her left.

"Thank you for sharing, Allison," said Mike. "That took courage."

Allison rested her face on her sweatshirt-covered knees. I could tell that she was quiet-crying. My stomach flopped with the nakedness of it all—this open sharing, the spilling of the secret inner world. No one in my family talked like this. Ours was an inherited culture of letting things lie, of quietly accepting the things we could not change, like the prayer inscribed on the plaque that hung above the dining room table. With Soopie and Sindee, my closest friends, I talked about periods, about what it would be like to actually make out with a boy, about which member of New Kids on the Block was the sexiest. But there were certain topics we never covered, places I did not go.

Once, in science class, Soopie had passed me a note with a scrawled drawing of my father. In the doodle, he wore his thick glasses and a ball cap, and a bottle hung from each hand. From his drooping mouth, a speech bubble held the words, "I'm drunk." When I stared at it, my throat felt sucker punched, like I'd been found out, like the door of a locked room had been pushed open and the lights thrown on, revealing everything that lay in darkness. Soopie nudged me and snickered, so I rolled my eyes and snickered, too, then picked up my pen and added to the picture, circling my dad's eyes until they bugged wide.

What I couldn't say to her, or anyone, was that his drinking wasn't funny anymore, that it never had been, even though as a child I'd loved the way he let me sip from his beer bottle and lick the dregs from his glass of rye-and-Pepsi. Even though he'd store up his empties for my brother and me so that we could cart them to the bottle depot and take home the cash. What I couldn't say was that only a few nights before I had found him drooped at the dining room table, nodding over a half-eaten supper, and for a reason I couldn't explain, had stalked outside to the fifth-wheel camping trailer and dug out a hidden bottle of vodka. I sat in the RV and drank tumbler after tumbler, eyes stinging, throat burning, thrilling at the singe on my tongue. I stared at the logo on the cup, a black-ink outline of a tiny house, stark as a child's drawing, until it shivered and blurred. When I stumbled back through the front door, my dad was still in his chair, but now he was snoring, his plate pushed to the side. He lay with his arms folded on the table and his head resting on them, like a child asleep at his desk.

Who my father had been as a boy was hidden knowledge, rarely spoken of, but I'd heard hints of him sneaking behind the barn with his brothers and cousins, smoking their home-rolled cigarettes and drinking whatever liquor they could scrounge. Some guy in a hot rod would show up with a brown paper bag and pass another bottle to my dad, who'd crack it open, take a swig, and joke about the rules of a kingdom that was going up in smoke. And then he was the one with the fast car, driving everyone to the party. He was the party. He was the one tipping the bottle, filling the empty cups of those around him until they overflowed. *I could be him*. The thought had poured through me like light as I'd watched his slumped-over form at the dining room table. His lips riffled and sputtered with every exhaled snore. *I could be him*. In the bathroom, I'd stood before the mirror and blinked until my face came into focus. With the cabinet doors pulled open, I saw myself in triplicate. On the left, on the right, and in the center, I looked the same, but had the feeling of being split, offered three versions of myself, as if there were a choice to make and I had to make it in that moment.

AFTER THE divorce girl, the candle moved more slowly, made more stops, the spilling of secrets growing contagious. One boy admitted that he smoked dope and didn't want to do it anymore. One girl was picked on by her classmates because she was fat, but she didn't want to be fat, or she didn't want to care what other people thought of her fatness. Another just held the candle and sobbed until a counselor put an arm around her. The closer the candle came to me, the faster my heart beat. Of all the things I could confess, my father was the one who kept rising, who stood breathing at my back, asking to be let in, the way he leaned against my locked bedroom door and called my name.

When the boy beside me nudged the flame toward me, I picked it up and held it in front of my face. With the flickering thread of light brought close, the rest of the room fell to shadow, the way the stage's spotlight sank an audience in darkness.

"Sometimes," I said, lifting the flame, "my dad drinks too much."

The words tasted strange. In the quietness of that waiting, while I still held the candle, I felt the surge of my confession, the quick heat of adrenaline from saying something so true my hands were shaking. The words hung there, illuminating that room at the center of our house where my father sat in darkness, pouring another drink.

If, in some time-warp version of the world, my dad could have sat in his own circle, clothed back in his teenage-boy body—if someone had passed him a burning candle and coaxed from him what needed to be said, surely the words spoken would have been light in darkness, too. *Mein Fader*, he might have said, *my father is a hard man. Won't look me in the eye with love.* But to speak the words was not enough. To say the secret aloud and let it light the moment didn't change the truth. We lit a flame that would briefly shine, and then be snuffed. Our circle in the dark gymnasium held nothing at its center. I felt like I was cheating on my dad, who had no way of knowing that he was always with me, beside me in the sharing circle, inside my brain, in my heart, like God, ever-present, even when I didn't invite him here. I wanted to bring him further in, to sit him in the center and say, "I'm sorry," to hand my father the flame and hear him speak back through the darkness, "I'm sorry, too."

"Thank you for sharing," Mike the counselor said, faceless in the dark.

I set the candle down and passed it to my left. The girl beside me paused a moment, as if searching for a worthy secret, then took a deep breath and pushed the candle along. "Pass," she said, and the flame moved on to the next one who sat in shadows, the next one ready to speak.

HELLO

ʞ ✕ ʞ ✕ ✕ ✕ ✕

THE TELEPHONE WAS MAGIC.

As a child, I believed it fully. Too small to reach the wall phone when it rang, I'd run to stand beneath it, and wait until my mother set down her knife or spoon, wiped her hands on her apron, then picked up the receiver, held it to her ear, and said, "Hello?"

By how her face and tone changed in the seconds that followed her "hello," I could guess whose voice was on the other end. If she brightened, then it must be one of her sisters. If her voice went higher, polite, it'd be a woman from the church. If brisk, if quick, my dad. If soft, then Grandma Funk.

"Ask her for some candy!" I'd say, tugging on my mother's arm. She'd furrow her brow, shake her head, and keep speaking to Grandma. I'd picture a stick of Juicy Fruit gum in its yellow paper jacket and silver foil sleeve sliding out the mouthpiece and into my hand, direct from Grandma's candy cupboard. Telephone as provider, deliverer of goods. Telephone as transmitter of pleasure, transporter of the physical realm.

Even after I realized that the telephone didn't operate like a vending machine, I understood that it had power. Its sudden jangle in the middle of the night shot my mother from sleep into a scurry down the hallway in her night-gown. Sometimes, from my room, I'd hear her go quiet, then sigh, and yawn and slow-shuffle back to bed. Other times, her voice deepened with dread. Then, in the morning, there'd be a story to go with the ringing in the dark, and in the days ahead, the long drive through town, over the river, and up the hill to the cemetery, where we'd stand with the family around a freshly dug hole in the ground, watching the casket descend.

Soon, I was old enough to answer the telephone on my own, to say the practiced words: "Hello?" and "May I ask who's calling?" and never "He's on the toilet right now." Soon, I was old enough to fall in love with the phonebook, all those names, all those numbers. I'd trace my finger down the alphabet of our town's directory, looking for the ones I knew, and feeling pride over the plentiful Menno-nites, to whom I was likely related through blood or mar-riage. Through the Banmans, Bueckerts, Dycks, and Esaus, to the Friesens and Froeses, Giesbrechts and Neufelds, Penners, Peters, Reimers, and Rempels, to the Thiessens and Toewses, Ungers and Unrahs, Wiebes and Wienses, I traveled the lists, coming back always to my name, to the column of Funks, all of them kin, all of them reachable by simply picking up the telephone and dialing the number that matched the name. Uncle Corny. Uncle George. Uncle Jake. Uncle John. Their voices on the other side of town saying, *Hello, I'm here.*

—HELLO?

The man's voice on the other end of the line lilted the question, the "huh" swooped down and the open vowel of the "low" swung up. Then, quiet listening followed, and the breathing through the receiver like a breezy heartbeat. I pictured the mouth—lips slightly parted, the whiteness of the top teeth visible, like a movie close-up. Clenched jaw. Stubble on the chin. The hot huffing.

—*Hello?*

The voice now brusque, insistent, the volume dialed up a notch. A demand for action and answer.

—*Who's this? Anyone there?*

If I had enough courage, I spoke the prank script with perfect solemnity.

"Is John Wall there?"

—*Nope, sorry.*

"Is Pete Wall there?"

—*I think you've got the wrong—*

"Are there any walls there?"

—*No.*

"Then what's holding up your house?"

Before the man on the other end could holler, I pressed down the receiver switch and—*ta-da!*—made his voice disappear.

I had other scripts too, often practiced with slumber-party friends after their parents had gone to bed and the telephone was unguarded. There was the one where we called the Pagoda and asked for Jimmy Wing, then Johnny Wong, and after being told they didn't work at the restaurant, apologized for "winging the wong number," always thinking ourselves so clever with words, but never thinking of how those words, and the ones who spoke them, cut.

There was the one where I pinched my nose and said in my best telephone-operator voice that I was calling from the telephone company, and we were doing some testing on the line, and would the person please stand ten feet back from the receiver and sing very loudly. *Sing?* they'd ask. It was the best way, I told them, to test the wires, and so they sang, often whatever song I requested. Sometimes "Frosty the Snowman." Sometimes "Three Blind Mice." I'd picture a farmer singing from his barn out at Braeside, surrounded by the cud-chewing cows in their milking stalls, or a white-haired grandma warbling from her kitchen in the Riverview subdivision. *Louder, please,* I'd say, *sing louder,* and they'd always comply, belting out the tune from their corner of town, while my friends and I tried to keep our laughter quiet.

"CALL IF you need anything," my mom said, and wrote down the number of the house where they'd be that Friday night while I stayed home alone.

As soon as the red taillights of my dad's pickup disappeared from the top of the driveway and down the road, I picked up the phone. When I released the cradle's switch, a dial tone purred a high A note, like a vibraphone's pipe, struck and held. I placed my finger in the wheel and dragged it to the metal stop, then released the spring action that whirred the circle back to the starting number. For each digit, I repeated the drag and release, the spring's whirr and return, until all seven numbers sent out their collective signal, a current that fired through the wires above me, traveling down Macdonald Road, onto Derksen Road, down Highway 16, over the tracks, the river, maybe to Loop Road, perhaps up Braeside, and then, pulsed into the cables that ran down the wooden pole and through a hole drilled in the side of a barn, into the case of a black telephone screwed to the wall. It started to ring.

In my ear, through the receiver pressed against it, the ringing sounded faraway and small, punctuated by silence. The drawn-out ringing. The silence. The ring.

"Hello?"

His voice on the other end of the line, small and surrounded by bales of hay, cows in their milking stalls.

"Hi," I said.

"Oh, hi," he said.

"Hi." My throat cinched. "Sorry. How are the cows?"

A sound like the broken first breath of a laugh. "They're dumb," he said. "Dumb as cows."

And then we were off and talking, about cows and their dumbness, their soft, vacuous eyes, how once on a field trip to an experimental farm in Prince George I'd seen a cow with a window in its stomach—a clear plastic covering through which we watched its food digest. Clots churned and fizzled in what looked like a tiny washing machine while the cow's jaw worked the grass in its mouth, chewing and chewing the cud.

In a pause within our talking, a sound came through the line. A sniff.

"Hello?" said the boy.

"Hello?" I said.

Between our breaths, another breathing. An invisible presence strung on the wire. How long the ear had been joined to our voices, listening in on our talking, we didn't know.

"Mrs. Martens?" said the boy. The breathing stopped. "You can hang up already," he said, impatient now.

A woman's voice, scraping and indignant, butted in. "I need to use the line!"

The farther out of town a person lived, the more the phones were strung together, with groups of rural numbers sharing the same circuit in what was called a party line. For those who liked to eavesdrop, the line was better than television. Out at my cousin Jennifer's farm, we could listen in on her next-door neighbor Mrs. Eggert. Together, with our heads conjoined, we'd press our ears against the receiver and take in whatever news and scraps of gossip we could get, hoping for some vivid secret to leak out in what we overheard. But mostly, her neighbor only talked about weeds and weather and how the chickens weren't laying as many eggs as they used to.

From his perch in the dairy barn, the boy told Mrs. Martens we'd get off the phone in a few minutes, so could she please just hang up. Then came a loud crack, the sound of her receiver slammed back in its cradle, leaving us alone on the line.

"Stupid party lines," the boy said.

"Yeah," I said. "Not cool."

"But I better go," he said.

We waited, breathing, for what words came next, making of that awkward pause a practice room for future heartbreak, the inevitable end to every hello.

"See you at school," I said.

"Yeah," he said. A cow lowed through the line. "See you."

Okay.

Goodnight.

Goodbye.

IN THE lobby of the high school gym, on a Saturday in between games of the Senior Vikings basketball tournament, Sindee, Soopie, and I huddled around the public payphone. We punched in random toll-free numbers, trying out various 1-800's that cost us nothing in quarters, and took us away from Vanderhoof for free.

Most of the time, the ringing eventually gave way to a sales desk operator on the other end of the line, a man or woman whose voice monotoned a greeting and company name, and then, "How can I help you today?" Once the person figured out that we weren't buying the Ginsu knives, or the Flowbee vacuum haircutter, or weren't about to book a cruise on the Mexican Riviera, the call went quickly dead, and we'd be left with the purr of a dial tone. But sometimes, the voice, perhaps bored of requests for credit card information and mailing addresses, kept us on the line, willing to talk. When we reached a concierge at the front desk of a hotel, we couldn't believe our luck.

"Would you like to make a booking?" said the man, smooth-toned as a radio host.

Soopie, Sindee, and I crushed together toward the receiver, three ears sharing the news.

"Um, where are you?" I said.

"We're located in Waikiki," he said. "Hawai'i."

The way he said *Hawai'i*—with the "ah" and "ee" split into two distinct syllables—made us sure he was telling the truth. Everyone we knew said "huh-WHY-ee," including us.

"We're in Canada," said Sindee. "In British Columbia."

"I've always wanted to visit Vancouver," said the man. "Are you near Vancouver?"

We sighed and admitted that we were nowhere close, and then explained how our town was a pinprick at the center of our province, a tiny speck whose name didn't make it on most maps of our country.

"Do you have snow there?" he said.

When we looked through the windows of the gym lobby doors, we could see winter's tilt, the snow-dust cindering down at a slant, late November's wind icing us over into the next four months of subzero weather.

"Yeah," Soopie said. "There's snow."

"Wow," said Mr. Waikiki. "I've never seen real snow."

We took turns speaking into the receiver, asking him about the beach, palm trees, luaus, surfers, shark attacks— our collective mind's-eye montage of Hawai'i. It felt like we'd won a small, brief ticket out of town, an almost-holiday to a dream destination. After we said goodbye to Mr. Waikiki, and I set the receiver back on its hook, Sindee, Soopie, and I agreed that it was the coolest phone call we'd ever made—to end up in Hawai'i from some random numbers was like playing the lottery on a whim and winning the jackpot.

"I mean, seriously," said Sindee, "what are the chances?"

"Where next?" Soopie said, as she picked up the receiver, her hand hovering over the buttons, and ready to dial us out of town.

PRAYER IS *like a telephone*, the preacher had said. *You can call God anytime, free of charge.*

On my bedroom carpet, I knelt. With the lights out and the curtains drawn, I knew no one could see me, but still, I felt exposed. Naked, even while fully clothed.

I clasped my hands like when I was a kid in Sunday school. Unclasped them. Pressed them flat against the rug. I swore I heard my Bible breathing in my nightstand's bottom drawer.

Hello? Is anybody there?

As a child, I'd held an empty tin can to my mouth and talked to my brother, who stood on the other side of the yard, his own can pressed to his ear. That he heard what I was saying through vibrations over a long, white string was easy to believe, an act of childhood faith.

Prayer is like a telephone. God's line is never busy. And He always answers when you call.

Upstairs in the kitchen, the telephone rang. My mother's footsteps flew across the floor above me, the joists creaking. Through the metal vent that blew hot furnace air into my room, her voice muffled down in mystery syllables.

To start with asking, to lay out my petitions like a Christmas wish list, seemed wrong. *First, I'd like to make out with Manuel.* I struck it from my mind. Dialed again. *Our Father, which art in heaven.* But all I saw was my own dad leaning on the pigpen fence, watching the hogs wallow in their mud. *Hallowed be Thy name.* I wanted my body to be whittled down, ivoried to bone. I wanted to be sifted like wheat, picked clean, all my chaff blown away. I wanted that voice again to tell me how to turn my ear, to lift my head. A psalm flew back to me from childhood. *The sun shall not smite thee by day, nor the moon by night.* I fed the words like coins into the air.

IT WAS important to be ready when the call came.

If a boy at school said, "Yeah, I guess I could call you tonight," and you said, "Okay! That would be awesome!" and he said, "Huh? Oh, yeah, okay," and you said, "What time are you going to call?" and he said, "I dunno, maybe around eight or something?" and you beamed at him and said, "Eight o'clock would be perfect!" and then his head disappeared behind his locker door and the conversation ended, it was important to be ready when the call came.

By quarter to eight, I had brushed my teeth and reapplied mascara, because the phone call was practically a date, or at least practice for one when the actual invitation came. I checked my hair in the mirror, sprayed the roots of my bangs so that they folded back into a puff that was high, but not too high—not high like Lucie Louie's. *How do you get your bangs to stay up like that?* we'd asked her. Sindee, Soopie, and I clustered around, trying to resist the urge to touch the thin wall of hair that jutted a stiff eight inches straight up from the top of Lucie's forehead. She'd explained her technique—how first she moussed her bangs and then ironed them on an ironing board, and then spritzed them with extra-hold Sprunch Spray. *Wow*, was all we could say.

By five to eight, I lurked around the wall phone in the kitchen. If my brother or mom came near it, I said, "I'm expecting a call," in a voice that aimed to sound both authoritative and nonchalant, so they would know the call was important to me but that I wasn't stressing over it. And I wasn't nervous or anything. Even though my left kneecap kept twitching.

If they asked who was supposed to be calling, I said, "Oh, just someone about some homework or something," which was true in that I could always ask the calling boy about quadratic equations, or what the word count for the English essay was.

When the short hand of the clock marked eight, and the second hand ticked to meet the long hand over the twelve, my throat began to ache with a pulse that felt heavy and hot. I sat on the wooden chair beneath the phone, math binder spread open on my lap, as if I were studying the formula that would make the numbers all come out right. But I couldn't stop watching the clock on the dining room wall. One minute past eight. Two minutes past. Three. Maybe the clock was wrong. Maybe the boy's clock was wrong. Maybe he didn't even have a clock in the room where he was. Or maybe he wasn't even in a room. Maybe he was outside in the dark, shoveling snow, or standing at the curb waiting for a ride home from basketball practice, or stuck in a ditch. Maybe his phone had stopped working. Maybe he had a party line and someone else kept talking and talking and refused to hang up the phone. Maybe he had forgotten what time he said he'd call me, or even that he'd said it at all.

SOOPIE, Sindee, and I huddled around the desk phone in our basement, the number jotted in blue ink on a slip of paper.

"You do it," said Sindee, and jammed the phone at me.

We were on the verge of chickening out, all of us, but the idea's greatness swelled our nerves. This part of the plan seemed the next logical step in our progression, which had begun with us finding our teacher's number in the new phonebook, then calling him on weekend nights when we stayed over at each other's houses. We took turns heavy-breathing into the receiver and listening to his reaction. First, he was baffled and full of questions. *Who is this? Why are you calling me?* Then, he grew frustrated, sputtering like he did when the jerk boys in the classroom's back row lipped off.

Out of all the male teachers in our school, Mr. Peltson was probably the most handsome, especially compared to the burly, mustached gym teacher who wore the same T-shirt and polyester basketball shorts every day of the week, and the shop teacher with a combover coiled to cover his bald spot—a combover that was rumored to have caught in a woodworking lathe that nearly ripped off a chunk of his scalp. Mr. Peltson was clean-shaven and sported a thick head of curls. Even though he had hairy nostrils, even though his dark-blue underwear was visible through his pleated, off-white slacks, Mr. Peltson was young and single, which heightened his allure, and made the girls in class ask questions about his personal life, like was he dating anyone, and what kind of woman was his ideal type, and had he ever been in love? He'd blush, stammer, try to change the subject, or turn back to the chalkboard and keep writing out our lesson notes about Samuel de Champlain, the fur trade, the coureurs de bois.

When we finally got up the nerve to say words into the phone, Mr. Peltson softened his response, speaking back, wanting to know the identity of this breathy young woman on the other end.

"Just tell me your first name," he said. "Please."

His "please"—tender and pleading—just about did us in. I clamped my hand over the mouthpiece so that Soopie, Sindee, and I could sink to our knees and let the stifled hysteria drain from our bodies. When we could breathe again, we skidded back into the fantasy.

"I—I can't," I whispered, deepening my voice and channeling my best Ashley from *The Young and the Restless*. I pictured Mr. Peltson sitting in his blue briefs at a bare kitchen table, the newspaper spread out and headlines circled and underlined like he had us do for our assignment, connecting current events to what we were learning in social studies. *Compare and contrast*, he'd say. *How does the local connect to the global?*

On one side of the snowy train tracks, in a windowless basement room, we were girls, bored and full of hormones, and with a tool in our hands that strung us to the other side of the tracks, to a man smoldering in the crucible of our valley town, a man alone in his apartment on a Saturday night, speaking to a disembodied female, begging her name.

When he finally said goodbye and hung up the phone, we lay on the rug and let the tears stream down our cheeks and our throats grow hoarse from laughing. At school on Monday, we could hardly look at him.

"HERE'S THE number," said Soopie, and she pushed the piece of paper toward me, the next part of our plan.

I took a deep breath and dialed: *1-800 . . .*

When the operator answered, I smoothed my voice to sound as sincere as a woman genuinely ordering the K-Tel eight-album compilation of *Love Songs Through the Ages.*

"Will that be charge or COD?" the operator said with a twangy drawl.

"Cash on delivery," I said.

"Your name?" said the operator.

"You can put it under my husband's name," I said. "Harold Peltson." And then I gave the mailing address we'd found on the label of a magazine Mr. Peltson had left on his desk.

"Expect delivery in four to six weeks," said the operator, her voice on the other end of the line small and trebly, like a woman speaking through a tin-can telephone, the string between us stretched over thousands of miles, over frozen rivers, mountains carved in ice, over borders drawn between our countries.

Someone on her side of the continent would read our order, pull a box set from a warehouse shelf, package it, label it, and send it all the way to our part of the world, into our town in a truck that unloaded its cargo at the back of the post office for the mail ladies to sort. Mr. Peltson would open his tiny mailbox door, see the slip of paper that told him he had a parcel to pick up, and when he went to the counter to collect it, the mail lady would hand him a fat cardboard box and then ask him for payment.

Forty-nine ninety-five, plus shipping and handling.

He'd stare at the package, see *Love Songs Through the Ages*. He'd wonder how the music found him. How "Earth Angel," "I Got You Babe," "Unchained Melody," and "Ain't No Mountain High Enough" had made the journey all the way to him.

"CAN I call you?" The dark-haired boy leaned from the driver's seat and hollered through the rolled-down passenger-side window, his car idling at the curb along the front of the school. Around me, bodies funneled out of the auditorium and into darkness. The dance, with its sweat and thumping bass and slow-dance musk, was over.

I moved closer to his car, bent down to the window, and told him yes. Said my number. He said it back to me.

"Tomorrow," he said. "I'll phone you."

I didn't ask what time. I already knew I'd make myself be home all day, waiting, guarding the telephone, checking my hair in the window's reflection as the hours slid by.

I'd be ready for the call when it came, if it ever came at all.

*"Arise, go out into the valley,
and there I will speak with you."*

EZEKIEL 3:22B

SLENDER
SILHOUETTES

✗ ✗ ✗ ✗ ✗ ✗ ✗

BEFORE THE PHOTOGRAPH SEALED behind a plastic sheath in the album marked "1980," I was the girl shimmying into the new swimsuit, a blue one-piece printed with black-and-yellow-striped cartoon bumblebees. The suit's slippery polyester made me sleek as a trout. I ran across the hot, pebbled beach to the lake's edge and splashed into the water.

From the houseboat edged up on the beach, Sparky, my dad's welding buddy, called out.

"It's Blondie!" he said. "Chubby little Blondie!" My dad and the other men on the boat deck chuckled.

"Smile," my mother called from shore, and held her camera to her eye.

Mid-thigh in the cool lap of waves, I looked up to meet the lens. I smiled. But those words—*chubby little Blondie*—slid like a key into a lock, teeth into the tumbler—*snick*, and the pins released, opening. I sucked in my stomach. Held my breath. Waited for the shutter's *click*. After I'd been captured on film, I let go, exhaled, and kept wading on tiptoes up to my belly button, my shoulders, my neck, my mouth, letting the lake swallow me bit by bit until my body disappeared.

"WELCOME to Slender Silhouettes," I said, in a friendly and upbeat voice, like I'd been instructed to do. I stood from my chair at the reception desk and stuck out my hand to greet Trudy Penner, my first client.

Like most of the clients who came to Slender Silhouettes, Trudy was not slender. She was soft-bodied, fluffy around the middle, and her hair was cut short and permed in a style worn by so many church ladies I knew, a sort of Mennonite afro that some of the men even sported during the early 1980s, when Tom Jones sang the top hits. To hug a woman like Trudy Penner was to be enfolded in a thick wool blanket and pillowy bread dough, all comfort and warmth. She was older than my mom but younger than my grandmother, a woman of in-between age whose body had begun to hormonally rebel in a kind of second adolescence. At any given moment, the face of a woman like Trudy could surge to a bright pink, sudden sweat beading on her forehead and upper lip. In their church pews, even in winter, women like her could be seen frantically peeling off their cardigans, then fanning themselves with their bulletins while the preacher droned on.

I took Trudy's winter coat and hung it on the rack, and showed her where to store her purse, then led her into a private tucked-away room where the scale was kept. This was my first solo shift of my first real job. On the day I turned fifteen, my mother had announced that I was old enough to find some part-time work, and if I couldn't, she'd find some for me, a gentle threat that meant she'd volunteer me again as a babysitter for the neighbors' kids, my nightmare, and so I applied for a job at a new business opened by the wife and daughter of my dad's trucker buddy.

The sign above the storefront displayed the outline of half a woman's body, and in a flourish of cursive, the business name: *Slender Silhouettes Toning Salon.*

"Not a *tanning* salon," I learned to respond to those inquiring by telephone. "A *toning* salon." Then, as Diane, the manager, had trained me to do, I explained what made Slender Silhouettes unique.

Our toning tables allow for exercise at your own pace, I'd say. You can tone your muscles, lose weight, *and* gain flexibility, I'd say. Every so often, I'd add the word "isometric" to my sales pitch, so that I sounded like an expert. Beyond the memorized script, I learned the routine of how to welcome a client, making a check mark beside her name in the appointment ledger and then ushering her into the curtained-off room directly behind the reception area.

"Let's start with the weigh-in," I said to Trudy, tuning my voice to a cheery brightness.

The scale wasn't a punishment, Diane had coached me; it was a tool to help the client achieve her health and fitness goals. Trudy slipped off her loafers and stepped warily onto the column scale's platform. I pushed the metal slider high, so that no matter what her actual weight ended up being, the numbers always appeared to be descending as the judgment came. Down, down, down, I nudged the slider, until it teetered and stilled to a balance.

"Excellent!" I said, and checked the stats in Trudy's file.

Whether she was up a pound, or down a pound, or stayed the same, everything was "excellent!" To be slightly up in numbers meant "muscle gain!" To be down meant "fat

loss!" And to stay the same was to have achieved a "temporary plateau!" More than a pound of gain was always
blamed on water retention, or perhaps the need for a slight
change in diet, such as cutting back on bread, potatoes,
and cream gravy, the staples of the Mennonite table. Every
pound not lost was also an opportunity for me to sell a
bottle of metabolism-boosting herbal tonic, an expensive
brown sludge that looked and smelled like the fish fertilizer
my mother poured on her greenhouse tomato plants.

"Calves first," I said, and pulled out the measuring tape.
As I knelt on the carpet, I drew the tape around the wid-
est part of her lower leg, noted the numbers in her file, and
then moved up the body, part by part, thigh to hips, waist
to upper arms, and finally, to the bust. The whole ritual
felt uncomfortably intimate, like when my brother and I
were watching TV and a tampon commercial flashed on the
screen. I tried not to look Trudy in the eye as I arranged the
strip of plastic so that it lined up straight across the nipples,
as Diane had demonstrated, then cinched the tape snug.

"Another half an inch off the bust," I said, which was
a line repeated often at Slender Silhouettes, to the disappointment of the clients. Of all the areas from which to lose
inches, it was always the bust whose measurement consis-
tently fell, even though no woman seemed bothered by its
extra flesh and fat.

Trudy sighed an "oh well" and shook her head, then slid
back into her shoes.

"Let's get started on our first machine," I said, and led
Trudy through a swinging saloon-style door into a carpeted
cubicle.

She climbed onto the sandbag table, then lay back and
adjusted herself into position so that her buttocks rested

on the machine's two pads. I hoisted a vinyl sandbag from the corner of the cubicle and draped it over Trudy's belly and hips.

"We'll do eight minutes today," I said, and set the dial on the base of the machine. "This time, try tightening your hips and thighs and holding for a count of twenty."

Trudy tucked her ankles against the padded footrests and braced herself for the action.

"Here we go," I said, and flicked the switch.

The two pads beneath Trudy's bottom started their rhythmic firm-and-tone action, like some sort of industrial bakery apparatus designed to knead vast batches of dough. As her body jiggled back and forth, back and forth, Trudy clutched the sandbag draped over her pelvis, its weight keeping her from slipping off the table.

"Count to twenty," I said. "Tighten and hold."

"YOU'RE built like a Shenk," my mom always said, meaning her side of the family. Meaning short and shaped like a pear. Wider of hip, thicker of thigh. "We come from peasant stock," she said, meaning I should be thankful for my sturdy heritage and for my low center of gravity, which served a female well when it came to the important things, like giving birth and digging potatoes.

Our bodies were simply part of the Mennonite package, my mother said, though I could tell that she fought it, regularly pulling from her purse a miniature booklet called *Count Your Calories* so that she could consult its tables and charts before mealtime. Sometimes, the booklet lay hidden in the drawer with the phonebook and old sets of keys, as if she'd given up on trying to change genetic destiny. But then, when one of my aunts or a neighbor lady convinced her to start the cabbage soup diet or the grapefruit diet or the Dr. Atkins diet, out came the booklet again.

Why was it, I wondered, that every girl and woman tried to whittle down her body to a smaller shape, while all the boys and men worked to make themselves bigger? In the evenings after supper, my brother ran through a series of push-ups, bench presses, and sit-ups. Over and over, he stretched the springs of a chest expander across his torso, sweating and trying not to let his nipple-skin catch in the metal coils. While he flexed in the window's reflection, eyeing the bulge of his biceps, I hid behind the locked bathroom door, holding my breath and angling sideways in the mirror for whatever vantage lessened me.

FOR MY first training shift at the new job, Diane had led me on a tour of the shop, showing me the operational side of the business—how to book new clients, take payments, answer the telephone, and sell products. But it was the second shift that really introduced me to what Slender Silhouettes was all about.

"Isometric exercises," said Diane.

That word "isometric" was new to me, but from the number of times Diane repeated it, I understood it to be important, a key selling point for the clients.

"Like this," said Diane, lying back on one of the tables and positioning her arms above her head, hands pressed against a bar. "Tighten and tap. Tighten and tap."

She was a petite, perky woman with flawless makeup and black, shiny hair that curled back from her face in the style of a country-music star. Her tanned biceps bulged as she demonstrated the exercise on a table that moved beneath her while she tightened and tapped. After Diane toured me through the workings of all eight toning tables, showing me how to increase the speed of motion, set the timer, and hit the emergency stop button should something go wrong when a client was exercising, she handed me a towel and told me to try a circuit on my own.

Machine to machine, I dialed in the timer, set the speed of repetition, and then laid my body down, strapping in whatever part needed securing. On the tummy-hip table, I lay on my front, upper body propped while the machine raised and lowered my legs, gently twisting my middle at the same time as Diane had demonstrated, so that the inches could melt off my waist. I didn't feel the melting, but I enjoyed the sensation of easy exercise, of my legs being moved for me, flexed and stretched as if I were a doll manipulated into various shapes by someone else's hands. Up and down, again and again, my limbs played along with the tummy-hip regimen, which was effortless and, according to Diane, isometric.

On the sit-up table, I reclined and allowed the machine to raise and lower me into an abdominal crunch, as if my body were being tipped back into the earth and then resurrected, over and over again, in a mechanized miracle. After the side-to-side, the body bender, the leg toner, the stretch toner, the arm-and-chest toner, I finished with five minutes on the circulation table, the reward for the client at the end of the circuit. This final machine was meant to improve the flow of blood to surface skin cells, thus removing toxins that led to cellulite.

"On this table, you just lie back and relax," Diane said, "and let the machine flush you out."

I closed my eyes as the table began its slow undulation. The gentle tilt and vibration made my body feel as if it were floating, bobbing with the lap of the water, the way it did at Fraser Lake when I lay back and practiced the starfish, arms out, legs out, splayed in the water like a creature of the deep. The voices on shore drifted away. The laughter of the men calling out to me from the deck of the boat glided into silence. The machine's soft *shush-shush-shush* repeated like a wave until it was singing away my cellulite, flushing out those cottage-cheese dimples on my thighs and butt that made me envy the mini-skirted girls at school and hate putting on my bathing suit in summer. Let it all be flushed away, I thought, imagining the tilt of the table draining off my fat like the grease off the gravy.

I'D ALWAYS avoided weighing myself, not wanting to face the numbers, but when it was time for our Canada Fitness unit in gym class, I hadn't been able to dodge the mandatory fat test. When Ms. Olds called my name, I took my turn inside her office.

"Pull up your shirt," she'd said to me, and I offered my belly to her metal calipers. Starting with my stomach and moving to the underside of my upper arm and down to my calf, she gripped my flesh in between thumb and forefinger, then pinched it between the cold prongs, noting the inches it measured. After she'd written down the numbers, she set down her calipers, picked up her clipboard, and ran her finger down a column of digits and over to the results of the body mass index: *Overweight.*

"But not by a whole lot," she said. "Now step on the scale."

Overweight. Though I didn't need the official verdict to clarify my thicker-than-average shape, the word settled like a stone in my throat. Back in the gym, my classmates milled. The skinny girls stood in a clutch, their Barbie legs gleaming beneath the overhead fluorescents. They laughed with each other over how much water they'd had to drink in order to get their weight up, speaking that secret language of the thin. On the other side of the gym, behind the vinyl curtain drawn to separate us from them, the boys with their deepening voices hollered and slammed their medicine balls at each other. Thinness, I knew, wasn't the only bait to drag in the waters of a boy's affection, but it was a very shiny lure.

When Soopie asked if I wanted to join Weight Watchers with her, I agreed, as long as we kept our membership a secret. I didn't like the idea of anyone at school finding out that I, too, wanted to be thin, or at least, thinner. Every Wednesday evening at suppertime, Soopie's mom dropped us off at the Village Inn, and we snuck into the side door of the banquet hall at the back of the restaurant. With a group of women who looked like our mothers and grandmothers, we lined up for the weigh-in. One by one, we took our turns on the scale, the mood in the room shifting with the gains and losses we penciled into our member booklets. Then, while the smells of the deep-fryer and the grill wafted from the kitchen, we sat in plastic chairs and listened to Brenda, the Weight Watchers leader, cheer us on with tips on how to avoid late-night snacking and ways to add flavor without fat. The whole thing felt like a version of church, but without singing and potlucks and God. I quit after a few months, too embarrassed to return every Wednesday and see that the scale hadn't budged more than half a pound, if at all. "Could be water weight," said Brenda, patting my hand.

I DIDN'T want to be Rudine, the anorexic fifty-pound woman featured on the Oprah show. Rudine's cheeks were sunken, her hair thin, her voice slurred when she answered

Oprah's questions. Yes, she still saw herself as fat. No, she didn't want to die. It started with grapefruit and salad and Diet Coke. That's all she ate every day, trying to lose weight, until she was eating nothing but grapefruit, and then only drinking water.

"Anorexia nervosa," said Oprah somberly, staring at me through the screen like an oracle as she explained the condition.

It was the hot topic in all the magazines geared to teen girls. The word itself, buzzy and new, had become a way of degrading the skinny girls in school. *She's totally anorexic,* I'd whisper to Soopie, when stick-insect Lindsay or bone-rack Mandy walked by, and then we'd roll our eyes and laugh. It was easier than professing my envy at the way their thinness snagged a boy's gaze, and sometimes even his hands. These were the girls grabbed around their waists by boys, whether or not they asked for it. These were the girls twirled in the middle of the school hallway until they grew dizzy and couldn't walk straight, or hoisted piggy-back-style for a lift to the next class. *You weigh nothing,* the boy would say, and the girl on his back would giggle and drape her arms around his neck.

When I looked in the mirror, I saw my body for what it was: imperfect, dimpled, generous with flesh. But now, too, a research project. For an English-class essay on a topic of my choosing, I read everything I could find about anorexia, scouring magazines and microfiched articles in the library, making notes on the nuances and variations of the disease. *Anorexia nervosa* meant "nervous loss of appetite," but the only part of it I wanted was the loss of the desire to eat all the foods I loved: potato chips dragged through thick, creamy dill pickle dip, J & S Drive-Inn cheeseburgers sweating grease in their foil jackets, soft-serve ice cream dipped in hot fudge that hardened to a shell.

If, as suggested by the articles I read, the body starved of fuel cannot sustain itself and sheds the weight quickly, efficiently, then I, too, could apply these principles to myself. I snuck my mother's *Count Your Calories* booklet from her purse and began to track and tally everything I ate until each day became a ledger with estimates and long addition. One small apple: eighty calories. Carrot sticks: seventy-five calories. Two plain rice cakes: thirty-five each. For supper, I piled a plate with leaves of iceberg lettuce, sprinkled it with a saltless seasoning mix, and doused it in white vinegar—sixty calories.

"You can't eat just that," my mother said, but her concern only sharpened the pleasure of the vinegar's sting.

In the one lost pound, I could see the future, the numbers dropping—two, three, five, ten. I could imagine what it would feel like for my ribs to emerge from beneath the soft roll of flesh. I'd run my fingers over them, feel that concave scoop at the bottom, the flat belly beneath, and the jut of hipbones. When I shimmied into my tight jeans—two, three sizes smaller—then turned a slow circle before my bedroom mirror to see myself from every angle, I would remind myself that a real anorexic is never satisfied with the loss, but instead sees it as a dare to keep going.

You gotta eat more food, my dad would say, waving his steak knife above his dinner plate. But still, I'd push away the mashed potatoes, the pork chop smothered in mushroom-soup gravy.

"Not hungry," I'd say, defying the gnaw in my empty stomach.

I DIDN'T want to be the one on shift at Slender Silhouettes when Lori Mason arrived. In the appointment ledger, her name was marked down for the same time slot every week, always the last hour of the Friday shift, so I told Diane that I'd prefer to work other evenings, but she told me I had no choice—working the weekend shifts was part of the job, take or leave it.

"You'll be fine," said Diane. "The friend who drives her knows what to do. Just be available to help where needed."

Lori was a woman who'd been in a wheelchair since her teens. I knew her enough to smile and say hi when I passed her on a sidewalk in town or when I saw her at church, but I'd never really talked to her, and didn't even know why she was partly paralyzed. When she talked, her words came out slow and slurred and hard to understand, her head nodding as she worked to speak. She was friendly, almost always smiling, but still, I felt awkward around her, unsure of what to say and how to say it.

Out of the late-winter darkness, Lori arrived on time for her appointment, wheeled through the door by the man who helped her.

"Good evening," he said, smiling as he stomped his boots on the mat.

He brushed the snow from Lori's shoulders and hair, and then wiped the dampness from her cheeks. He unzipped her jacket and tugged it off her, lifting each of her arms in turn. He knelt on the wet rug in front of her wheelchair, pulled off her boots, and set them beside his own.

"Where would you like to start?" I said to the man, who had wheeled Lori to the reception desk, and now stood waiting for my direction.

He looked down at Lori and offered my question to her. "What do you think?" he said. "The sandbag?"

Lori shifted in her chair and mouthed a "yeah."

"To the sandbag, then," he said cheerily, and wheeled her toward door number one.

Lori had very little control of her arms, and almost no control of her legs, but the toning salon was good for her muscles, my boss had explained, telling me to skip the weigh-in and measurements and focus instead on her movements while on the various machines.

The man instructed me on how to stabilize Lori's legs as he transferred her from wheelchair to toning table. He drew his arms around her, and then hoisted her sideways. He wasn't a large man, but he was strong, and even though Lori couldn't support her own weight, he lifted her. Together, we positioned her body on the machine, and I draped the sandbag over her hips.

"Ready?" he said to Lori. She nodded slowly and beamed up at him.

My regular script didn't fit in this cubicle. To say, "This will help you lose those stubborn inches," or, "Tighten and hold" didn't seem appropriate. Lori lay waiting to be moved, but not for the same reasons as Trudy Penner or any of the other women who came to the toning salon.

I set the timer, then flicked the "on" switch. The machine began its rhythmic kneading of Lori's backside, and in response, her whole body tremored.

"I'll sit with her," he said, settling into the wheelchair. "Keep an eye on her so that she doesn't try to make the machine go faster." Lori made a sound like the first syllable of open-mouthed laughter, a long, sung O.

Machine to machine, the man led Lori, lifting her on, lifting her off, and I followed along, helping when asked, but feeling uncomfortable and in the way. Hers was a body unable to move—to walk, stand, even sit upright without some support. Hers was a body soft at the thighs, soft around the hips and middle, not strong, not able, and yet, beside her, with his arms around her and lifting her, was a man who deemed her worthy.

When he picked her up off the circulation table, he held her like a groom about to carry his bride over the threshold. He settled her back into her wheelchair, then wiped the saliva from the corners of her mouth.

"We'll see you next Friday," he said, and I handed him the receipt.

I followed them to the front door and said goodbye, like I did with every client, but after the door shut behind them, I locked up and drew the blinds down over the glass and watched through the slats. He lifted her again from her wheelchair and settled her into the front seat of his car. He drew the belt across her body, leaned over her to click it in place. He smoothed her hair back from her face, and for a moment, it looked like he might kiss her. She smiled up at him, her head tilting, her mouth shaping words I wished I understood.

I watched them drive away, their headlights receding out of the parking lot and down the snowy road toward the ice-locked river, across the bridge to where she lived with her parents. When they arrived at her house, he'd lift her again, bearing her body in his arms. I held that weightless image in my head as I dusted and vacuumed and emptied the trash, readying the salon for the next morning's clients.

Like I did at the end of every shift, I made my own circuit of the machines. I cranked the action to its highest setting, adding in crunches on the sit-up machine, and butt clenches on the sandbag table, combining extra twisting action on the bender, until I was breathing hard and sweating, doing what I could to make my body smaller. After the final machine, I slipped behind the curtain of the weigh-in area. Even in the silence of the empty, dim salon, I felt like someone was watching, gazing at me through a crack in the ceiling as I bent to unlace my sneakers. That eye following my every move, lighting me up, as if luring me to lift my head, see the way it looked at me, the truth of what it saw. I turned from it, stepped on the scales, and waited for the metal slider to find its balance.

I let the numbers teeter and tip slightly to the right, pointing the way to lightness. Then I stepped off. I took off my sweatshirt, my T-shirt, my pants. I stepped back on the scale. I let the counter-weight fall heavy to the right, then nudged the numbers lower, lower, searching for the balance. I closed my eyes. I breathed out until my lungs were light, the way it felt when I was swimming in the underwater dark, my body reaching for the bottom, for as low as I could go.

MIXTAPE

⚔ ⚔ ⚔ ⚔ ⚔ ⚔ ⚔

THE SONY SPORTS WALKMAN, canary-yellow and the size of a junior Bible, cost me eighty dollars at Radio Shack, and cramped my hand when I carried it for more than a mile, but still, I carried it everywhere, volume blasting through the hard-plastic headphone nubs jammed in my ears.

"You listening to that junk again?" my dad hollered. Inside the coolness of the detached garage we called "the shop," he stood, puffing on a cigarette, nursing a can of Pepsi spiked with rye.

I saw his lips moving, but I pretended not to understand his words. I sat down on the steps of the back porch, unclipped the locking mechanism on the Walkman, and clicked a cassette into place—a new mixtape I'd made from borrowed music, some loaned from friends at school, some snuck from my brother's secret stash.

In my bedroom, behind a locked door, I'd recorded from a stack of master cassettes onto the blank tape in my double-deck ghetto blaster, working hard to smooth the transitions so that the *clunk* of the Stop button wasn't audible in the space between songs. With both cassettes in place and the master song cued to start, I'd release the Pause of the left deck's Play button and simultaneously press Record on the right. The ribbons of both decks geared into motion and somehow, by a mystery I couldn't explain, the song unspooled from its original source into the blank, turning what was silent into sound. The music reproduced as compilation, a mix that matched the range of emotions brooding in the teenage heart. A driving, hook-heavy tune gave way to the riff-crunch of glam-metal electric guitar, which swelled to a power ballad's canned strings and sentimental soaring, then leapt to the dance-pop beat of a sunny feel-good romance, all of it curated to carry me, the listener, elsewhere and away from the ordinary rhythms of our yellow-and-brown split-level house where the radio crackled with local news and country hits.

I tightened the laces on my white high-tops, stood up, and slid on a pair of sunglasses.

"Where you goin' now?" my dad called.

I pointed up the driveway toward the road. "For a walk."

"What for?"

"For anyhow," I said. "For exercise."

"You want exercise, you can do some work around here." He dropped his cigarette butt on the shop's cement floor, scuffed it with one foot, then kicked it to the gravel.

I knew the litany of options that would follow: *You can detail my pickup. Go help your mom in the kitchen. Mow the lawn. Sort the empties. Clean the shop.* But before my dad could even launch into the list, I pressed Play and started walking.

As soon as I crested the driveway and hit the asphalt, I rolled up my knee-length shorts—vivid red cotton with rows of tiny white flowers, a fabric I chose, and a simple pattern sewn by my mother—shrinking them into almost short-shorts. Then I tucked up the bottom band of my white halter-style top, leaving my midriff bare. The chances of an aunt or uncle driving by were high, but I resolved not to care about what they'd think if they saw me this exposed, my pale flesh too much on display, flaunting itself to the *thwack* of the drum beat. At least I was less flesh now than I had been a few months ago, down eighteen pounds on my diet of bran, lettuce, and rice cakes. When I'd asked one of my phys ed classmates to find out what his best friend Graham thought of me, he came with the news: "Graham says, 'she's not as fat as she used to be.'" Morning, afternoon, and evening, my mother's bathroom scale gave me the results of my calorie counting. Every time the scale's needle fell a little further, I felt the new number's rush, and savored the descent out of the 140s, to the 130s, and now limboing down into the 120s—*how low could I go?* I weighed Graham's words in my mind, trying to decide if they were compliment or insult, and whether I could make him ever want to kiss me. I looked down at my stomach and sucked it in flat. My legs were not as fat as last year, but still jiggly and spidered with thin violet veins.

"They're hereditary," said my mother, who lay nightly with her legs elevated on the back of the couch, trying to improve the circulation in hopes of preventing future varicose veins, and the arrival of more cellulite.

On my left, along the road, birch and fir and poplar trees grew in gangly stands, ceasing only when the ditch banked up into a driveway, which opened to a yard and the house where Soopie used to live. Past her old house, past Andy and Mary's trailer and their giant boulder painted to look like a doghouse though they had no dog, and over on the right, the Rempel house. A sheet of plywood covered what would have been a large living room window, and a second-story door opened into air, no stairs yet built to reach the ground. Loreen, five years older than me, lived there with her dad. Loreen with hair frizzed out over her shoulders like an isosceles triangle, and with a mother dead of cancer. "What kind of cancer?" I asked my mom, wanting to know if it was like Grandpa's tarry lungs or Aunt Linda's brain tumor. "Breast," she answered, with the same quick hush as when she said words like "period" and "brassiere" and "pregnant."

Where the road split right and led to the Markay subdivision, I followed the curve left toward the highway with cowbell and the crunch of an electric guitar riff in my headphones. On the corner, across from the Klassen house, the Vanderhoof Mennonite Church had just released its students from classes. The boys ran into the field that adjoined their parking lot. The girls walked together in clusters. This was one of seven or eight Mennonite churches in town, but one of the few that still forbade radios, musical instruments, and the flash of chrome on vehicles. Every Sunday, the girls and women sat on one side of the sanctuary, and the men and boys sat on the other.

"I bet they still sing in four-part harmony," my mother said when we drove past on our way to the Evangelical Mennonite Church, which did allow radios, TVs, chrome, and modest jewelry, and even pants for women outside of Sunday services. It was hard to know which of us had it right and who, at the end of all time, might be penalized. I wondered if heaven might be divided into the "okay" and the "really good," the way they divided the females from the males, us from them.

As I passed, the older boys—the ones with baseball gloves ready for a game of scrub—stopped what they were doing and turned to look my way. They stared at me— my midriff naked, short cuffs rolled way up—with blank, unsmiling faces, the way the cows across the road gathered at the barbed-wire fence and surveyed me as I walked on by. The tallest boy, dark haired in black pants and a white shirt buttoned to the throat, stood with his hands at his sides, his leather baseball mitt like a giant tawny paw dangling from his wrist. His mouth hung half-open, as if on the verge of utterance, as if when I passed by the chain fence that swagged the perimeter of the church property, he might call out, "What's your name?"—to which I'd raise an eyebrow, shoot a flirty smirk at him, toss my hair like a shampoo commercial.

I could see it all—how I'd woo this tall, dark boy, lead him away from his austere family, lure him into midnight sneak-outs in the bushes along the road, and teach him how to kiss as deep and full-mouthed as a movie star, as if I knew these magic tricks. *Jacob*, I'd say, *Jacob, if you love me.* But his parents would find out, flip out. Call an all-church meeting. Drag us both to the front of the sanctuary, me on one side, Jacob on the other, and when we confessed our sins, the elders would slam down their Bibles in judgment. And the shunning would begin. Jacob, now the outcast, and me, the cause of his excommunication. Or worse, instead of the shunning, a demand for us to marry.

Carla, do you promise to honor and obey Jacob? I'd stand in my white prayer cap, my black wedding dress, and say, "Yes." Tears rolling down my cheeks, but I'd say it. "Yes, I do." Then Jacob would drive me home in his chromeless gray passenger van large enough to hold our future brood of plain dresses and black pants, girls on one side of the vehicle, boys on the other.

In the parking lot, the girls eyed me too, standing there in pastel dresses all cut and sewn the same—long-sleeved, elastic-waisted, high-collared, and zippered up the bodice back, with the hemline falling a few inches above the ankle. Their long hair braided or bunned, their heads covered either with a kerchief or a prayer cap, the kind their mothers wore, the kind both of my grandmas still wore over their thinning gray hair, and the kind my mother had slowly stopped wearing years ago.

I left them behind—those girls standing like a mirror that showed an alternate version of my future, what my life could be if I zipped myself into the shapeless dress, tied on the apron. Did they see me the same way, like a portal into a possible life, a doorway to the flesh? None of those girls would ever sit inside a darkened movie theater waiting for a boy to slide his hand over the armrest and take her hand in his, so that the grip and sweat of their entwined fingers lit a pulsing ember below the ribcage, the heat spreading to the hips, chest, up into the neck and jaw, and to the mouth where the lips ached to be kissed.

And did they even kiss—these long-hemmed, straight-spined, prayer-capped girls? Did the tall, buttoned-up boy even know how to take a girl's face in his hands and press his mouth to hers? In Grandma Shenk's Amish heritage, they had something called bundling, a courting ritual in which the boy and girl slept side by side in cloth bundling bags, full-body safe sacks. Only their heads remained exposed, which meant they could look at each other while they lay together in bed, talking, and even kissing if they were rebels.

"Some bundled, yes," Grandma Shenk said warily when I'd asked her about the tradition. "But I never did." She told me about how Grandpa Shenk came courting with a '39 Chev, green, not old, but not new, and how he'd drive her and all the Sheridan Mennonite girls who worked at the glove factory into McMinnville every Sunday night. That was how they dated back then.

"Okay, but what about the bundling?" I pleaded, eager for details. But Grandma claimed to know nothing much of the practice, except that to some, it had seemed like a practical way for a young man and woman to find out if they'd be a good match in marriage. I thought of all the boys with whom I'd want to bundle—not for holy matrimony, but rather for the heat of the experiment. I walked the school hallways in my head and chose my bundlers from the rows of lockers—icy-eyed Sean who slumped in his back-row desk in social studies, know-it-all Tim who rivaled me in every class and wore the same white T-shirt too many days in a row, and Graham, sharp-tongued Graham, who'd never see my hidden fat within the cotton sack.

Past the Hansens' log house on my left, and on my right, past the trailer where the Pennsylvania Dutch family lived, I started to jog. The handmade wooden sign at the end of their driveway read, "Count Your Blessings." In phys ed class, the skinny girls gazelled laps around the track like it cost their lungs nothing, their cheeks flushed in a way that seemed to make the boys perk up, puff out their chests, as they sped by. I ran with Soopie at the back of the pack, and we traded physical ailments like foreshadowings of our future care-home selves, citing weak knees, a sore back, burning lungs.

"I think I have asthma," Soopie huffed.

"I think I have PMS," I said.

Please excuse Carla from running today. She has her period. In clean, fine-tip blue ballpoint, I sometimes forged my mother's signature, mimicking her neat, pert cursive. When I handed the note to Ms. Olds, one of our gym teachers, I made sure to press my hand to my lower gut and add a wilt to my posture, so that I looked the part of the afflicted female. I'd learned early that this was our secret weapon, the get-out-of-almost-anything-free card. To any of the male teachers, all one of us girls had to say was, "I have cramps," and Mr. Kelly or Mr. Lloyd would raise both hands as if in surrender, nod, and then quickly excuse us from burpees or running bleachers.

When, at age eleven, I called to my mother from the bathroom, told her, "I think this is it," said, "I'm pretty sure that, you know, I've got my, well, you know, my first," and then finally blurted, "I started my period," she gasped and clapped a hand over her mouth. When she spoke, all she said at first was, "No!" And then, "Already? Are you kidding? But you're only eleven!" And then she drew in a deep breath, straightened her shoulders, and exhaled.

"It's as natural as falling off a log," she said, and patted me on the arm. She stood framed in the bathroom doorway, her face full of roller-coaster panic, eyes like those of a woman readying for the track's next drop, the ride's big loop-de-loop.

As natural as falling off a log. On the screen of my mind, my mother's words projected a memory: me, balancing on a fallen fir tree in the back acres of our old house on Kenney

Dam Road. I was a girl in rugby pants and a T-shirt, trying to keep up with my brother and the other boys who scrambled through the woods, inventing war games. When Ivan, the oldest, said, "I gotta take a dump," my brother told me to stay back and not to look. But I peeked through squinted eyes, and saw Ivan sitting on the fallen log, his bare butt hanging over the edge. "Your sister's watching," he called to my brother, his toothy mouth wide and loud, his pink lips stretched tight. *As natural as falling off a log.* "She likes it," he kept saying. "Your little sister likes it." I shut my eyes and tried to burn away the image of Ivan's huge chimp teeth, his black hair, the round white curve of his rump.

As the road sloped down into the dip before the climb, I gave myself to gravity, racing the beat of the kick-drum and the singer's soaring *whoa-whoa-whoa*. A tool and a weapon. A blessing and a curse. That was the body, swinging on a hinge between beauty and crudeness. But a girl had to keep pressing, pushing away from the shame and filth, never swaying too far from being sweet and clean. A guy could drip with sweat, hock and spit, belch, fart, scratch his crotch, but any girl caught doing that would earn herself a reputation, be called butch, a pig, a piece of trash, or worse. In Algebra, while we solved for variables and balanced our equations in quiet study time, I watched Cole Shepard, the star of the basketball team, squeeze the pimples on his back. Cole's hand groped along his bare shoulder, the neckline of his jersey, feeling out each cyst, then pinching it between his thumb and forefinger until the white head burst. Then, still bent over his textbook, his other hand still penciling out the answers, he'd wipe the pus on his shorts. I couldn't look away, shuddering and marveling at how he could do such a thing and still have girls who longed to hold his hand. That was the body, if you were free to be vulgar and unashamed. At mealtimes, my dad would pick his nose, burp, slide his false teeth out and set them on the table, expecting that my mother would swing by with her dishrag and her soap and bleach to clean up any mess. "You get what you get," my mother would say, meaning that we didn't always get to choose, about the body, and what it could and couldn't do. All of us were bound by the laws of nature, which were part potluck, part lottery, part grab-bag gift from God.

"You look just like your dad," an aunt had said at one of our Sunday-night barbecues, eyeing me across the picnic table. Her words snagged like barbed wire. My father sat separate in his wooden chair, a cigarette in one hand, a beer can in the other. He wore a ball cap stitched with a LORDCO logo, the name of the shop where he bought parts for his logging trucks. His face was stubbled, his cheeks jowled, and his mouth rested in a frown. Sallow and tanned, his skin had an oily sheen. His eyes, sad and watery, held the early-evening gleam of the afternoon's whiskey. When he spoke, his speech came slow and slid together, like words without space between them. His sentences ended with a laugh and an *eh?* or a *huh?* He talked in one-liners, comebacks, wisecracks, eager for an audience response and the laugh track that never came.

If I looked too long at him, I wanted to run, find any reason to get up from the table, leave the room, hide away, turn up the music, like I always did when he thumped on my bedroom door and called out, *Aren't you gonna come say hi to your old man?* I pretended not to hear, cranked the volume louder, let the music be my excuse for why I didn't answer. When he came late for supper, heavy-footed on the stairs, sock feet sliding on the linoleum, I picked up my stack of textbooks and loose-leaf and left the dining room table. *What? You're gonna leave now 'cause I'm here?* he'd say, and I'd reply with silence and absence, weapons meant to hurt him but ones that would only end up carving out an absence in my own heart, cheating me out of love.

At the top of the hill, sucking lungfuls but trying not to look out of breath, I waved to Uncle Corny as he passed in his pickup, giving me a wide berth. With a hand still on the steering wheel, he waved back with two fingers, the trucker's salute. Past the stop sign, across the highway, lay the J & S Drive-In with its low roof and yellow paint and gathering row of cars for soft-serve vanilla ice cream. One night a week, they cooked Mennonite food—*Wareneki* and sausage with *Schmaundtfat*—and though Mennonites could have that food at home any night of the week, they still drove to the J & S to eat it, someone else's filled dough pockets, someone else's sausage. The men all looked the same— ball-capped, snap-front shirts with the sleeves rolled up, and work pants or blue jeans. The women, too, permed or kerchiefed, depending on where they fell on the spectrum, which Mennonite church they belonged to, whether radios were unrighteous and females wearing pants allowed.

I'd never be one, I swore. Never be a J & S wife. Never, I told Soopie, would I marry a man from Vanderhoof. Never a Mennonite. Never a guy who drove a chromeless van. Never a kerchief. Never an apron with the strings tied tight and a baby crawling up my calf, crying for my breast. Never this small town. Instead of the gravel shoulder of this potholed asphalt road, I'd take the freeway. Instead of the double-wide trailer, the city high-rise. Instead of the buttoned-up churchyard boy, I'd take the boy I hadn't yet met, the one becoming a man elsewhere on a street with a proper sidewalk, whose last name wasn't Wiens, or Dyck, or Giesbrecht. A man whose idea of traveling meant more than a weekend stay at Esther's Inn, the Prince George hotel everyone called "Mennonite Hawai'i" for its indoor swimming pool flanked by palm trees.

In the ditch, weaving parallel to the road, a trail dipped into a gully and rose at a tilted angle up a scrubby clay bank. Only a few years ago, I was riding those trails with Soopie and her sister, Theresa. On summer days, before any of us were old enough to have jobs, we tore off on our ATVs and raced across the acres at the back of our adjoining properties, weaving through the forest and along the barbed wire fence that divided the land. In spring, when the snow melted and left the earth soggy, we went out in search of bogs and deep puddles. Though there was no prize or title, we all competed to create the most epic spray and splatter, but to enter with a splash and part the muddy waters wasn't enough. You had to make it through to the other side without getting stuck. To be the one revving, leaning forward across the handlebars and willing the ATV to pull through, to be held there in the mire with a hot and steaming engine against your flank, tires spinning clay and muck and spatter until sputtering to a stall—this was the fear. You had to wager smartly, make sure you'd fly through, or risk the great humiliation of having to stand on the side of the road, waiting for a man to pull over in his pickup, ease out from behind his steering wheel, laughing the whole time over some girl too weak or dumb to figure it out. Then the man would climb on the stalled, stuck machine, rock it back and forth, cock the choke, and fire it back to life, shaking his head and chuckling as he rode it free from the suck of mud.

Beside me, the empty trail rose and fell, paralleling my steps as I passed the Siemens driveway and saw the dog straining on its chain. I unrolled the cuffs of my shorts, bringing them back to their regular length just above the knee. I tugged the band of my halter top lower on my ribcage. Ahead, farther down Macdonald and across Highway 16, Sinkut Mountain stood as a dusky blue triangle still peaked with white. At the turnoff to Sinkut, on Blackwater Road, a driveway veered right to my grandparents' house, where Grandpa Shenk likely leaned back in his recliner by the woodstove, the newspaper unfolding its headlines and the radio talking politics, and where Grandma stood in the kitchen in her dress and apron, stirring and chopping what would become their supper. If I kept walking on this same road, I'd reach her in no time.

When I turned down our driveway, Tiny, a black-and-white terrier we'd inherited from a dead woman, came scrambling, her barks sharp and shrieky. The bay door of the shop was still raised, and my dad sat hunched on the bench seat of a picnic table by the cold woodstove. In the yard, beneath the cocked hood of his beater Celica, my brother leaned, pouring in another liter of oil to feed the leaky motor. Whenever I rode in the passenger seat, if I peeled up the floor mat, I could watch the road go by beneath my feet, a blur of asphalt, the miles flying. I bent to the dog, scritched the top of her head. On commercial break from her afternoon soap opera, my mother stood framed in the kitchen window, peeling potatoes at the sink. Always potatoes for supper.

The music in my head ripped a final round of synthe-sized descent, and over a steady, snare-heavy drum beat that sounded like gunshot, the electric guitar riff ascended into air, hung in reverb like smoke. With a *click*, the tape ended. In the space where the music had been, the out-side world sang in. Through the poplar leaves, a shirring of wind. The clear-water whistle of a robin. The car engine's chug. I unlocked and hinged open the door of my Walkman, lifted out the cassette, and flipped it to the other side. My father's radio, twangy and blue, drifted into the mix. The dog at my feet wagged and whined. I locked the Walkman back up, pressed Play, and listened through the crackle for the next song to start.

THE NEWS
FROM HERE

ꭗ ꭗ ꭗ ꭗ ꭗ ꭗ ꭗ

VANDERHOOF—A high school student with lightning-fast typing skills was recently awarded a job at the local newspaper. Carla Funk, who clocks a typing speed of just over 100 words per minute, will be working as a part-time typesetter at the *Omineca Express*. When asked how she feels about the new role, Funk said that she's "looking forward to the challenge." In joining the newsroom team, Funk leaves behind her job at Slender Silhouettes, the toning salon, where she measured the bustlines and thigh girth of local ladies. Funk hopes to "type as fast as she can" to ensure the paper goes to print on time.

I sat down in the squeaky, padded steno chair at the desk assigned to me and surveyed my new surroundings. Desks and filing cabinets lined the walls of the cramped newsroom. Off to one side was the publisher's office, and connected to it, the reception desk, where a woman named Gail answered calls and collected ads for the classifieds. Across the narrow hallway in the production room, two women leaned over workstations with X-Acto knives, slicing printed copy into columns and headlines, and arranging them on master sheets of paper that would eventually go to press. These women looked like middle-aged versions of the black-purse girls from school, the ones who spent every recess in the smoker's pit with the skaters and headbangers. But they smiled at me when they looked up from their work. The one named Patti tucked her cigarette in the corner of her mouth and waved at me through a whiff of smoke, then went back to her slicing.

The narrow window above my desk looked out to the alleyway, and beyond it, to the Village Inn, a restaurant whose front door swung open and shut with a steady flow of diners. If I leaned forward and craned to my right, I could see the edge of the low-roofed police station, and across from it, the corner of Ferland Park. That park, when I was a kid, had always been a shiny attraction, a reward for when my brother and I didn't scrap in the back seat while my mother ran errands in town. If we behaved, Mom might pull off along the road beside the park and let us out to climb the monkey bars and squeak down the slide in what felt like a brief holiday. Now, though, the playground seemed small and dingy, its structures rusty and flaking paint.

Jim, a narrow-faced, mustached man who looked more like a cowboy than an editor-in-chief, rolled his chair beside me. "Let's get you started," he said, and pushed a button on the side of the computer. Dust covered the monitor and the keyboard letters were smudged, but the machine hummed on, and a blinking white cursor flashed onto the black screen. After Jim explained how the program worked and how to make sure I saved all my work on a backup floppy disk, he handed me a sheaf of loose papers.

"I hear you're fast," said Jim.

Speed was the reason I'd been offered this job in the first place. A week earlier, my high school typing teacher had called me to her desk after class.

"You hit 103 words per minute today," Mrs. Powell said, her finger pointing to a printout of my day's performance at the keyboard. She eyed me in a way that made me uneasy. "How would you like to compete at the provincial high school typing championships?"

Mrs. Powell assured me that this was a real competition, and that each year, students from secondary schools across British Columbia traveled to a designated city to compete. "Like volleyball or basketball," she said, "but instead, well, typing."

I envisioned a floodlit gymnasium full of students in rows of desks, each one hunched over a typewriter. I saw myself there, jittery and with palms sweating, as my fingers pecked out the competition script amid the clack-and-clatter of other teenage typists. Machine carriages dinging and zipping back into place. Metal keys hammering text onto paper. I asked her what the prize would be if I were to win the contest, trying to gauge whether the reward would outweigh the humiliation of being sent as a delegate. Mrs. Powell wasn't sure exactly, but she guessed a small amount of money, along with a trophy or plaque—plus, of course, the title of Provincial High School Typing Champion.

"You might even make it to the nationals," she said.

Always, the fantasy of traveling somewhere beyond Vanderhoof made me swoon, but stronger even than the pleasure of a free trip out of town was the stigma of a title like "typing champion." That one wouldn't be easy to shake. *Meet the province's fastest teenage typist,* the headline would read on the front page of the local paper, with my name and photo magnified. Titles like MVP, or Student of the Month, or even Bull-a-Rama Rodeo Queen seemed to hold more cachet, especially when it came to boys, but if I had to trudge down from the bleachers during assembly, shake the principal's hand, and smile for the camera in front of the whole school, I was sure I'd die of shame, or worse, never get a boyfriend.

"Thanks," I said to Mrs. Powell. "But no."

She looked at me with a mom's disappointment. "Well," she said, "then how about a job at the newspaper?"

The *Omineca Express*, our local paper, had called the school looking for someone who could type—and type efficiently—and Mrs. Powell put forward my name. After a ten-minute interview with the publisher, a jolly barrel-chested man named Terry, he offered me the job of part-time typesetter. "Six twenty-five an hour," he said. "Can you start this week?"

VANDERHOOF—Two weeks into her job as typesetter at the *Omineca Express*, Carla Funk continues to strive for record-high words-per-minute speed. Every Thursday and Friday after school and on Saturday mornings, she reports for typing duty amid a newsroom haze of cigarette smoke. When asked what part of the job she most enjoys, Funk coughed and then replied, "I really like the people I work with. And it's always fun to see what makes the front page of the paper." Though Funk dreams of one day writing "a novel or something," she hopes to continue as a typesetter through the summer and into the next academic year. She plans to use some of her earnings toward a possible trip to France with the school's French Club, which is holding its first fundraiser, a Rock-a-Thon, next month. Participating students will gather pledges to rock all night in rocking chairs. To financially support a Rock-a-Thon rocker, contact the high school office and ask for Monsieur Murphy.

Each week, I worked my way through the stack of paper on my desk. Whatever was set aside for me, I clipped to the typing stand and transcribed into the computer program that would eventually spit out content for the production-room ladies to carve into columns. Some of the texts I typed were press releases faxed over from the Ministry of Transportation or Finance or some other wing of the government. Others were brief reports from local community groups, like Ducks Unlimited, or the Nechako Valley Fall Fair, or the Women's Hospital Auxiliary. But most were handwritten pages in various states of legibility—obituaries, birth announcements for "The Stork Report," results from the latest golf or bowling tournament, seasonal recipes sent in by readers, and columns submitted by guest contributors. In shaky scrawl and inky smudges, the words embodied a cross-section of Vanderhoovian viewpoints and voices.

Each week in "Good News," a different local pastor wrote a short sermon on topics like "mourning with those who mourn," or "the power of the tongue to bless or curse." Katherine Woolsey contributed "Our Daily Bread," a food column in which she ruminated on everything from the best hot dogs to tips for successful microwave cookery. In "A Look at the Past," Bill Silver, one of Vanderhoof's pioneer historians, presented excerpts from the archives of the *Nechako Chronicle*, an earlier iteration of the *Omineca Express*.

But it was the Cluculz Lake News that made me work for my minimum wage. Each Friday, Ida Cutler dropped off her weekly column reporting the goings-on in Cluculz Lake, a rural settlement about a twenty-minute drive south of town, off Highway 16 and onto gravel roads that wove through forest and toward the water. A small clutch of folks had houses in the Cluculz area, and they all seemed to be the backwoods type, the sort who hunted and fished and kept traplines, well prepared for the end of the world.

Most of the time, Ida Cutler's report was submitted as a folded stack of paper in various sizes—letter-writing stationery, yellow notepad paper, and scraps of loose-leaf held together by a paper clip. Always, though, I recognized her handwriting: looping, slanted cursive in the same blue ink. At least one word in every sentence seemed to be lifted from a foreign language, encrypted and difficult to read.

"Do the best you can," said Jim, who seemed relieved that it was my job and not his to crack Ida Cutler's code.

"The new fall root?" I said. "Or the new hall roof?"

I carried Ida's writing from workmate to workmate, asking for help. Was this word "heart" or "heat" or "hearth," or maybe even "death"? Patti would set her cigarette in the ashtray and squint at the page, then shrug. Gail at the front desk would pencil out possibilities on her yellow notepad, as if working through a puzzle. Terry would lean back in his swivel chair, scan the page, exhale a puff of smoke from the side of his mouth, and then shake his head. "Good luck with that."

As I deciphered the Cluculz Lake News, I learned that Guest Road was having a third coat of tar and gravel, and that Mrs. Lenora Buchan was out of hospital now. Also, the young man who flew off his snowmobile didn't suffer brain damage as originally believed, and Cody Bryan, three years old, caught a one-pound, three-ounce trout in the lake, as witnessed by Tom McMaster. I recognized almost none of the names Ida Cutler mentioned, which made Cluculz Lake seem like an entirely unknown community, only connected to Vanderhoof by rural off-roads and shared space in the newspaper. But the more I deciphered and typed, the more it grew in my imagination. As I recorded the ordinary details of Cluculz, from the merganser nesting in Ida's duck box, to R. Martinson getting stuck while excavating for footings, to the results of the Ladies' Spike-Hammering Contest, the lakeside community I'd never visited became as real in my mind's eye as the setting of a novel, one I was reading in real time.

Though my job was only to type the given text and to check the spelling and punctuation to make sure I stayed accurate to it, I couldn't help but want to embellish the stories, to crack open the possible glorious details that lay hidden inside. I was hungry for controversy, drama, and suspense, a narrative with more excitement than what I believed my small town could hold. As I typed out the happenings in town, I saw the surface of the story, the information and the facts. The school board was considering switching spring break to coincide with bush-camp spring break-up, the time when the season's snow and ice began to thaw and turned the bush to mud, and loggers stopped working until the ground dried out. The Kinettes won second place at the Annual Humbug Dance with their lip-synch entry of "Black Kids on the Block." The Tribal Council voted against Alcan. Fred "Beer-Bottle" Bernie was on his way to Alberta to manage the new Co-op store.

FALHER, ALBERTA—The Co-op welcomed a new manager this week. Fred Bernie stepped into the role after working as an assistant manager at the Co-op in Vanderhoof, BC. Knowing that ninety percent of Falher residents speak French, Bernie says he is "brushing up" on his high school "Français" to better communicate with his staff and customers. Bernie, a bachelor, also looks forward to making new friends and possibly even finding himself "a special lady-housekeeper" who knows how to "maybe iron and cook a good pot roast." Bienvenue et bonne chance, Monsieur Bernie!

Occasionally, a few letters to the editor would be tucked into my weekly stack. As I typed them up, I felt as though I were listening in on a town-wide party line, the voices speaking over each other as they thanked, argued, and scolded. One praised the community for coming out to clean up the river shore. One begged readers to consider the effects of the upcoming Supreme Court vote on abortion legislation. One chastised Vanderhoovians over the rash of drunk drivers causing mayhem on the roads. One passionately endorsed a renegade politician and appealed for the construction of a public swimming pool.

They all began the same—*Dear Editor*—and then veered into a specific concern, but when I began typing one letter's words—a demand for Bill Vander Zalm, our province's premier, to be publicly castrated—I took the paper to Terry's office and asked how to proceed.

"Ah, yes," said Terry, scanning the page. "Hazel Kafsky." He shook his head and made the same *pffft* sound my dad made when his truck driver called in sick for the fourth shift in a row. Terry led me across the newsroom to a cabinet. He opened a drawer and pulled out a file stuffed full of paper and labeled with one word: "Hazel." Terry handed me the folder.

"All from Hazel?" I said.

Terry said that these letters were just from the past year. They were keeping a paper trail in case she actually did anything dangerous.

I'd seen Hazel around town but didn't know much about her other than the fact that she wore her ankle-length skirts pinned between the knees as makeshift culottes. It was hard to tell how old she was, but I guessed between my mom's and grandmothers' ages. Her thick, black hair hung to her shoulders in a blunt, scissored bob that swung forward to hide most of her face, except for her heavy-browed glower. Once, as I was heading into the post office to get the mail, I passed her on the sidewalk, close enough to hear her muttering in what sounded like a Slavic language.

Hazel's file full of letters to the editor spilled out a host of topics, from the danger of icy sidewalks, to the horrific noise pollution of her neighbors, to a request that her last name be pronounced with a long "A" instead of an "ah" sound. But the dominant theme of her submissions was a zealous concern for the animal kingdom. In one letter, she threatened to throw a brick through the window of Woody's Bakery, because the baker used butter, not vegetable shortening or margarine. Hazel's voice seemed to shout from the page in hand-printed letters that shifted to capitals for emphasis—EGGS, BUTTER, EVIL, DEATH!

When I asked Terry if Hazel had ever done anything truly violent, he said that other than breaking some glass and screaming at a few meat-buying shoppers in the grocery checkout line, she hadn't done real damage. No one really knew the whole story on Hazel, Terry said, but clearly, she had some problems. There were rumors she'd survived the war. Spent time in one of the camps. Hated men. It was hard to know what was true and what was just juicy small-town gossip.

VANDERHOOF—A group of teenagers were in for a big surprise this past Saturday night when a local woman known for public acts of violence attempted to castrate one of the male youths. Police were called to Redmond Pit Road where they apprehended a knife-wielding female of unknown age and origin. When questioned as to her motive for the attack, the perpetrator, who goes by the name Hazel Kafsky, screamed, "All meat-eaters must pay the price." She had reportedly witnessed the victim eating a stick of pepperoni outside Circle 7 Foods and had followed him to the gravel pit, a location frequented by rebellious Vanderhoof young people. The victim, though shaken up, suffered only minor lacerations to his acid-wash jeans.

A few weeks into my job as typesetter, when I showed up for an after-school shift, Terry asked if he could see me in his office. Other than the odd typo, I didn't think I'd done anything that would get me fired, but still, I was nervous when Jim, the editor, followed me into the meeting.

Terry sat back in his chair and took a deep breath. "You're in big trouble," he said. Then he and Jim started to laugh. "I'm only kidding. But we do have a bit of a problem."

He explained that the journalism student they'd hired to be the summer reporter had been—and here, Terry paused and shared a look with Jim—"let go."

"Which means we don't have a summer reporter anymore," said Jim.

"Listen," said Terry, flatly. He folded his arms and leaned on the desk. "The guy drank too much and we had to fire him. Do you want the job?"

I hadn't told Terry and Jim that I fantasized about seeing my name and my words in print. Though I'd long ago stopped recording random thoughts in the red pocket diary I'd kept as a young girl, I had begun a new ritual, spurred on by an English teacher who talked about the private lives of writers like Anne Sexton and Sylvia Plath. They wrote in notebooks and kept journals, confessed their darkness and their secrets on the page, and then turned those words into poetry. The whole thing seemed pretentious, which I liked, but I wasn't sure how to make a poem, so I started with a form I understood. Each night before I went to sleep, I opened the blue vinyl three-ring binder in which I'd once kept my sticker collection, flipped to a clean sheet of looseleaf, and wrote a letter. Always, I addressed it to the same person, my dream dad, Bill Cosby.

Dear Mr. Cosby. I'd spill out the notable events of the day. How Dallas passed me a note in science, and maybe I kind of liked him now, but not really. How Chad looked cute in his denim shirt, except he smelled like a crawlspace. How Amy was a total flirt, and how Sindee and I had this idea about sneaking into her bedroom and cutting off her huge pouf of bangs while she slept. How my new goal was to weigh 110 pounds and wear size-five jeans by the time I graduated.

How my father needed my help untying his bootlaces when he stumbled in the front door, late again for supper.

Dear Mr. Cosby, I wrote, *where did you learn to dance like that?* and *What's it like to be famous?* and *I wish I were your daughter, I wish you were my dad.*

Though I never mailed any of the letters, I admitted on paper all my sins and secret desires to him, as if he were a kind of priest, a holy TV father endowed with wisdom and goodness, capable only of being cool and fun, like he was in every episode as Dr. Heathcliff Huxtable. *Dear Mr. Cosby, One day I'd actually like to be a real writer, maybe even a journalist who works for a really big newspaper, maybe even in New York City.*

"As summer reporter, you'll have your own byline," said Jim. He held up his hand and traced across the air. *"By Carla Funk.* Sounds pretty neat, huh?"

"And we'll pay you what we would have paid the other guy," said Terry. "Same wage."

VANDERHOOF—The *Omineca Express* welcomed a new full-time writer to its staff this week. Carla Funk, a local student, steps into the role of summer reporter. Though she holds no professional credentials and possesses no journalism experience, she shows up at work on time and sober. Funk admits that at Town Council meetings, she has "no clue what is going on" and that the "shorthand notes" scratched in her coil-bound steno pad are "mostly doodles and squiggles." For her first front-page feature, Funk will report on her high school's dry grad festivities. When she shows up at the decked-out gymnasium with a camera strapped around her neck, she will feel like a celebrity voyeur, snapping photographs, interviewing students and teachers, and scribbling the facts in her notebook. She will write down as many adjectives as she can–"dazzling," "fun-filled," "exciting"–all the while thinking to herself, "One day, this will be me, posing in front of a fake palm tree with the most popular boy in my class. One day, my name will be drawn from a raffle box and I'll win a mostly restored 1982 Chevy Cavalier donated by a local auto body shop."

Throughout the summer, I walked around town with my notepad and pencil, on assignment to ask the right questions, get the quotes, take down the facts, and then build the story from the details I was given. I tried to start every story with a strong lead sentence, as instructed by Jim. I learned to save the least important information for last, in case the production ladies had to slice it off if space in the paper was scarce. But all the stories I reported on—tourism numbers at the visitor center, billets needed for crew members of the upcoming airshow, plans for the next Hooterville Hoot classic car show—seemed bound to the limits of the town, as narrow in scope as the window I looked through each day as I sat at my desk: the alley, the Village Inn, the edge of the police station, the corner of the park, my view the same every day and constrained by the frame I couldn't see beyond. The first few times my byline appeared above a story—*by Carla Funk*—I felt a jolt of pride, but it faded quickly, the same way our weekly newspaper was printed, read, and then chucked into the woodbox by the fireplace, ready to be crumpled into a nest of kindling and burned.

"Have you thought about studying journalism?" said Jim, one afternoon as we sat side by side at our desks. "Then you could come back here. Take over the paper."

It was one way the story could go. But I was already imagining other facts, figuring out my own five W's, who I was and wanted to be that summer in Vanderhoof, at the heart of it all. The *why*, the niggling question mark like a hook, tugged me. I could feel it, the pull away from my hometown, the urge to live a different story.

"I don't know if I ever want to come back," I said.

It was the first time I'd spoken those words aloud to someone other than Sindee or Soopie. To each other, we regularly lamented our hometown boredom, how we just wanted to get out of the Hoof, move to a city, and live the kind of lives we saw in movies. Glittering lights. Posh parties. Fresh faces. Soopie wanted to study fashion design, or maybe dental hygiene. Sindee wanted to be a teacher. But they both figured they'd probably move back when they finished college or university, because where else would they live?

PARIS, FRANCE—A young Canadian woman took home the grand prize at the International World Typing Championships this past weekend. The competition's clear front-runner was the renowned Japanese typist Hayai Yubi, who came into the finals as the World Record holder for highest words per minute. However, Carla Funk, a short, stocky, fair-haired Mennonite, shocked the judges and her fellow typists with her speed and accuracy. When asked how she will spend her one-million-dollar prize, Funk replied that she hopes to donate some of her winnings to her hometown of Vanderhoof, BC, so that they can finally build a public swimming pool. The rest of the money, Funk says, will pay for her dream of traveling the world, which will include a stop in New York City where she hopes to meet her TV dream dad, Bill Cosby.

"I've got a story for you," said Jim. "A feature, if you want it."

It was August, and the Vanderhoof International Air Show, our town's biggest week of the year, was a few days away. The newsroom was in high gear, pumping out promotional ads and adding extra pages to the paper. Jim was booked with photo ops and preview stories on the Snowbirds and the Blue Angels, and this year's confirmed fly-by of an F-16 fighter jet.

"There's a woman pilot landing here tomorrow," he said. "The interview's yours, if you want it."

The big news was that Joann Osterud, a pilot from Oxnard, California, was attempting to set an International World Inverted Flight Record, and Vanderhoof would be her touchdown destination. Osterud was determined to break the current record of four hours, five minutes, and twenty-two seconds, set by an American named Milo Burcham. Her plan was to first fly right side up from California to Vancouver, where she'd refuel and do a final maintenance check. Then, following the Fraser River from Vancouver to Hope, Williams Lake, Quesnel, and Prince George, she'd fly upside down all the way to Vanderhoof, our town, at the heart of the province.

On a sunny Thursday afternoon, I stood inside the Vanderhoof Flying Service headquarters with my aunt and uncle, who were the owners and operators. Through the crackle of the CB radio, a woman's voice broke through, giving coordinates and asking for the conditions.

"Wind out of the west at ten miles an hour," said Aunt LaVonne into the radio. "No reported traffic in the area. Land at your discretion."

"Cleared to land," came the woman's voice through the static.

With the rest of the staff and onlookers who'd come to witness the spectacle, I made my way to the edge of the runway. Before we heard it, we saw it—a dark speck moving across the blue.

"There she comes," someone hollered, pointing to the sky and the upside-down biplane drawing nearer.

Before the plane began its final descent, it barrel-rolled right side up. As the wheels touched down on the runway, they smoked, bounced, then rolled to a stop at the end of the asphalt strip.

As a crowd, we pressed toward the plane, toward this vessel bearing a woman who'd come from far away. When Joann Osterud climbed out of the cockpit, I was ready with my notebook and sharpened pencil and my camera looped around my neck.

"Excuse me, Miss Osterud," I said, and edged to the front of the crowd. "I'm from the *Omineca Express*, and I'm here to ask you a few questions about your flight."

"RECORD SET," said Jim, when I showed him a draft of my story. "That'll be our headline."

We'd aim to keep it positive, explained Jim, focusing on what this woman had accomplished, how far she'd come—not on her failure.

"Congratulations," I'd said to her, this short, blonde woman who'd just climbed out of a cockpit, her face red and puffy from the blood-rush of her flipped-over flight. A man in a pilot's jumpsuit held out his hand to her as she hopped down from the plane. Someone offered her a glass of water.

Inside the flying service headquarters, I drew up a chair across from her for a brief interview. "What made you want to attempt this flight?" I said, my pencil ready to record her response. "When did you realize your plan would not succeed?"

She sipped her water, answered my questions, but when she smiled for the photograph, only her mouth looked happy. Joann Osterud had come from California's palms-sway and beachy surf froth, from orange groves and vineyards and theme-park dazzle. She'd followed the river flowing from the Pacific and curving through the Fraser Canyon toward my town. Upside down in her Ultimate 10-300S, she flew in a way that flipped the story, turned the river into sky, the Cariboo plateau with its hayfields and horses into a new horizon.

And yet her eyelids, heavy and swollen, were those of a woman exhausted, tired of trying.

VANDERHOOF—A daring attempt at a world record fell short of expectations on Thursday, August 23, due to a mechanical malfunction. Joann Osterud, professional pilot and stunt flyer, attempted to fly inverted in her "Ultimate 10-300S" airplane, from Vancouver to Vanderhoof, in order to capture a title in the Guinness Book of World Records. In order to break a previously set record, Osterud was attempting to fly inverted for 4 hours and 30 minutes. However, due to engine difficulties, Osterud was only able to fly for 1 hour, 25 minutes and 4 seconds. Shortly after an hour of inverted flight, "The engine started to make strange noises,"

Osterud said. "The indicators appeared to be normal, but the oil pressure was dropping rapidly." When asked where the next attempt will be, the energetic Osterud replied, "It will be from Vancouver to Vanderhoof, of course. We're not defeated yet!" Although Osterud was not successful in her attempt, her time of 1 hour, 25 minutes and 4 seconds is a world record for inverted flight by a woman.

As a child, I used to lie on the sofa with my head and shoulders hanging off the cushion edge. From that vantage, the ceiling became the floor, and the shag rug and linoleum became the ceiling. I played out the inversion in my mind. Saw myself walking beneath a skyscape of furniture—the armchair, love seat, lamps, and coffee table anchored overhead. As I'd tiptoe across the stippled white paint, the sparkles embedded in its spackle would snag and stick to the fibers of my socks, but it didn't matter, because I was walking on stars. Above me, my dad asleep, stuck by gravity to the shag rust carpet, snored like an old planet. Before me, my mother's legs whooshed past, scissoring through the air, defying the laws of nature as I knew them. I could almost feel myself rising, leaving the ground of my making. Away from it, I'd fly—out of the narrow frame of the town, out into the wider sky of the new world, appearing as a speck on the horizon, a contrail in the open blue, a brief scrawl vanishing like smoke in the wind.

DRIVE

✗ ✗ ✗ ✗ ✗ ✗ ✗

IN THE SCHOOL PARKING LOT, they gathered in conference, young men practicing for future parking lots, like the truck stop café, or the tire shop, or gas station. They surrounded a chosen vehicle—a car or pickup belonging to one of them— and kicked the tires, then moved toward the hood, which the driver cocked. They craned over the engine, leaned in to touch cables, rattle a few parts, then stood back with their hands in their pockets or their arms crossed over their chests. Those wearing ball caps adjusted them.

Jesse stood on the back bumper and jumped up and down to get Clint's beater Chev bouncing. Then Norm or Ed or one of the other rebel Mennonite guys would let fly an insult, and the gang would laugh, and Jesse would punch Ed in the arm, and they'd start their mock-scrapping, horsing around in a way that drew an audience. The jocks shooting hoops in the gym paused their free-throws to stand in the open double doors. The skaters carved over on their boards. Girls leaning on the fence and sipping their cans of Diet Coke turned from their gossip. We all turned to watch. Bodies locked together, a grappling of sweat and muscle in high-top sneakers and faded denim, until one pulled away, ran his hand through his hair to smooth it back into place, his eyes darting toward the girls and then to the motor, the wheel rims, the horsepower, and the laughter of the other boys.

Guys who'd graduated the year before drove past the school on the lunch hour, slowing to a crawl as they eyed the girls on the sidewalk or huddled in gossip. My brother's friend dubbed it "the panty parade," as in, "If you're free at noon, let's go do the panty parade." That squeal of rubber on the asphalt as the Chev or Dodge or Ford cranked the corner at the stop sign was like a buck's snort and grunt in rutting season, a call meant to lure a mate.

I rolled my eyes along with Soopie and Sindee. "Pervs," we said, pretending that we didn't want to be the girls for whom they slowed, then revved, then popped the exhaust. The tailpipe's gunshot crack made me jump and my pulse quicken. I couldn't help but crane to see who was in the driver's seat. To see if he was cute. If his hair was something other than a mullet. If his upper lip was free of that stubbled smudge of a mustache that seemed to be a badge of manhood. To see if there was already a girl sidled over on the bench seat, tucked against him like an extension of his body, or an accessory for his truck, like the fuzzy dice hanging from the rearview mirror, or the gun rack over the rear window, or maybe even the gun.

SPARK PLUG. Rad hose. Timing chain. Crank shaft. These words my father spoke often into the telephone, listing the names of parts he needed for his logging trucks. Though familiar, the language of automotives was one I didn't speak or fully comprehend, like the Low German my dad spoke with his mother and siblings. Piston. Cylinder. Fan belt. Wires, valves, and heads.

"How much horsepower?" he'd always ask, and if the vehicle wasn't a Ford or a Kenworth, his next question was, "How much did you pay for that piece of junk?"

What I knew was that the driver with the most horse-power won—both the traffic-light drag races and the envy of men. To be left in the dust was the loser's shame and could only be compensated for by having a speaker system that out-blasted the other cars, which is why my brother spent his paychecks on tweeters and woofers and subwoof-ers that made his '75 Toyota Celica shudder and thump with Metallica.

When he was still in school, he'd let me ride with him some mornings, as long as I didn't complain about his music or comment on the dorky cut of his jeans and the way he styled his hair. He'd speed around the tight corner by the Mennonite church, flying down the dips and up the slopes as long as the road was clear, so that it felt like we were kids again, me on the back of the Big Red three-wheeler, and him at the throttle, both of us secretly pretending we were in an episode of *Knight Rider* or *The A-Team*, in pursuit of the bad guy.

For a teenager in a town like ours, which was spread out over the rural miles, a car was transcendence, granting freedom to go where you wanted and when. On weekends, my brother could drive out to the gravel pit or down the backroads for a party, cruise the town at two in the morn-ing to see what pranks the guys were up to, or even head an hour east on Highway 16 into Prince George for a concert

or a movie. Without a car, you were still a child, only going
as far as you could walk or ride your bike. When you exited
the movie theater with the boy who'd almost held your
hand, you didn't want your mom, parked and waiting at the
curb, to honk and call your name. You wanted to walk with
the boy to your own car, to pull the keys from your purse,
and offer him a ride.

If I couldn't have my own DeLorean with a flux capaci-
tor to shatter time and space and break me free from 1990,
Vanderhoof, then I'd take whatever vehicle I could. Even
though I didn't understand the world of cars, I wanted the
keys to that kingdom, to be the one who decided when to
brake and when to rev. To be the one who cranked the wheel
hard at the stop sign and spit gravel in my wake. To leave
the gawkers coughing in my cloud of dust.

Grandma Funk had never learned to drive. Until Grandpa
was too sick from the cancer to take her into town, he
was the one behind the wheel. In their maroon Ford LTD.,
Grandma sat always in the passenger seat, purse on her
lap, content to be taken where she needed to go. Grandma
Shenk drove, but whenever she and Grandpa went anywhere together, he was the driver. It was the same way with
all the men and women in our family, and even in the town.
Only when my parents returned from a late night of playing
cards did my mother drive, so my dad could rest his drooping head against the window and snore. But after she'd
helped him out of the pickup and through the front door, he
held out his hand, and she gave back the keys, restoring the
old order. In the morning, when my father came to the table
for his coffee and cigarette, the sound of him walking was
a metallic jangle, the keys in his pocket ready to take him
wherever he chose to go.

WITH Theresa behind the wheel of her black Dodge Daytona, and Soopie and I as passengers, we headed into town to check out the Friday-night action on our way to Diamond Jim's to rent a movie. As long as Soopie and I promised not to be idiots, Theresa drove us where we wanted to go. She was two years older and two years cooler than us with her blue eyeliner and black mascara, her tight jeans and blond, feathery perm. Plus, she was friends with the older boys, all of whom seemed to want her, even though she was tough and could skate as fast as any of them on the hockey rink.

We cruised over the tracks, past the gas station convenience store we called the Chevron Town Panty, because that word always made boys laugh, and toward the Co-op mall. The grocery store was closed and the parking lot was empty, except for a few cars at one end. The drivers stood beside their running vehicles and leaned on their cocked-open doors, enwreathed in exhaust clouds and lit up in the high beams that caught the falling snow. Theresa knew them, these boys with cars, boys with names like Kurt and Rob and Wade. When she pulled into the lot, Soopie and I cranked down our windows to get a better look.

None of the boys had as sleek or new a car as Theresa, but still, they started the game, a contest to see who could spin the most donuts in a single slide across the snowy parking lot. First one boy, then the next, revved and sped across the asphalt, slammed on the brakes, and cranked the wheel hard. As the car spun, we counted each rotation, tallying the score. Car by car, the boys one-upped until the hoods steamed and the air smelled like rubber and metal, gasoline and heat.

When Theresa shifted her Daytona into first and told us to hang on, I slid my new cassette single into the tape

deck and cranked the volume. As the hiss-and-clap beat of
"Ice, Ice, Baby" began, Theresa hit the gas. Along the edge
of the parking lot and across the ditch, the railroad ran parallel, and I had the feeling of being on a train veering off its
tracks, U-turning and circling, like the Gravitron carnival
ride whose g-force belted my body to the metal and plastic
as it spun and spun.

When we came out of the final donut's rotation, all
the boys who stood beside their own cars nodded, gave a
thumbs-up. "Not bad" and "pretty good," they said, and I
was sure this was what it meant to be cool. Through the
Daytona's open windows, the cold air whipped in and
the music pumped out, rapping about girls in bikinis and
Lamborghinis. The song's hook looped with the beat, and
Theresa's foot revved the pedal, readying for another slide
across the ice and snow.

WHEN Theresa turned sixteen, her parents gave her the
Daytona. Soopie's sweet sixteen was coming up, only a few
days after mine, and already, she'd picked out her birthday
car—a red Mustang—which I mentioned repeatedly to my
father when I caught him in a good mood.

"A Ford Mustang," I said, knowing it was his favorite
make, but he only nodded and tapped his cigarette in the
ashtray, showing no sign that he understood what I was
hinting at.

My mother insisted that having my own car was imprac-
tical, unnecessary. "Where do you need to go?" she wanted
to know.

"Places," I said, picturing myself cruising the main
strip with my music cranked—Bryan Adams or Richard
Marx, something hot on the charts that would catch the

ear of any boy standing on the corner by the Reo The-
atre, or outside Circle 7 Foods. I didn't care about the
car itself.

The morning of my sixteenth birthday, my gift lay waiting on the counter in the kitchen. The box was small, no
larger than a bar of soap, and wrapped in silver paper. My
hands trembled as I opened it and my heart thumped, as if I
were five years old on Christmas morning, anticipating that
one toy I'd circled and underlined in the Sears Wish Book.
I told myself that if it was a car, it wouldn't be brand new.
Secondhand was fine. Even a car like my brother's—a rusty
beater with an engine that guzzled a liter of oil every few
days—would be good enough.

As my mom looked on, I lifted the lid of the small box.
Inside it was another box, hinged and velvet—and too
small. I cocked it open. A thin gold ring with a tiny red gem
in its band glinted.

"It's your birthstone," said my mother. "Garnet."

I could tell that she'd put thought into the gift, considering "sixteen" a milestone worthy of commemoration. It
could be a keepsake, she explained, something to hold onto.

"Does it fit?" she said.

I slid it on my ring finger and held out my hand like a
bride-to-be. "Perfect," I said, but I didn't mean it.

"I didn't even know if this was something you'd like,"
she said, which was my cue to tell her it was a good gift,
that I would wear it to school that day and show it off to my
friends.

But instead, I ran my finger over the garnet and said,
"Red. Same as the new car Soopie's getting for her birthday
next week." If my mother flinched, I didn't witness it. "Can
I least get my learner's today?" I huffed.

During my lunch break, my father met me at the insurance office so I could write the test and get my permit. He wouldn't let me drive his pickup back to the school, so I walked, carrying the folded slip of paper in my hand as if it were a golden ticket, the permission slip that would grant me access to a higher realm, or at least, the roads that led toward it.

That night, my mother surprised me with the news that she was taking me to dinner at North Country, the town's log-house restaurant.

"Just the two of us?" I said, hoping she heard the disappointment in my question.

I was still wearing the garnet ring. Throughout the day, I'd studied it, twisted it on my finger, let the gold band clack pleasingly against my desk when I flipped through my math textbook. It wasn't a car, but I couldn't help but like the way the ring made my hand look. Delicate. Feminine. Strange. Even my nails, bitten almost to the quick, seemed longer. I thought I might finally paint them with the clear polish my mother had bought in hopes it would help me stop chewing them. "Don't you want to grow them?" she'd say, reaching to tug my hand from my mouth, but I'd only pull away from her, keep biting.

When we arrived at North Country, Soopie and Sindee were waiting inside the door. "Surprise," they said, and handed me the string of a foil balloon bearing the number 16.

It was supposed to be a fun girls' night, my mom's treat, but I didn't know how to act or what to talk about in front of her with my friends around. In my mother's company, I felt squeezed, caught between two ways of being, two versions of myself. I couldn't relax like I did at Soopie's house, or even at Sindee's. At their dinner tables, I cracked jokes that made their families laugh, found out that I could be funny, not just inappropriate or harsh. At my own dinner table, I whined to my mom about the pork chops and said that meat was gross and I was vegetarian now—what didn't she get? I stiffened when my dad stomped up the stairs, late again for supper, and rolled my eyes when my mother brought him a glass of milk at his demand. "You have a piano tied to your butt?" I'd say to him, hoping she would catch the hint that I would never be a wife who catered to a man.

After the waitress took our orders, we sat and sipped our water in near silence, awkward in our small talk, as if practicing to be adults, not children. My mother straightened her fork and knife and spoon. She folded her paper napkin.

"So," she said to Soopie. "Soon you turn sixteen."

"Yep," said Soopie. "Eight more days."

"And then you'll get your car," I added.

My mother folded her napkin again.

"Lucky," said Sindee. "You can be our chauffeur."

"And we can cruise the main drag every Friday night," said Soopie.

I cleared my throat and pleaded with my eyes for her to say no more, especially about how we begged Theresa on weekends to drive us around so we could scout for boys. A solid line divided who I was at home from who I was with friends, but with my mother at the table, I felt the danger of a swerve across that line, as if our talk might drift to boys we liked, the R-rated movies we'd rented, that rooftop party where we'd somehow ended up after the MuchMusic video dance party, swigging peach schnapps bootlegged by the older guys who lived above the post office.

Who I was apart from her, I was sure my mother wouldn't like, or at least, would not approve of, and so throughout the meal, I tried to steer our conversation toward what felt safe, benign, like the dressing on the Caesar salad, the softness of the garlic bread, and "Hey, when's our socials essay due?"

In childhood, my birthday table had been full of neighbor kids and cousins who came for potato chips and hot dogs and a cake baked by my mom in whatever shape I asked. A butterfly. A teddy bear. A rocking horse. We played the party games she planned, like the blindfold one where we fed each other popcorn with giant wooden spoons, or raced to stomp balloons and win a prize. I knew she'd never had those kinds of parties as a girl, her family too big to celebrate every child, every year. Even now, she was trying to give me something she'd never been given, a night away from our own family table, but I cared more about what I didn't yet have and still wanted.

"Can I least drive home?" I said, as we were zipping up our winter coats and tying on our scarves. When her mouth cinched at one corner, as if she was about to say no, I pleaded, "Come on. Mom. It's my birthday."

She sighed and handed me her keys.

In the back seat, Soopie and Sindee huddled, joking as they buckled up that this could be my last birthday, our last night on earth.

"Go slow," my mom said. "The roads are slippery."

"They'll be fine," I said. The snow was falling fast and thick. As I eased away from the curb, I felt the tires spin for traction, but I tried not to let my panic show.

"Signal," said my mother. "Left."

"I know," I said, fumbling to find the lever.

"Wait," she said. "There's a car coming."

"Calm down," I said, sounding like my father, whose constant refrain to her was, "Don't be so hyper," as if that helped at all.

"Stay in your lane," she said, her voice rising.

"I'm fine," I said, swerving back on course. Whatever yellow lines existed on the road were covered by the hard-packed snow. But I could see the tracks of those who had gone before me, two dark grooves running parallel on each side of the main drag. As I found my way into them, the roll of the car smoothed out, as if I were being carried on a conveyor belt, my foot on the pedal keeping the machine moving forward.

"Your wipers!" My mother reached to turn them on.

Through town, with winter's banner of blue-black night over us, I drove, guided by my mother's directions to turn here, tap the brakes lightly, take my foot off the gas when rounding the corner, check the mirrors for what's behind, and keep my eyes on the road ahead. As I revved through the light where the overpass cut to the highway, the car fishtailed, the back end sliding sideways down the hill, and my mother quietly reached for the steering wheel and pulled it into the direction of the drift. The Probe straightened out, the tires found their grooves, and up the hill toward home I drove. In the back, Soopie and Sindee laughed and murmured. My mother gripped her seat belt with her right hand, but her left hovered between us, ready to take the wheel if I needed her help.

EVERY ROAD became new. With my windows rolled down and the stereo blaring, I turned down streets I was sure I'd never traveled before. I was surprised to find out we had a

Campbell Avenue, a Hunter Lane. Parts of the town seemed to open like a secret portal, as if allowing me entrance only now that I was the one behind the wheel.

The bridge, when I drove over it for the first time on my own, seemed like a bridge belonging to a completely different town, the river beneath me wider and deeper and sparkling like a scene from a movie in which I was the heroine. Sometimes, in the storyline that played through my mind as I drove, I was the detective in search of a missing person. Sometimes, I was the missing person, on the run for a crime I didn't commit, hiding in a valley town in the middle of nowhere. Soon, I'd fall in love with a tree-planter, one of summer's tribe of tanned, scruffy guys who wandered the town on weekends, waiting for an empty machine at the laundromat and hunting for a girl to woo with his patchouli and thrift-store guitar.

When my foot pressed down on the accelerator, I pretended this was not my mother's car. This was my ride, my new Ford Probe. I felt the turbo of the 145-horsepower engine, all four cylinders, and let the rev punch me forward with a jolt that made me think "fuel injection" and "torque," words my father used, the language of men. With one quick jerk of the steering wheel, I could veer clean off the bridge, smash through the metal railing, and crash into the current below. If I looped past the fairgrounds and the airport, past the old Mennonite graveyard, and cut through the farm roads, I could swing back to the highway, drive until the sun embered down into the river. There was enough fuel in the tank to take me all the way out of the valley. I was in control, one foot on the brake, one on the gas, and my eyes fixed on the widening road ahead.

Even though I walk through the valley...

PSALM 23:4A

✗ ✗ ✗ ✗ ✗

ONE FOOT
IN THE FIRE

ꭙ ꭙ ꭙ ꭙ ꭙ ꭙ

ON A SUMMER SATURDAY NIGHT, as the dusk sky deepened to the blue-gray bruise of twilight, we stood at the edge of my front lawn—Sindee and I, and the boys who'd come from down the road, listening to Steve tell his story.

"That idiot almost hit me in the stinkin' head!" said Steve. His voice, indignant, revved. "Seriously, I could have wiped out. Got killed!"

Steve was ticked because the neighbor who lived two houses up had hurled a beer bottle at him when he smoked by on his Honda Hurricane. Sure, Steve agreed, he probably shouldn't have been riding a motorbike on the road, but the guy didn't need to chuck an empty Molson at his skull.

"Someone should chuck a bottle at him," I said. "See how he likes it."

"Or a rock," said Willie, the freckled one whose smile flashed a missing tooth. "Right through the dude's window."

"With a note in it," I added, "that says 'moron' or something."

I kept eyeing Phil, worried that he might dampen the mood, go full Sunday school on us and say, "Hey, guys, we're not being very Christian." He came from a stricter

Mennonite family than mine, one that still spoke German in the home. That was why his voice carried the familiar Mennonite lilt, the deepening of the long o, and the other vowels all slightly tilted, so that "Elizabeth in her red dress is dead on the bed" would sound out of Phil's mouth more like "Alizabath in her rad drass is dad on the bad." His way of speaking made him seem like someone more tuned to my dad's generation, more like a chaperone than a comrade.

Phil didn't normally hang out with us, and though he wasn't saying much, he was at least smiling at our plans for payback. When someone suggested a stink bomb lobbed into the neighbor's backyard. Phil said, "Yah, totally, you batcha!"

Our indignation brewed and brainstormed. From a rock through a window to slashed truck tires, or a freshly slaughtered chicken dripping blood on the neighbor's front step. We tossed ideas like tinder into the center of our circle, our words, as they met the air, chemical with revenge.

Only half an hour earlier, before Steve, Willie, and Phil had wandered down the driveway, Sindee and I had been sitting in my basement bedroom, trying to figure out what to do with our Saturday night, whether to rent a movie from Diamond Jim's, cruise the town looking for drunk people to mock, or keep doing what we usually did—complain about how there was nothing fun to do. We were boyfriendless, and we cared more about making honor roll than going wild at a gravel pit party, not that we'd been invited to one. The Sunday-school classes of childhood kept us from fully leaning into the rebel life. If we were stoners, we'd be smoking dope behind the bowling alley. If we were skateboarders, we'd be spray-painting fat cusses on the back of the post office. If we were Viqueens, the elite jocks of the basketball team, we'd be wooed by Vikings and making out in back bedrooms with our weekend flings. At least, this is how I imagined our alternate realities, if we were cooler, and better at being bad.

As a child, I'd stood dutifully in the children's choir with the other kids, my knee socks bright white, my dress ironed smooth. Every Sunday before church, my mother sent me to the bath, from which I emerged shampooed and scrubbed. In her bedroom, I sat on the floor beside the electrical outlet, and she fitted me with the vinyl cap of her hair dryer. She clicked the little silver switch to "on," and through a hose attached to the plastic motorized console, hot air began to blow. At first, it was a cool, light wind, but as she turned the dial higher, the air intensified, moving toward storm, tidal wave, a rocket with boosters blazing. The plastic cap inflated with the heat, so that my head ballooned into a fat, white bulb, an incandescent flare. My scalp tingled and my hair grew so hot I wondered if my brain might boil.

"Too hot! Too hot!" I yelled over the blowing wind, and my mother came running from the kitchen to adjust the dial. When my hair was dry, she brushed it until it gleamed, then curled it and pulled it back with barrettes in the shape of butterflies. With the other Sunday-school girls, I glowed, clean and pressed and keenly listening to our teacher, one of the church dads, tell another Bible story meant to make us good.

And I wanted to be good. I didn't want to burn in hell. Who did? I reminded myself of this in the dark hours of my own bedroom, when my thoughts teetered on a line that seemed to lean toward heat. Always, I felt the tug toward it, the glitter of its thrill and danger, the way a candle's flame would make me want to pass my finger through it, quick enough to not be burned, but slow enough to feel the singe.

I'd been taught that evil lurked in the world, seeking to devour me and lure me to the shadows. But I was starting to see that the trouble also lived inside me, as if I'd swallowed a seed of darkness and learned to feed it, and let its thirst and hunger be my own. When, on the last day before summer break, I snuck some of my dad's gin to school in an empty shampoo bottle, I expected a swell of pleasure, a quenching of some desire to be bold and bad. Instead, each soapy, floral Ivory swig tasted to me like a message. *I see you*, that inner voice intoned, that quiet eye that watched me always and argued with the dark in me. When I cut classes with Sindee and Soopie to go smoke cigarettes down at the river with some of the party kids, the burn at the back of my throat smoldered with the same warning.

"Hey," said one of the guys, taking back his Du Maurier. "Don't you go to the EMC church?"

"No," I said, and tried not to cough. "I mean, yeah. Sometimes."

Truth was, I went every Sunday, not because I wanted to, but because that was the way it had always been. Once a month, I even played piano for the worship service, plonking out the chords while the hymn leader stood behind the pulpit and waved his pinched-together fingers up and down in time to the beat, conducting the congregation as they sang. Mostly, though, I sat in my pew trying to look like I belonged, like what the preacher preached meant something to me. Only when a Bible verse contained some mention of sex did my eyes unglaze, my ears perk. *For the flesh lusteth against the Spirit, and the Spirit against the flesh*, the preacher would read, and with "flesh lusteth" my brain would rouse. *Fornication. Sexual immorality. Passions of the flesh*. The words snaked and sizzled, sparked a neon theater of thoughts in me—that boy, his mouth, my mouth, our hands—and then, like the residue of a naked-in-public dream upon waking, shame came flooding. Surely, I'd think, no one else who sat in church burned with thoughts like mine.

I'd tried attending the Friday-night youth group for a few months, after the new assistant pastor invited me. Pastor Reginald, a short, squat man with a face as round as a baby's, except a baby with a full black beard, had sidled up to me in the foyer with crinkly eyes and a too-huge smile.

"I'm Pastor Reg," he said. He tucked his Bible beneath his armpit and stuck out his hand to shake mine. "Have you ever thought about joining the youth group?"

I'd thought of it, yes. My older brother, Richard, had been part of the church youth group before he graduated and moved away for college, but the group had been different then, overseen by a young married couple who organized hayrides, barbecues, and games nights. But the thought of belonging to a social club where, instead of booze and dope, teenagers were encouraged to embrace mottos such as, "There's no high like the Most High!" and "No pill like the Gos-pill"—well, it seemed like the opposite of cool. The only real bonus to the church youth group, as I saw it, was the possibility of sanctioned time with boys. Even if my Mennonite bloodline did cross genetic paths with several of the guys in the group, the thrill of sitting next to one of them, while the length of our third-cousin-once-removed legs touched, held some appeal. But after a series of Friday nights mostly involving huge bowls of popcorn, Bible charades, and the occasional game of capture the flag, I gradually stopped attending. I faded away with excuses of being busy with school, work, family obligations. When Pastor

Reg flashed his bearded-baby smile at me from across the Sunday-morning sanctuary, I pretended not to notice.

More than being boring and uncool, youth group made me feel guilty. I sat in the circle of chairs in the church basement with Bev, Sarah, Sherry, the two Keiths, the three Steves, Phil, and Willie, and when Pastor Reg asked if any-one had any prayer requests, they all offered up heartfelt needs: healing for an aunt with cancer, courage to share the good news about Jesus with a friend at school, help with a big math test coming up.

As soon as I closed my eyes in prayer, a list of all the ways I missed the mark scrolled into focus, my sins glit-tering onto the stage of my heart's darkened, private the-ater, hidden from any audience, except, of course, from God's relentless, spotlight eye. I wondered what it might be like to be the kind of person who spilled out all the truth— who confessed her sins like a Catholic did, tucked inside the safety of a booth with a priest to listen from behind a screen. In our tradition, we had no confessional, no pri-vate vestibule into which our secrets could be spoken. The closest thing we had to confessing was Testimony Sunday, which happened only a few times a year, and in front of the whole congregation.

On Testimony Sunday, the senior minister at our church, a thin, bookish man called Pastor Bergmann, set up a microphone at the front of the sanctuary, and instead of preaching a sermon, he invited people to come forward and "share what God has put on your heart." It was the only service I simultaneously looked forward to and dreaded. The unpredictability of who would come forward and what might get said, coupled with the long minutes of waiting for a congregant to get up the nerve to rise and walk slowly down the aisle toward the microphone in silence, made me cringe and itch and want to crawl beneath my pew. But when someone finally did stand at the mic and start talking, I grew eager for what sin might be confessed, what secret exposed. When Shawna Olson sniffled into her Kleenex and spoke of her hard-heartedness and unforgiveness, when Matthew Toews rose to say he battled with believing in God's goodness after such a season of struggle, when Alf Wiebe shared of his wife's poor health and need for healing, I leaned forward. With every confession I could almost imagine myself up there, spilling my iniquities, confessing a host of secret sins—and not just the bootlegged peach schnapps, the smoking on rooftops, or the hot tub parties when Soopie's parents were out of town, but that thing inside that made me do the things I didn't want to do, knew I shouldn't do, but couldn't seem to stop myself from doing. Like winking at the boy from the Remedial English class, only to see him blush and stammer. Like inking on the door of the Co-op washroom Tasha Hockley's phone number and "For a good time, call." Like bribing Stephanie, the Mormon beauty queen, with a fistful of money to slow-dance with John Dyck, the boy who'd just moved into town from the backwoods bush and had no clue what to do with a girl's hands sliding into his back pockets while a Whitesnake power ballad blasted and a crowd of spectators laughed from the edges of the floor. I couldn't stop the wick from sparking, that surge of fire from thrilling with its heat.

But I vowed I'd never stand at that microphone on Testimony Sunday and confess it all—not my elation at another's shame, not the hot pulse of power that surfaced when I saw John's sweaty, awkward face as he clutched Stephanie's tiny waist, not the pride at my own conniving. To spill what lived inside me felt more dangerous than containing it. To pour it out risked losing control, threatened to turn me into a girl who desired nothing more than weakness, who'd sooner stand inside the fire until her darkness burned away than be the girl who stoked it.

SINDEE and I stood with the boys in the front yard, the lightless house at our backs and my parents asleep inside it, oblivious to the plans hatching on their property. The trees shot a jagged row of shadows into the sky, darkness on darkness.

"My dad has a jerry can full of gas in the shop," I said. "And a box of matches."

Steve said something about how that would sure teach the neighbor guy a lesson. We all laughed, and then we grew quiet. Willie and Phil kicked at the gravel.

"Maybe just a lattle bat of fire," said Phil.

We headed down the driveway, trying not to crunch the gravel loudly for fear we'd wake my parents, whose bedroom window looked out over the backyard. We snuck into the coolness of the shop. Along the walls were my dad's tool cabinets, compressors, hooks hung with chains, lengths of rope, electrical cords. At the far end was the woodstove, ashes cold in the summer months. And tucked in the corner by the woodpile was the red jerry can full of gasoline.

On a shelf by the woodstove, we found a box of wooden matches, the strike-anywhere kind. Steve hauled the jerry can, which sloshed with every step. I pocketed the matches. Up the driveway, soft-shoeing over the gravel, we crept.

"Are we really doing this?" said Sindee. We stopped at the top of the road where the newspaper box leaned on its metal pole. Steve set down the jerry can.

"Okay," he said, "we need to think this through."

We needed a swift method of fleeing the scene in case the neighbor came running out with another beer bottle in his hand, or a rifle. We didn't think he'd shoot. No one had seen him with a gun or anything.

"But yeah," said Steve, "that'd suck if he killed us or something."

"What we need is a gataway car," said Phil.

Sindee offered to park her Jeep farther down the road, to have the keys ready, the doors unlocked, so that we could light the fire, then run to the vehicle, jump in, and take the hill toward town, maybe deke down the overpass and head to Sandy Beach. No one would ever suspect us if they found us at the river. The plan was solid, we agreed.

After Sindee coasted the vehicle a little way down the road, we regrouped in a huddle at the end of my driveway to plot our method. We'd only pour gasoline on the neighbor's driveway, just at the end of it, so that when it lit up, the neighbor would definitely be able to see it from inside his house. By the time he got outside, the flames would already have died down. We didn't have to use a lot of gas, said Steve, just a little, just enough to get the fire going. We'd light it. We'd run. We'd make a clean getaway.

"It'll be hilarious," said Willie. We all tried to laugh. We laughed the quiet laugh of those looking over the edge of a high, steep cliff to the water below, all while eyeing the sign that warned of sharp rocks and strong currents and possible death.

Up the dark road, we tiptoed to where the turnoff to the neighbor's house met the asphalt. The first thing we all noticed was that his driveway was not very long. In fact, it was more of a parking space than a driveway. The distance from his front door to the newspaper box was barely the length of my dad's logging truck—without the trailer attached. Parked in the very short driveway was the neighbor's pickup, which left us very little ground on which to pour our gasoline.

"Maybe this is a bad idea," said Sindee.

Even Steve, ever laid-back, had a nervous edge in his voice when he said we'd just have to be careful, really careful about where we poured the gas. I took the matches out of my pocket, and Steve unscrewed the cap of the can. We looked at each other a moment, as if teetering on a fulcrum that might tip one way or the other. All it would take was one of us to say "wait," say "stop," say "no." But none of us said the words, and then Steve was pouring—a splash, and then a stream spilling and running in small rivulets over the gravel. As Steve walked backward, the fuel flowed with him, onto the road, over the yellow line, and trickling toward the neighbor's pickup truck. To top up the puddle, Steve tossed a couple extra splashes. And then he set down the jerry can and screwed the lid back on.

"Now who's gonna light it?" he said.

In my hand was the box of Redbirds, the tray slid open, the matches lying in uniform rows, red and white tips sulphurous for the striking. I held out the box to Phil. "You do it," I said.

Phil put up his hands in surrender and took a step back.

"You can run faster," I said, making my pitch. "That way you can drop the match, and Sindee and I can get a head start to the car." Something in me knew that Phil was glad to have been invited into our evening, and because of that, he couldn't say no. His entrance to the confines of our group demanded that he light the flame.

He let out a long breath.

I pushed the box at him again. "Come on," I said. "Do it."

Phil took the box from my hand and slid it open. He drew out a single match. With a *snick* against the scratchboard, he lit it.

Someone hollered, "Go!"

Sindee and I began to run, with Steve and Willie right behind us. Though I didn't see Phil drop the match, didn't see the tiny glow hit the ground and ignite the fuel, the moment of illumination was sudden and vivid. What had been the blackness of night—so dark it was hard to see the looks on each other's faces—was now a wall of light. Behind us, all around us, overhead even, the sky crackled orange and gold. A whoosh of brightness and heat pushed at our backs. My torso leaned ahead of my lower body, and as in a dream, my legs were unable to create the speed needed to run as fast as the rest of me wanted to move.

"You guys!" I huffed, as Willie and Sindee overtook me, and then Steve, too, with the gas can glogging against his flank. Then Phil tore by, arms pumping, knees high like a track-meet sprinter. "Wait!" I called out.

The flash behind me became in my mind's eye the backdrop of a film, the kind of movie designed for a group of church teenagers, a cautionary plot meant to scare them away from sin. At my back, the flames licking the edges of the bottomless, fiery pit, and the crackle and roar of hell trying to suck me in.

As I huffed and ran to catch up with Sindee and the boys, I felt the heat at my back, otherworldly, an illumination that prickled my scalp and the hairs on the back of my neck, my arms, my legs. My whole body felt the fire, not only in the air that surrounded me, but inside, too. As I scrambled into the passenger seat of the getaway car, as I fumbled with the buckle, as the boys ducked down in the back seat, and Sindee hit the gas, and we sped away from the scene, the heat thrummed within me, adrenaline and sweat and that dark well of fuel that never seemed to run dry.

THE NEXT MORNING, as my mother revved the car up the slope of the driveway, she glanced to the right up the road to where the asphalt lay blackened with a swath of soot and char.

"What on earth?" she said, slowing to get a clearer look.

From his front window, the neighbor whose driveway had shot into a wall of flame would have seen no proof of our jerry can, the spark, or the dropped match. He may have been sitting on his couch, remote control in hand, clicking through channels to find a better story than the one he started with. He may have had a Molson in the other hand, and just as he was taking a swig from the bottle— the same heft of bottle tossed at Steve's head as he flew by on his Hurricane—the man's living room may have brightened with a surge of light. By the time he made it out his front door, the fire would have been gone. When the smoke cleared, he'd have seen the charred road and hurled his curses at the air, swearing that this world was going all to hell.

My mother turned to look at me. "Do you know anything about that?"

"Me?" I said, keeping my voice cool, tamping down any notes of panic threatening to surge. "Why would I know anything about it?"

My question was not a lie, I knew. It wasn't quite the truth, but to ask it kept me leaning toward goodness, away from guilt. One foot in the fire, but the other firmly planted on unscorched, holy ground.

"I heard sirens in the night," she said.

"Sirens?" I kept my voice even, flashing to our careening escape, Sindee gripping the steering wheel and trying not to hyperventilate, Steve and Phil and Willie ducked down in back, and me, fiddling with the radio dial and staring straight through the passenger window, playing the part of one who was blameless and pure, even while the smell of gasoline clung to my hands, the same hands that would soon rest on the ivory of the church piano, ready to accompany an old, familiar hymn. Mr. Klassen would stand behind the pulpit microphone and call the congregation to rise and open their hymnals. He'd look over at me, and nod. Like I'd practiced, I would chord out the prelude that led the voices in, following the words that sang of the cross and the blood and that cleansing, holy fire, playing back and forth over the white keys and the black.

IS THIS LOVE?—A QUIZ

ｘ ｘ ｘ ｘ ｘ ｘ ｘ

TAKE EVERY LYRIC, EVERY POEM, proverb, and cliché. Take the plotline of every paperback teen romance, variations on a theme in which small-town Juliet moves to ritzy Manhattan and meets Craig or Chad or Rick at an upscale athletics club and worries she won't win his heart because she's just not the champion tennis player that the wealthy, glamorous Cassandra is, and Craig-Chad-Rick likes winners best, and how will Juliet win the biggest prize of all—his heart? Take *Flashdance, Footloose, Top Gun,* and *Pretty Woman,* all the love scenes in your VHS rental repertoire. Take everything you know of love and lay it out, the way your dad before he builds a fence lays tools on his workbench, the way your mother lines up scissors, pins, needle, thread before she starts to stitch. Love is modern, endless, here to stay. Can't be hurried. Can't be faked. It can, however, be crazy, shaken, stolen, or made. Can be given a bad name. Love stinks. Love bites. *O, Love that will not let me go.* In every hymn, love haunts with thorns and blood. *Love is patient, love is kind, it does not envy, does not boast.* Love's a shack, a freeway, a warm puppy, a battlefield, and it's in the air tonight. Onto the stereo's turntable, you slide the 45 and let

Whitney Houston sing your burning question. You crank the volume and side-step to the clap-clap-clap of the pop dance beat, imagining as you close your eyes that another body grooves in synch with you. *How will you know when it's love—true love?*

1. In socials class, the boy whose hockey jacket all the grade-nine girls are vying to wear passes you–you!–a note. You wait until recess to read it, until you're alone in the bath-room stall, where you unfold it, fingers trembling, and see the message he has written, a message that tells you:

   A. His favorite band (*Metallica*), his favorite movie (*Rambo* III), his favorite player in the NBA (*Michael Jordan rocks!*);
   B. He's been watching you and really likes your hair;
   C. He's having a party Friday night and you can come, just bring your own stash and whatever else you like, *hint, hint*, cartoon eyewink, and a doodle of a thick-lipped girl smoking a fat cigarette, a girl who looks like you but whose name is scrawled as Mary-Jane;
   D. He spells love in lower case, l-u-v, and prints his name like a child.

2. There's a new boy in town for the summer who has all the girls talking. When you meet him at the lake, you pretend you've only vaguely heard of him, that you don't really notice his lean, tanned torso as he lounges near you on the sand, then asks to share your towel. Later that evening in the moonlight of the park, he sits on the swing and pumps so high you think he might fly away. As the chains slacken and slam, you stand beneath him, uncertain of his muscular hum, his eager hands, and why he's chosen you. Higher and higher, he swings, and through the darkness, says:

A. *Do you want to be my girlfriend?*
B. *I think that you're my soul mate.*
C. *I'm so horny right now.*
D. *How do you spell your name?*

3. And after he has scraped himself against you in a way that makes you think of Patrick Swayze, of *Baby*, of all those dirty dancers, and also, weirdly, of your cocker spaniel locked in the garage and waiting in heat for the stud, after he has left you in the flash of his mother's rearview mirror motoring east and away from summer's sweat and sun, you find out:

A. You were not, these last few weeks, his only soul mate;
B. "Sucker" is another word for "soul mate";
C. "Soul mate" is the kind of thing a boy will learn to say when his brain is damaged from sniffing too many paint fumes and he cannot think beyond cliché;
D. Cocker spaniels, though adorable as puppies, are not the smartest breed.

4. The Swiss exchange student who plays trumpet and speaks five languages and smokes coolly in the school's snowy courtyard asks if you like jazz, and though you know nothing of the genre, you say, "Totally. Absolutely, it's my favorite kind of music." That night, you shift the radio tuner to CBC and on the blue shag carpet of your bedroom, listen to what sounds like a wounded animal crawling back and forth across the piano keys, like a dying swan, like engine trouble. Still, for the Swiss trumpeter, you join the Columbia House record club and order all the jazz cassettes in the catalogue. When the Swiss boy walks past your locker, you flash a copy of *Tutu*, your newest Miles Davis tape, and he

moves in closer. Next thing you know, you're playing piano with him in the jazz ensemble, your hands clueless to the sudden, unpredictable chord changes, everything you studied of Bach and Beethoven now diminished and dissonant, swinging from the minor seventh to the eighth, syncopating, augmenting, blowing changes in broken time, but the trumpet solos keep you at the keys. After "Take Five," after he leans on the piano and blows the spit from his valves, he squints at you in a way that makes you hopeful, and he asks:

A. *Can you feel vhat jazz is now?*

B. *Do you vhant to sometime practice together, the two of us?*

C. *This veekend, vhat are your plans?*

D. *Are you—vhat is that called here—an albino?*

5. At Friday-night Young Peoples, you slouch in your wooden chair in the church basement, one of a dozen yawning teenagers enduring "Apathy Night," the youth pastor's attempt to make a point about the state of the adolescent heart. You sit in silence, eyes closed, hands in your lap, taking in that familiar musty-carpet, cold-concrete smell, all the Sunday-school classes of your childhood floating back to you now, all the glue pots and glitter, crayons and play-dough, and that flannelgraph storyboard where paper cutout figures illustrated miracles and parables. In this holy moment, more than anything, you desire:

A. To pay more attention to Jesus;

B. To pray, to read your Bible, to put God first;

C. For Luke Toews, who sits behind you, to lean forward in his chair and sniff the vanilla perfume on your neck, a smell that he says reminds of him cake, a smell that makes him hungry;

D. To have a boyfriend, *Please God, just let me have a boyfriend.*

6. When you pass the lanky, dark-haired boy in the empty
   school hallway where he leans against his open locker and
   you ask him for the time, he looks up from his textbook and
   answers, *Ten to four.* He smiles. You smile back. Though this
   is the first time you've ever spoken to the boy, you are sure
   that:

A. He would never answer back unless he wanted more;

B. The numbers—*ten to four*—are a code by which you'll know
   what more he wants, what move is next, and when to make it;

C. When you get home and sneak to your bedroom with the
   telephone book to look up the boy's number and find that it
   contains not one zero, but two, like the zero in the number *ten,*
   but doubled, this is more than coincidence, this is a sign;

D. At the end-of-the-school-year dance, his hands will settle
   on your waist and you will sway to a song by Roxette whose
   words in that moment sing for you, only for you as you turn
   slow circles and feel his hipbones graze your hipbones and
   you are close enough to catch a waft of his cologne through
   the dry ice and sweat of musky other-slow-dancers and you
   will know it instantly—*Colors by Benetton*—a scent for both
   women and men, and that, too, you will take to be a sign.

7. After the movie whose plot you cannot recall because you
   were too focused on the armrest on which your arm was
   draped just so, the length of your sleeve brushing his, your
   hand sweating and ready and aching to be held, after he
   finally laced his fingers through yours, after your whole arm
   went numb from the odd angle of its position, after you
   endured the pleasure and the pain, he takes you for a drive
   in his mother's old Volvo. Out of town, up the highway, he
   turns onto a dirt road, the station wagon humping over
   washboard ruts, a cattle guard, potholes until you arrive at

a stream. You sit in the car, too nervous to speak, and stare through the rain-streaked windshield at the blur of birch trees and the mountain on the other side of the water and the plywood outhouse whose cocked door is spray-painted with a neon-pink happy face. This, the boy tells you, is his special place, a secret place he goes sometimes to be alone, and now, with only the rain and the stream and the woods all around, you are alone together. When he unbuckles his seat belt, leans toward you, and pulls you close, your first thought is to:

A. Close your eyes;

B. Suck in your stomach;

C. Swallow your wad of spearmint gum;

D. Push from your mind your father's wild, magnified eyes and your mother's shock and scolding, push away your brother, your grandmothers, your aunt LaVonne's oracle warnings, push away all the ancestors breathing from the chasteness of their Anabaptist wedding nights, to push away, away, away the Bible verse whispering that the body is a temple of the Holy Ghost and shall not be defiled.

8. You've made your vows. To friends, you've sworn aloud you just don't want the man, the marriage, the procreated brood. That shape of life won't fit, and never will, you've claimed. But now, finally, you have a boy's arm around you, hallelujah, and you're walking side by side along the shoulder of the road like living figurines from atop a wedding cake, so when he turns to you and tells you one day he wants to have two children—one boy, one girl—you, with your brain brined in hormones, echo his desire. *One boy, one girl—me too!* When he kisses you beneath the porch light,

you ignore the swarm of blood-hungry mosquitoes, pretending you defy cliché, you rise above all hackneyed high school romance plots, you are immune. Alone, by lamplight in your basement bedroom, you:

A. Ink your future self to him, doodling your names until their syllables join and woo you with their music;

B. Pull out *The Book of Names* and choose your son and daughter—Wolfgang and Emily, or Benjamin and Kate;

C. Lie on your bed in the dark and listen to the mixtape he made for you, each Heart, Richard Marx, Wilson Phillips, and U2 song picked with you in mind;

D. Strip down to your underwear, stare at your body in the full-length mirror, and believe the boy *is* the mirror.

9. Each day, the boy sends you postcards in the mail, photographs of sunsets from the fishing lodge where he works all summer. He writes:

A. Clichés you swallow hungrily;

B. Poetry that rhymes;

C. How much he misses you / how in his dreams he kisses you;

D. That one day soon, he'll make a lucky Mrs. of you.

10. The boy, back from a term at university, invites you to spend Christmas Eve with his family, which tells you this is serious, this is for real, this just might be it. At the table, wedged between him and his mother, across from his father and younger brother, you feel like a peg slotted in the wrong spot, ill-fitting. No one speaks much. The family's pet rabbit nibbles at the toe of your sock and you startle, kicking it in the head. No one laughs when you tell the story of how you killed your own pet rabbit, by accident, completely by

accident. Neither does the father hold up an empty glass and demand to be served. The mother doesn't sigh and push back her chair with a force that hints a hidden message. The brother doesn't call you a dumb hag. Nothing interesting happens. After you clear away the plates, as you stand at the kitchen sink, drying the last dish, the boy:

A. Smells different than he used to smell;

B. Tries to kiss your neck when his mother isn't watching;

C. Keeps talking about his new friends at university, all of whom have names like Megan, Annaliese, and Kayla;

D. Whispers over your shoulder, "Want to see my bedroom?"

11. He gestures like a salesman at the small, tidy space. With a bed tucked against the wall, a chest of drawers, a desk, a closet, it looks like any room. He sits down on the mattress and pats the space beside him. Shoulder to shoulder, you sit. The air smells like laundry and lemon soap and hair. From a bookcase, he pulls an atlas, opens it, and finds the continent of Europe, then narrows in on Germany. He points to a dot on a map and says, *Schwangau.* He'll take you there one day, to the top of a high, rugged forest hill in Bavaria, to Neuschwanstein, the fairy-tale castle built for a mad king. *Close your eyes,* says the boy. You feel him sliding off the edge of the bed, hear rummaging in a drawer, the crackle of plastic. When you open your eyes:

A. He's taking a knee on the creaky hardwood;

B. He's holding out a small, pink velvet box;

C. He's cocking open the tiny hinged lid;

D. He's asking you to promise him to one day be his wife.

12. But not yet, the boy explains. Obviously, not right now, he says. Eventually. One day. Maybe in a few years. Four, or maybe five. When you're both done university. But he loves you, he insists, as he tugs the ring from the box's velvet slit. You offer:

A. Your left hand to him;

B. Your fourth finger to him;

C. Part of your heart to him;

D. To keep the whole thing secret, so none of his friends find out, and definitely not his parents, or your parents, or anyone at all, to keep this just between the two of you.

13. You will yourself to hold his gaze, to not flinch from the eye contact. This is what real romance is about, staring into each other's dilated pupils, getting lost in them, like the pop songs sing. In his eyes, you can almost see:

A. Yourself, a tiny, inverted girl shining in the darkness, a far-off version, years away from arriving;

B. Hints about the future you can't yet know;

C. The telephone ringing and ringing and ringing, but no answer, and the voice, when it comes, like a dull blade;

D. The ring slipped back into the box, and the box thrown back at its giver.

14. Like the tiny diamond chip glued in its thin setting of gold, the story's tropes glitter. When you say goodbye on his front porch, the snow drifts down like:

A. Confetti;

B. Pathetic fallacy;

C. False prophecy;

D. A fairy tale shotgunned to bits and already beginning to fall.

15. As you drive the slow road home, the snowflakes fly at you in streaks of white, like shooting stars in a sky lush with wishing. The crystals shatter as they hit the windshield, and then are swept aside by the wipers, the wipers, the wipers. You blink hard, try to shake off the trance of their rhythm. The ring clacks against the steering wheel's plastic as you shift your grip to two and ten o'clock, like the driver's handbook says to do. Keep the wheels aligned. Stay in control. But you can't even see the lines anymore, the road covered by a thick white layer. The only light in the sky comes from the falling snow that feathers onto the windshield, flake on flake on flake illuminated by the high beams. In the blizzard's cast spell, your eyes glaze to the middle distance. Before you, the road blurs until it seems you might be going nowhere, held there, shaken inside night's starry globe.

The tug of the snow pulls toward the shoulder. You tap the brakes, like you've learned to do, when everything feels out of control. The car fishtails in a slow-motion *shoosh* that spins the back end out and leaves you sliding sideways over the road, headlights shining on a fence, post after post, and lines of barbed wire gliding by. You take your foot off the gas and brace for:

A. The slip, the ditch, the smash and crack, the glass and bone, the wound, the blood;

B. The world to swerve back on course;

C. The end;

D. All of it, everything, all of the above.

Every valley shall be lifted up,
and every mountain and hill be made low;
the uneven ground shall become level,
and the rough places a plain.

ISAIAH 40:4

CLEARING TRAILS

ᚷ ᚷ ᚷ ᚷ ᚷ ᚷ ᚷ

DOWN THE KLUSKUS LOGGING ROAD, over potholes and ruts, the pickup rattled and bounced. The early-morning July sun streaked the treeline of fir, spruce, and lodgepole pine. We were heading toward our first site and the first full eight-hour day on the job. In the stuffiness of the back seat, wedged between crew mates, I was carsick and jittery with nerves. As a kid, I'd watched my dad leave for work in his dark-blue work pants and shirt, carrying an industrial-grade lunch kit and thermos. Into his Kenworth he climbed, morning, afternoon, and in the middle of the night, depending on his hauling schedule. The rumble of the truck engine, the hiss of the air brakes, and the tangy bellow of the horn were the soundtrack to his shiftwork comings and goings.

Back then, I'd ridden along on the occasional trip with my dad, with the promise that the drive would be an adventure, wouldn't take too long, and that "yah, we'll see, maybe if there's time," we could stop for fries and gravy at the Pine Country on the way back, or soft ice cream from the J & S Drive-In. If he was in an easy mood, if the weather was clear, if the radio was playing a tune by Randy Travis or

George Strait, if I asked with the right dose of kindness in my voice, he'd let me call the miles. As we guttered down the gravel road, I gripped the transmitter of his CB radio, and when we passed a mile marker, I pressed the button on the side, held the speaker to my mouth, and announced our location: *Kluskus, up, nineteen.* Other logging trucks coming toward us heard my voice crackling into their cabs and spoke back through the static with a *Ten-four, Roger that.* If they were close, they called their location, too, so that we always knew when to slow down and pull over to the shoulder to a let a load go past.

Those ride-alongs always seemed to stretch past what he'd promised. My anticipation over what the journey might hold—the possible drama of a sudden swerve and near-accident, or a small brush fire being doused by a forestry crew, or the sighting of a grizzly and her cubs—fizzled with the familiar drag of slow time. My dad would wander the clear-cut, puffing on a cigarette and talking with the other loggers who were also waiting for their trailers to be loaded. I'd be sulking in the hot, stuffy cab, too paranoid of the horseflies to climb out and explore, too bored to care about the world beyond the rolled-up truck windows.

Daughter of a logger, I grew up with words like axle grease, monkey wrench, bush camp, and tire gun. That world was full of horsepower and fuel, smoke and sap and sawdust. That world was full of men and their machines. Whoever entered it came out dirty, grit beneath the fingernails. Grease perpetually creased the lines in the palms of my dad's hands. He smelled like his work—coffee and sweat and trees and engine oil, capped off with the tang of beer or rye whiskey's amber sweetness. It was the musk of all my dad's buddies who stopped by for drinks after their own long shifts, a kind of trucker-cologne vividly whiffed upon entry to their gatherings. That odor was as familiar as the Saturday-morning fragrance of my mother's domestic to-do list—the kitchen's yeasty rise of the bread dough mixed with the cool chemical waft of bleach from the basement laundry room. The two realms—blue collar, red apron— existed in a sharp binary: either/or, here/there, male/ female. But finally, I was beginning to feel the untethering, the loosening of restrictions, and a rising sureness that I'd dodged the inherited narrative of tying on my own apron and kissing my trucker husband good morning before he called his own miles down a dusty bush road.

Only a few weeks earlier, I'd shuffled across the local hockey arena wearing a royal-blue robe and cap, making my way with the rest of the graduating class in stuttered toe-step rhythm to the relentless plod of "Pomp and Circumstance." After all the teacher speeches and awards, I stood at the podium microphone and read out my valedictory address, which I'd infused with words borrowed from a book full of inspirational quotes. I ended with the final lines from Tennyson's "Ulysses," a poem whose iambic pentameter pulsed with a momentum that seemed significant, hinting prophetically at something I couldn't quite grasp. *To strive, to seek, to find, and not to yield,* I recited, thinking not about the poem's restless, worn-out hero at the end of his mythic life, but only about what lay beyond my high school life. Channeling the energy of an Oprah Winfrey pep talk, I looked out over the audience and urged my fellow graduates to strive to make a difference in our world, to continue to seek knowledge, echoing sentiments I'd heard before, ones that sounded crucial for the future,

however vague. Then one by one, in our ceremony's closing
ritual, we walked across the stage, each bearing a flickering
candle meant to symbolize the light of knowledge. Three
years earlier, my brother had passed his flame to me, both
of us somber and awkward as we stood and posed for the
camera flashes while we held the candle. Now he was gone,
married to his college girlfriend and studying at a university far from home, as if that fire, once given, could blaze
the way ahead for the one who gave it. When my name was
called, I took my place in the spotlight's beam and handed
my candle to Jennifer, my younger cousin, and hoped that
flame would set me free, too.

Now I was riding in the back seat of a forest service
pickup, dressed in coveralls and a yellow hard hat, ready to
swing an axe. Along with a few dozen other grads and college students who'd returned home to work for the summer,
I'd been hired as part of a government-funded program.
In the week leading up to my first day on the job, I completed the required industrial first-aid course. Like everyone in the class, I took my turn blowing into the mouth of
a scuffed-up resuscitation dummy named Annie, performing chest compressions against her springy ribcage. I practiced how to splint a broken bone, and stanch a chainsaw
wound with a tourniquet fashioned from duct tape and a
sock. With my fellow crew members, I also learned how to
use—and not use—the various tools we'd be assigned. Both
the long-handled axe and the maul could easily cleave a foot
if swung without care. The Pulaski, with its double-blade
hatchet head, worked well to hack out stubborn roots when
clearing trails, but pulled back too hard could split a skull.
The backpack-style pressure sprayer filled with pesticide

would kill off the scourge of purple thistle, but if the spray wand weren't handled correctly, the toxic chemical mist could burn your skin with future cancer. In groups, we took turns practicing the techniques, how to swing the tool, how to clean the blade after use, how to not sever a limb.

After an hour on the logging road, with all those tools clattering in the back of the pickup truck, our crew foreman pulled over to the shoulder and cut the engine.

"This is it," Rusty said. "Time to get working."

We climbed out into the coolness of the morning and into clouds of blackflies and mosquitoes. Even after we took turns spraying each other down with industrial repellant, they swarmed us. "Suck it up," said Rusty. He unlatched the tailgate and told us to unload the tools, then follow him into the woods.

There were about a dozen of us in the group, most of which was made up of guys. I recognized the three other girls, but they were a few years older than me, and they belonged to different social circles, so I kept the appropriate distance, smiling if we happened to make eye contact, but quick to look away. Instead, I stuck close to Kyle and Calvin, two classmates who also came from Mennonite families. They were church kids, too, which made them safe, more like half-brothers or cousins than ordinary boys.

"This is going to be terrible," said Calvin. "I have a bad feeling about this."

His bad feeling was that we were going to be attacked by a grizzly. Ever since the forestry crew chief gave us all a lecture on how to deal with bears and other dangers in the wild, Calvin had been shaking his head and muttering the narrative of his tragic end by tooth and claw. Though

I didn't admit it aloud, I was nervous, too. After the group safety talk, Tami, one of the other crew leaders, had pulled all the female workers aside and called us into a huddle.

"Here's the deal," she said, her voice low. "Bears can smell when you're menstruating."

We snickered at the awkwardness of hearing Tami, a tough party chick with mean eyes, say the word "menstruating." It felt as if we were getting the puberty talk all over again. But when Tami told us to shut up and quit acting like toddlers, we quit laughing, and nodded that yes, we were we going to take her seriously. She explained the special feminine protocol for dealing with predators while working out in the bush.

"You gotta dig a hole," she said. She held up her hands and measured the depth. "A good foot or so." We had to bury used tampons and pads in the dirt, she explained, and we had to make sure to cover it up, too, or else the bears would catch a whiff, sniff out our scent, and come after us for blood.

Her warning played through my mind as I trudged the trail, close behind Calvin, and listened with low-level paranoia for bush crackle and branch snap.

"Ah, we got axes," said Kyle, who was carrying one of the Pulaskis over his shoulder. "We can take 'em." He began swinging lazily at an invisible predator.

As we headed deeper into the forest, we followed a rough path marked with neon-pink surveyor's tape tied to the ends of branches and the tops of saplings. Our job at this first site was to clear the trail, to make it passable for hikers and campers and anyone out exploring this patch of wilderness. Somewhere through this stand of trees was our destination—a small lake loaded with rainbow trout, a secret fishing hole and a water source for the wildlife in the area.

After a short hike, our crew stopped at a small clearing, and we stood in a circle as Rusty gave us an overview of the project. We'd begin by dividing into teams to tackle the first segment of the trail. All the deadfall brush had to be hauled off the path. All the stumps removed. All the roots hacked away. Each job would require a different set of tools, so we'd trade off on the tasks from section to section. If all went as planned, we'd be out of there in a week, two tops, and then we'd move to the next assignment.

To pick up branches and brush from a designated area of the forest floor and chuck them into piles seemed, in theory, straightforward, and a fair trade for the ten dollars an hour we earned. We broke off into teams, and I moved ahead with Calvin and Kyle to our section of the trail, where we began to pick up the limbs and boughs.

"There's a grizzly out here," said Calvin, shaking his head. "And I'm probably going to die today."

He sighed loudly, and then went on to describe in detail how the animal would attack, sink its teeth into the soft flesh of his neck, blood spurting from his jugular, and then the claws digging into the meat of his belly, which would be pathetic because he basically had no meat on him. As he lay bleeding in the forest somewhere down the Kluskus, the bear would sink its muzzle into his gut and make of him a quick meal. First day on the job, and he wouldn't even be able to collect the money he was owed. The whole thing sucked.

"There are worse ways to go," said Kyle. He picked up a pair of heavy-duty snippers, aimed them at Calvin, and laughed darkly as he flashed the blades open and closed.

As we worked, the conversation slid into talk of death. All the ways to die. Sucked into an undercurrent like Kevin Jantzen, his body hauled from the river last summer. Hit by a train coming home from a party the way Tyler Antonsen was. We'd cut class to attend his funeral, even though none of us knew him well. Sitting in the church pew between Soopie and Sindee, staring at the casket that held the boy who sat two rows over from me in social studies class, I'd felt suddenly like an adult, as if the future had arrived in force with the reality of a body gone before me, Tyler clearing the way toward my own mortality.

Eventually, we'd all die, said Calvin, but if he had a choice as to death's method, he wanted the whole thing over with before he knew what was happening to him. He wanted the opposite of a bear attack. Something clean and quick, taking him by surprise, like the train. If I could pick my own end, I told them, I wanted something interesting, the kind of exit that would make my life more epic, a headline-worthy death.

"Cannibalism," said Calvin. "That would make the news."

We'd all seen the movie *Alive*, based on the true story of a soccer team whose plane crashed in the Andes and whose survival depended on them eating the bodies of their dead teammates.

"Imagine," I said, "you're stranded on a desert island. You're either going to have to eat your companion or be eaten by them. What would you choose?"

We fleshed out the storyline as we dragged away the deadfall. Calvin, kneeling at the bloated body of a drowned Kyle, hacking away at his thigh with a shard of beach glass. Or Kyle, roasting a chunk of Calvin's left buttock over a driftwood fire. Scenes that hadn't even happened, would never happen, were now becoming real and vivid in the mind's eye as we built them together with words. I could see myself at the edge of the ocean, staring out across the water for a sign of rescue, my eyes sun-blind, my lips crusted with salt. This was how the future worked, I thought. I had to conjure the impossible until my mind jeweled into scenes from a life illuminated as possible. Only then, when the dreamed-up kingdom of the not-yet was imagined in technicolor detail, would I be able to get there.

By midday, we were all exhausted from what had seemed at first like simple, mindless work. In near silence, our crew sat in a patch of shade and ate our lunches, our backs slumped against tree trunks and our hard hats polka-dotting the moss and dirt. I was sweaty and already dreading tomorrow's shift. My new work boots, unlaced now, had left my toes numb with the steel-toed weight. When Rusty pulled off his sunglasses and checked his watch, we groaned collectively, rising sluggish into the afternoon heat.

Kyle and Calvin and I returned to our trail clearing to find that though we'd removed the easy and obvious debris and chucked it on a communal pile, the first layer of branches and broken limbs had only hidden a deeper level of obstacles. Roots gnarled the dirt, some growing from the old pines that leaned along the path, others snarling out in a tangle of tripping hazards from nearby stumps. Fallen trees and rotting logs lay like hurdles at various intervals across the forest floor.

Rusty, who'd wandered over to check our progress, swatted his ball cap at the mosquitoes around his head and surveyed the path. He nodded at the work we'd done so far, and then he kicked at the roots. "These gotta go," he said.

Snippers wouldn't cut through roots this thick, he explained, but he had something that would. He sauntered back down the trail, and when he came back, he was hauling an armload of safety accessories and hefting a chainsaw.

"I'll do it," I said, before Rusty or Kyle or Calvin could step up. "I can run the saw."

"It's pretty heavy," said Rusty. "You sure?"

I'd watched my dad buck logs my whole life, and when my brother was deemed old enough to handle the saw, I'd watched him, too. Never once had the tool been offered to me, but I wasn't sure I'd ever asked for it, either.

Calvin and Kyle looked on with curiosity as I stepped into the apron chaps and tightened the waistband. They were, essentially, a pair of bright-orange open-back pants. The fabric that covered the front of the legs was densely woven out of high-grade ballistic nylon, designed to stop the blade if it came in contact with the fibers. I didn't need them, I insisted to Rusty, but he told me I had to wear them.

"Guidelines," he said, and handed me the safety glasses and ear muffs. "Don't forget your hard hat."

By the time I was fully suited up, sweat was prickling my scalp and trickling down my lower back. I walked with Rusty over to the first trail-barring network of roots, and he set the chainsaw on the ground.

"You know how to start it?" he said.

I tried to remember all the steps our training supervisor had covered. *Place the saw on a flat patch of ground. Make sure the blade is clear.*

"I got it," I said, and tucked my foot into the rear handle to stabilize the saw. I took hold of the starter rope and pulled. The saw leaked a low, feeble *zhuuuuh.* I took a deep breath and pulled the rope again, harder this time, but still trying not to show that I was exerting all my strength. Another *zhuuuh* belched out.

"It's a cold start," said Rusty, and he explained that I needed the choke to warm up the motor.

"Right," I said, and slid out the choke, pulled the starter again. But the motor wouldn't catch. I asked Rusty if I should check the fuel, but he shook his head. He'd already topped it up. It was as if he was waiting for me to ask for help, to confess my weakness, to say I was just a girl, and I needed him, I couldn't do this on my own.

"I think I have short arms," I said.

"You want me to give it a try?" said Rusty.

I stepped back from the saw and let Rusty slide his toe-cap into the handle. With one fluid rip, he fired it up.

Thanks, I mouthed over the noise, then took the roaring saw he handed to me.

Rusty stuck around to supervise my first few cuts. He stood to the side of the trail, his arms crossed over his chest. When the first cleaved network of gnarled roots fell away, he nodded and gave me the thumbs-up, then ventured back to the other groups to check in on their progress. Calvin and Kyle were farther down the trail, eager to take a turn on the saw, but I had no plans to hand it over. The blade, as I eased it down at an angle, chewed through the bark and spit out the wood in a fine mist of sawdust. The scent of it brought back childhood—the Saturdays of piling lumber for whatever project my dad planned next. A picnic table. A sandbox. Our tree fort. The pigpen. The chicken coop. It smelled, too, like Christmas—the tree hefted up the stairs and into the living room to be glitzed with tinsel and garland and our crooked golden star.

From the tangle of roots, I shifted to a deadfall pine that partly blocked a section of the path. Down the log I shuffled, and it fell away in firewood-sized rounds. The saw grew heavier, but I didn't want to cut the motor and risk having to ask Rusty to come start it again, so I rested a moment and let it hang thrumming. I felt the vibration of the machine through the fabric of my glove, the power in my grasp. And I felt tough. Cocksure. Like my body was performing a small miracle, rising from its desire to be thin and whittled down, and hungry now for muscle and brawn. Tool in hand, I swelled with a quiet pride over the fact that I was doing a job normally reserved for men. And my mind flashed to my dad and the thought that if he saw me like this—standing in a world he understood—perhaps he'd understand me, too, his daughter who chose to be anywhere but near him, always a wary stranger shunning his love.

I'd applied for the forestry job because everyone else was applying. Because the pay was nearly four dollars more an hour than the minimum wage. Because Sindee was applying and I assumed we'd get to work together, instead of being split up and on separate crews. Because when I told my dad that the forestry service was hiring summer students, that we'd be out in the bush, out in the clear-cuts, out with shovels and pickaxes and chainsaws doing the kind of work he counted worthy, he'd looked up from his drink and cigarette with surprise. In a voice that sounded interested, almost proud, he said, "Is that right?" Because when I came home from the workwear store and walked into the shop to show my dad what I'd bought—my own pair of steel-toed boots, my new coveralls, my yellow hard hat, he nodded, giving me the approval I didn't even know I craved.

I angled the blade-tip and swung back into the bucking, grinding through another deadfall length. My forearms burned with the weight of the saw, and when I tried to adjust my grip, to shift how I was hanging on, I neglected to keep my eye on the running blade and to take my right finger off the throttle. Before I even had time to think about pulling the brake, the chainsaw bit into the top of my left leg, the blade vibrating against my thigh, chewing at the fabric of my safety chaps. Within seconds, ballistic fibers seized the teeth and killed the motor.

I stood a moment, looking down at my leg, at the blade stopped mid-cut, as if frozen in tableau. *Amputation, interrupted. Girl, altered. Girl, on the verge of no-going-back. Girl, going, going, gone.*

When they heard the motor stop, Calvin and Kyle wandered over with their tools. "Wow," they said, and Kyle whistled through his teeth as they inspected the almost-accident and marveled at the near-subtraction of my leg.

"Screw death by bear," Calvin said, as we worked together to try to free the saw from my pants. "Death by chainsaw. Like a frigging horror movie."

Rusty was ticked, and said it was going to cost a lot of money for repairs. Plus, the chaps were a write-off. He grumbled about how his supervisor was going to give him the gears for letting me, a girl, handle the saw.

"I thought you said you knew how to run the thing," he said.

I slid out of the safety apron, the chainsaw still attached to the fabric. I tried to look appropriately apologetic, told him I was sorry, really sorry, that my arms were tired, I didn't mean to let it happen. My heart was still thudding an ache at my sternum, and I couldn't stop the heat from rising in my cheeks.

For the rest of the afternoon, I stuck even closer to Kyle and Calvin, who storied forth about what it might feel like to lose a leg, to have an entire limb hacked off, which turned to the question of, *Would you rather have no legs or no arms, and why?* I swung the Pulaski at the stubborn roots that snaked across the forest floor, and imagined our futures with parts of ourselves missing, and how I'd move through life dismantled, humping along as I tried to strive, seek, find, and never yield.

What I'd been promised had not always come to pass, like Armageddon about to occur but the world still here, or a quick drive to the bush dragging sunrise to dusk, or a ring slipped on the finger as a pledge of true love forever, but then, months later, slipped off. In my mind, the problem lay with the promise, shaky at its heart, and the one who gave it, not with the one to whom it passed. When the story didn't go the way I planned, I could blame the elements around me. At summer's end, I'd unhitch from all that held me here—home, church, the small, small town. I told myself I could make whatever life I chose, like the plotlines of the *Choose Your Own Adventure* books I'd read as a kid, though with those stories, it seemed, I'd always picked the wrong path, chosen to climb out of the space-pod or submarine or cave too soon, and ended up devoured by an alien or giant squid or fire-breathing dragon. *The End*, the page would tell me, though I was only at the start.

Through the trees, past bear scat and mosquito swarms, a nameless lake shone with sun and the iridescent flicker of fish. I could almost see it. Somewhere, up ahead, when we

reached the shore, I'd take off my boots and sweaty wool
socks. I'd shuck my coveralls and leave them in the long
grasses, wade into the shallows and let the shine of it woo
me deeper. Around me, reflected, the trees and clouds and
blue. When I looked at myself in the warp of that shimmer
and light, I'd hardly recognize who I was, and would become.
Dragonflies and striders skimming the surface, sketching
lines across my cheeks, my eyes, showing me myself in a
strange, familiar light. I'd bend to wash the sweat and dirt
from my face, breaking the image. Then I'd rise from the
water and find my way back on a trail I'd cleared myself. *To
strive, to seek, to find, and not to yield.* The words hammered
their music in my head. With every downward swing of the
blade, another root sprang loose, another step on the path
opened up.

EVERY SHADOW
IN THE VALLEY

⤬ ⤬ ⤬ ⤬ ⤬ ⤬

THE SUN SPARKED ON THE SURFACE of the water, flashing it to a mirror. As I stepped from the weedy shore, I could see the far side of the river, and myself standing there. Three years ago, on those banks with Soopie and Sindee, I'd stumbled light-headed in the heat, pretending to be drunker than I was on my swigs of smuggled gin. Late June on the final day of school before summer break, we'd cut class to prove that we were good at being bad and snuck to a top-secret party at the cutbanks. There, I'd bummed a cigarette from the Pentecostal preacher's son, and we'd stood together smoking, avoiding eye contact, aware that come Sunday, we'd be quietly confessing these very sins in our separate pews.

Now, on the opposite shore, I stood with Wayne, that preacher's son. Throughout high school, we'd known each other from a distance, never moving in the same group of friends. But a month before graduation, when we found out that we'd both been dumped, we agreed to go to the grad banquet as each other's consolation dates. He was honest and kind, the sort of guy who was safe to be around, but the ease with which he talked about Jesus made me nervous, and hungry in a way I didn't like. God's will, God's plan,

273

God's presence—Wayne seemed to understand it all, and crave it, too. Though I'd heard those words my whole life, now, somehow, they sounded different, making me wonder if what I thought I knew so well, I didn't know at all. Both of us were on the verge of leaving town, our diplomas like tickets to the future. In a few weeks, Wayne was heading for Bible college to study theology. Finally, he said, he was surrendering to God's plan for his life. He'd sensed the call and was ready to follow it.

"You ready?" said Wayne.

We'd come to ride the river, lugging inflated inner tubes from the tires of logging trucks. Though all my friends seemed to have tubed the Nechako, I'd never done it. Neither of my parents had ever learned to swim. Ours had been a family who spent time on the water, but not in it. Only once as a kid had I been taken to a part of the river everyone called "Sandy Beach," a popular swim spot that was just a small patch of shoreline at the end of a gravel road. There I'd waded with my brother in the knee-high current while my mother sat on her blanket and warned us not to go any deeper. That river was strong enough to pull us under, she reminded, to sweep a person away.

"Ready," I said to Wayne, and stepped into the water.

The cool shallows sucked my feet into the silt, and the current washed against my ankles as it pulled toward the Fraser. I was ready to go with the river's flow—that southward tug through the Cariboo and the canyon, west to the Pacific, and then over to an island soaked with rain, licked with salt, and lush with cedar forests. I could already see my life across those waters. The one-bedroom apartment with a balcony overlooking a busy street, and strangers on the sidewalk, and lights shining from a gridwork of houses in a neighborhood bigger than the whole of my hometown. I'd dreamed myself cut loose toward that future, where a new lexicon of words would roll off my tongue—words like campus, professor, poetry, theater, the Fine Arts of Canada.

For months, I'd plotted the countdown on my calendar, X-ing off the days with Sindee, who was leaving with me for the same university, aiming for a degree in Education. But she already knew her time away from Vanderhoof would be temporary. She'd move back as soon as she could, then find work in a local school, fall in love, build a house, have kids, and stay forever. "It's home," she'd say. "I'd miss it too much."

If I closed my eyes and turned a slow circle in the spot where I stood, the river, the bridge, and the town on the other side of it rolled by. The streets and avenues I knew by feel and by foot, but not by name. The high school, the hockey rink, the ball diamonds, the railroad tracks. The train's whistle bending the air so that the color I heard was sunset, the sky washed in rust and gold, a sound that made me think of the Robert Frost poem we'd had to memorize in ninth-grade English class. One by one, each student had stood at the front of the room and recited "Nothing Gold Can Stay," like Ponyboy in *The Outsiders*, our novel study for the term. By the end of the hour, those repeated rhymes and iambs had worn a furrow in my mind. Every time the train passed through town and blew its whistle, the words—*Nature's first green is gold, / Her hardest hue to hold*—sang back to me.

I could feel the start of a burn on my neck and shoulders as Wayne and I pushed our inner tubes out to deeper water. Though the river was cold, the sun was high and bright, baking with the kind of August heat that veiled the horizon with a low blur. Behind us lay the old motel, once owned by a friend of my father, a German man named Fritz who worked as a stone mason. The concrete statues he'd crafted still stood on the patchy grass, among them, a deer, a lamb, a wolf. As a kid, I'd climb on the backs of the animals and pretend I belonged in Narnia, that this was the White Witch's courtyard full of creatures turned to stone by her enchantment. While my parents visited with Fritz and his wife, I'd explore the motel grounds and outbuildings, dreaming myself into a character from the book. The darker the sky, the greater the danger, and the more urgent my need for magic. Now, the stone flock was scraped and faded, smaller than I recalled. Missing chips of concrete notched the lamb's ears. The wolf's muzzle was wearing away.

When we reached waist-high water, we hoisted ourselves onto the tubes. The black rubber, tacky from the heat, squeaked against the top of my thighs as I pulled myself up and over, then flipped onto my back. I sank down in the center of my tube, body hammocked, hooking my arms and legs over the edges to keep myself above the water as it carried me.

The river was famous for spring floods. Once the thaw set in, spring dripped in with salt and mud, slushing and sleeting and velveting the willow branches, turning the world green and loud with machinery and birds and boat motors on the quick, high waters. Homes along the shores sandbagged and prayed the levels wouldn't rise. But by summer, as the long hours of daylight seemed to slow time, the river slowed, too, turning sluggish. Only by watching the shoreline could I tell we were actually going anywhere.

It wasn't always this way, Wayne explained. Sometimes there were eddies and fast undercurrents that could suck a person down. We both knew of the drownings, bodies washed up downstream, bruised and swollen. At least that wouldn't be us, he said, slow-motion down the river.

As the motel slid behind us, the old St. John Hospital came into view. The building loomed white on the hillside in a way that made it look larger than it really was, and just as haunted as I'd been told. Now, the hospital's rooms housed community education classes and a preschool, though people who worked in the building still heard strange noises in the basement where the morgue used to be, footsteps and slamming doors, even when the place was empty. I used to swear I saw faces in the upper-floor windows whenever we drove past at night. Beyond it was the new hospital where I was born, and behind it, the cemetery where I'd stood around the holes dug in the dirt. This aunt. That cousin. That sad and gray-faced man.

While Grandpa Funk faded in his hospital bed, Uncle Pete's dog Sophie had lain outside the window. Each time the nurses moved Grandpa to a different room, the dog moved too, Grandma said, following the scent of him to the next window, and the next, until his body was gone. Then Sophie trotted the shoulder of the road all the way from the hospital to Grandpa and Grandma Funk's house. Beneath Grandpa's bedroom window, the dog sat, her muzzle reading the wind for some sign of him, expecting his return.

At home, my bedroom floor was stacked with cardboard boxes, my hope chest emptied of all the things I'd take with me. Tea towels and dish cloths. The cutlery bought on sale from the hardware store. The coffee mugs pilfered from the camping trailer. I added it all to the pile of kitchen supplies started by my mother. Though I didn't bake or really know how to cook much of anything, she'd insisted

I needed cookie sheets, a pie plate, a bread pan, a casserole dish, and a good set of knives. "What about a skillet?" she wanted to know, and "Don't you want a toaster oven, too?" She kept a list of what she thought I needed, as if I were a bride-to-be moving straight from my parents' home into the marriage house, like she did on the day she wed my dad. The money she'd saved for nursing college he spent instead on furniture, surprising her with what he'd chosen—a black pleather couch and chair adorned with ruby-red brocade, and a glitzy floor lamp in a style she never liked.

"Why didn't you ever leave," I'd say, "and go where you wanted to go?"

She'd only shrug when I asked the question. My father had said, "Want to marry me?" and she'd said yes. Like a hook snagging the eye, a key into the lock, his question fit together with her answer, as was the custom. I never asked her if she'd hoped for a different ending to the story, or even for a different story altogether. This was the story passed down to her, and before her, to her mother, and to her mother's mother. Before and before and before, the storyline hummed, old as Eden, that first Garden where woman cleaved to man, because what else could she do? She was bone of his bone, a rib borrowed from his side, and ever trying to return to its source, to find the way home.

"You don't have to go so far away," my father kept telling me, even though he knew my plans were set, that I was moving in a matter of weeks. He sat at the dining room table before bed, heaping spoonfuls of sugar into a bowl of corn flakes and cream, and watched me fill another cardboard box with dishes from my mother's kitchen stash. He told me I should be like Soopie, go to Prince George for college instead, because it was only an hour away. "Then you can come home on weekends," he said.

"She'll be back at Christmas," my mother said. "And then again next summer."

I'd fantasized my climb out of this valley, vowing to be the girl who got out of the small town, and who got the small town out of her. To fly away, and away, and away, until home was a string of numbers and a taut wire stretched over miles, a speck on the map. I knew that the closer I came to leaving, the more I was supposed to feel the pull to stay. But already I saw the town growing smaller, and behind me, the bridge that crossed the river, the river following the train tracks, and the bowl of the valley hanging with early-autumn fog. Ahead, the highway rose and fell, curving south and west, the road signs flying by—*Bednesti, Prince George, Hixon, Quesnel*, a chain of villages, small towns, and little cities—*Clinton, Ashcroft, Cache Creek, Hope*—with names I knew by heart.

As we floated beneath the bridge that spanned the north and south sides of the river, we fell into the coolness of its shadow. The muffled thunder of a truck passed overhead. The water smelled silvery, like fishing as a kid in my dad's aluminum boat, like hooks and earthworms and wood-smoke and dirt, like my mother's hands holding a cup to my lips, like my brother reeling in the rainbow trout that flashed at the end of his line. I was a small thing growing smaller as I drifted. The river fed the dirt that fed the roots of all that grew inside the valley. What grew in darkness moved toward light, every shadow in the valley reaching for the gleam. Ahead, the river curved. What lay around its bend was hidden from my view. Ahead, the river narrowed and split and narrowed again, following a bed carved into the earth by time and ice and stone, forces of nature beyond my knowledge, generations before I ever entered these waters. When I slid from the shadows, blinded by the sudden brightness, the eye of the sun, wild and ancient and faithful, would find me again, fix me in its radiance, illuminating every part.

ACKNOWLEDGMENTS

✕ ✕ ✕ ✕ ✕ ✕ ✕

WHILE WRITING THIS BOOK, I reread *Vanderhoof: The Town That Wouldn't Wait*, by the Nechako Valley Historical Society and Lyn Hancock, and my fondness for my hometown only grew. Thank you, Vanderhoof, for being a town that keeps on giving.

Thank you to my great-aunt Mildred Schrock (1920–2012), who passed down the story of the little red apron, both through oral tradition and in her 1972 book, *For His Sake*. That book was later reprinted, and then reissued with additional historical notes in 2014, edited by Wilbur R. Shenk.

The form of "Is This Love?—A Quiz" borrows from the countless *Seventeen*, *Sassy*, and *YM* magazine quizzes I took as a teenager. Only after I wrote the chapter did I realize that I'd also been inspired by A. E. Stallings, whose poem "First Love: A Quiz" I read years ago and recently rediscovered.

Thank you, Greystone, for welcoming me into your community of writers. Paula Ayer, editor beyond measure, you've been a gift to me. Thank you for asking excellent questions, and for spending your own imagination on my work.

I'm profoundly grateful for the friends and family members who helped me write this book. You patiently listened to me yammer about bygone teenage days, offered your own coming-of-age experiences, and cheered me on in the journey.

Rob Trepanier, patron saint of this fumbling writer, thank you for your steadfast intercession on my behalf.

Thank you, Aunt Donna and Uncle George, for helping me with the Plautdietsch and the Funk facts.

Grandma Shenk, your memory astounds me, and I'm grateful that you've shared it with me.

To my mother: one day I'll try to write fiction, I promise; in the meantime, thank you for being generous, full of grace, and a good sport.

To my brother, Richard: thank you for your encouragement and for filling in the gaps of my own memory.

Soopie and Sindee, thank you for all of our nostalgic hivemind conversations that brought back forgotten parts of the stories, plus so much laughter, and so many fabulous photos of bad fashion choices, circa 1989.

And to Lance and Amelia, my great delights in life, thank you for bearing with me, being the most fun, and loving me so well, even when I'm writing.